MODERN RADIO
PRODUCTION

General

Media/Impact: An Introduction to Mass Media by Shirley Biagi

Media/Reader by Shirley Biagi

Mediamerica: Form, Content, and Consequence of Mass Communication, 4th, by Edward Jay Whetmore

The Interplay of Influence: Mass Media & Their Publics in News, Advertising, Politics, 2nd, by Kathleen Hall Jamieson and Karlyn Kohrs Campbell

Technology and Communication Behavior by Frederick Williams

When Words Collide: A Journalist's Guide to Grammar and Style, 2nd, by Lauren Kessler and Duncan McDonald

Interviews That Work: A Practical Guide for Journalists by Shirley Biagi

Mass Media Research: An Introduction, 2nd, by Roger D. Wimmer and Joseph R. Dominick

Communication Research: Strategies and Sources, 2nd, by Rebecca B. Rubin, Alan M. Rubin, and Linda J. Piele

Computer Graphics Applications: An Introduction by Kenneth Hoffman with Jon Teeple

Radio/Television/Cable

Stay Tuned: A Concise History of American Broadcasting, 2nd, by Christopher H. Sterling and John M. Kittross

World Broadcasting Systems: A Comparative Analysis by Sydney W. Head

Broadcast/Cable Programming: Strategies and Practices, 3rd, by Susan Tyler Eastman, Sydney W. Head, and Lewis Klein

Radio Station Operations: Management and Employee Perspectives by Lewis B. O'Donnell, Carl Hausman, and Philip Benoit

Broadcast and Cable Selling by Charles Warner

Advertising in the Broadcast and Cable Media, 2nd, by Elizabeth J. Heighton and Don R. Cunningham

Copywriting for the Electronic Media: A Practical Guide by Milan D. Meeske and R. C. Norris

Writing for Television and Radio, 4th, by Robert L. Hilliard

Writing the Screenplay: TV and Film by Alan A. Armer

Newswriting for the Electronic Media: Principles, Examples, Applications by Daniel E. Garvey and William L. Rivers

Newstalk II: State-of-the-Art Conversations with Today's Broadcast Journalists by Shirley Biagi

Announcing: Broadcast Communicating Today by Lewis B. O'Donnell, Carl Hausman, and Philip Benoit

Modern Radio Production, 2nd, by Lewis B. O'Donnell, Philip Benoit, and Carl Hausman

Audio in Media, 3rd, by Stanley R. Alten

Television Production Handbook, 4th, by Herbert Zettl

Directing Television and Film, 2nd, by Alan A. Armer

Sight-Sound-Motion: Applied Media Aesthetics, 2nd, by Herbert Zettl

Electronic Cinematography: Achieving Photographic Control over the Video Image by Harry Mathias and Richard Patterson

MODERN RADIO PRODUCTION

■

SECOND EDITION

LEWIS B. O'DONNELL
State University of New York College
at Oswego

PHILIP BENOIT
Dickinson College

CARL HAUSMAN
Free-Lance Writer and Producer

■

Wadsworth Publishing Company
Belmont, California
A Division of Wadsworth, Inc.

Senior Editor: Rebecca Hayden
Editorial Assistant: Tamiko Verkler
Production Editor: Gary Mcdonald
Managing Designer: MaryEllen Podgorski
Print Buyer: Karen Hunt
Designer: Stuart Paterson/Image House Inc.
Copy Editor: Steven Gray
Technical Illustrator: Shirley Bortoli
Compositor: Graphic Typesetting Service, Los Angeles
Cover: Stuart Paterson/Image House Inc.
Cover Illustrator: Edward W. Lawler

Printed in the United States of America 19

1 2 3 4 5 6 7 8 9 10---94 93 92 91 90

Library of Congress Cataloging-in-Publication Data

O'Donnell, Lewis B.
   Modern radio production / Lewis B. O'Donnell, Philip
Benoit, Carl Hausman.—2nd ed.
       p.   cm.—(Wadsworth series in mass communication)
   Bibliography: p.
   Includes index.
   ISBN 0-534-11622-1
   1. Radio broadcasting.   2. Radio plays—Production
and direction. I. Benoit, Philip, 1944–   . II. Hausman,
Carl, 1953–   . III. Title. IV. Series.
PN1991.75.036   1990
791.44'0232—dc20   89-33770
                                                  CIP

Preface

Modern Radio Production will introduce you to the fascinating and challenging field of radio production. Why was it written? Because we perceived a need for a nontechnical text that provides step-by-step instruction in radio production and an insight into the world of professional radio. For too long, the basic concepts of production have been shrouded in technical jargon, and the stress has been on the hardware, rather than on the product, the finished production.

The needless complication of radio production often results in gaps in the accumulated knowledge of both students and practicing professionals; it's all too easy to "tune out" when the terms and concepts become too ponderous. We mention this even though some readers, perhaps through experience in the campus radio station, may have picked up some familiarity with equipment and practices and may feel that portions of this book are too basic.

We don't think that is the case. Although hands-on experience is valuable, people working at campus radio stations aren't always exposed to a wide range of techniques, and they tend to rely on a mechanical, learned-by-rote approach, without understanding the theories behind the techniques. Modern Radio Production is structured to provide a balanced mix of techniques and theory, along with step-by-step instruction in hands-on production techniques. We believe that production is largely an extension of a particular station's programming sound.

Part One, The Tools, comprises Chapters 1 through 5. Chapter 1 introduces radio and radio programming and tells how the role of production fits in. Chapter 2 demystifies the workings and operations of the broadcast console, an integral but often-misunderstood tool of radio production, and introduces some of the concepts that relate to the equipment and production-technique chapters that follow. From Chapter 2 on, the text includes *applications*—problems posed and solved in relation to the material presented in the chapter—and exercises. The exercises provide opportunities for a mixture of production work and thoughtful problem solving. Chapters 3, 4, and 5 explain the operation of basic equipment and deal, respectively, with turntables and compact disc players, tape recording and playback units, and microphones and sound.

The next three chapters, Part Two, deal with the basic *techniques* of production. Chapter 6 explains the basics of splicing and dubbing. Chapter 7 outlines many of the basic operations used in recorded production in a studio setting. Chapter 8 deals with production techniques from the standpoint of doing a live radio airshift.

Part Three, The Applications, focuses on achieving effects to produce radio that creates a mood and puts across a message. Chapter 9 blends the mechanics of production with artistic elements of communicating an idea. Radio drama and dramatic elements in radio production are featured in Chapter 10; the purpose is not to deal with radio drama as such but to show you how dramatic scenes are incorporated into a variety of productions. Commercials—a very important product in today's radio—are discussed in Chapter 11, where the techniques of construction and persuasion are outlined.

Chapter 12 centers on production for news and public-affairs programming. Chapter 13 explains the intricacies of remote and sports production. Chapter 14 focuses on some of the more advanced aspects of radio production, such as multichannel production, music recording, and simple broadcast electronics. Chapter 15 investigates computer use in modern radio.

This sequence of instruction, we feel, provides a basic and well-rounded scope of knowledge to the student entering radio production. This knowledge will serve as a foundation for future experimentation, because in the fascinating field of radio broadcasting, a creative and energetic person never stops learning.

This book has changed considerably since the first edition. Technologies have advanced with startling speed, and new information was added to the second edition until almost the day it rolled off the printing press.

But while *Modern Radio Production*'s second edition may appear to be very new, it is still the same type of book: It is a work that stresses communication skills rather than hardware. *Modern Radio Production* still clings to the notion that the tools and techniques of radio are the mechanical methods by which a producer persuades, interests, entertains, and motivates a listener. Radio production is not the science of hardware; it's the art of entertaining in the theater of the mind.

So, having assured you that the premise remains the same, let's look at some specific areas in which coverage has changed. The second edition of *Modern Radio Production* includes the following:

▸ *Expanded coverage of digital recording.* Chapter 4 introduces the concept of digitally encoding information and discusses the pluses and minuses of digital recording with digital audiotape. Chapter 5 adds an extensive discussion of compact discs to the discussion of turntables and standard grooved discs.

▸ *Many pages of new information on satellite feeds and programming services.* We discuss what's available and how it is typically used. Chapter 8 has been supplemented with an extensive guide to syndicated services, with particular emphasis on how a console operator or station programmer interacts with these services.

▸ *An entirely new chapter on digital computer technology in modern radio.* Chapter 15 begins with an introduction to computer basics—defining and demystifying the vocabulary—and then demonstrates how computerized equipment can be used to generate radio production effects. Computer-assisted editing is described and demonstrated. The increasing use of computers for highly sophisticated automation is also discussed. Of particular interest are state-of-the-art techniques for automation-assist programming, whereby console operators can fire a series of operations by exercising one command.

Because *Modern Radio Production*'s first edition was used widely in classrooms across the nation, we have been able to garner some very valuable advice about what needed to be strengthened in the revision. As a result, we have included many and various revisions of drawings, photos, and text explanations. For example, the chapter dealing with microphones has been made slightly less technical; more attention is paid to announcing techniques in the chapter on on-air production; and the role of modern newsgathering technology has been more fully addressed.

Appendix A, a troubleshooting checklist, is a reference for tracking down the sources and causes of various problems commonly encountered during radio production. It is a self-diagnosing tool that will help readers answer their own questions. Appendix B, a listing of the most popular radio formats in current use, gives readers a brief guide to the distinguishing features of different modern radio formats. In addition, the glossary has undergone a major expansion, and the listing of recommended readings has been greatly enlarged to meet the needs of students and radio professionals.

We would like to express our sincere gratitude to a number of people who made valuable contributions to the book. First, our thanks to Frank (Fritz) Messere of the State University of New York College at Oswego. Fritz has served as our technical adviser on both editions and has made contributions far above and beyond the call of duty. The book is a better one because of his willingness to help and, of course, his seemingly endless knowledge of broadcast audio. He also prepared the instructor's manual, new to this edition, that goes with this text.

We also extend our gratitude to the following reviewers, who made many good suggestions based on use of the first edition or their careful reading of the manuscript for the second edition: David W. Anderson, Indiana University–South Bend; Julie Brady-Jenner, Saddleback College; David H. Champoux, Herkimer County Community College; William L. Hagerman, University of Southwestern Louisiana; Cynthia M. Lont, George Mason University; Deborah Petersen-Perlman, University of Minnesota–Duluth; Charles L. Rasberry, Arkansas State University; and Jack Summerfield, New York Institute of Technology.

Finally, we'd like to thank our editor, Becky Hayden, who again cheerfully helped us wade through mountains of manuscript and photos to turn out a more polished final product.

About the Authors

Lewis B. O'Donnell (Ph.D., Syracuse University) is Professor Emeritus of Communication Studies at the State University of New York College at Oswego. O'Donnell, president of a radio station ownership group, has worked in a variety of management and performance positions in radio and television. He has been awarded the Frank Stanton Fellowship by the International Radio and Television Society and the New York State Chancellor's Award for Excellence in Teaching.

Carl Hausman (M.A., Antioch University) is a writer and producer who has taught communications at several colleges in Massachusetts and New Hampshire. Hausman is the author or coauthor of eleven books, including six books on the communications media. He has worked in various news and news management positions in radio and television, and from 1977 to 1980 developed and produced Syracuse University's syndicated radio news service.

Philip Benoit (M.A., State University of New York College at Oswego) is director of communications for Dickinson College in Carlisle, Pennsylvania. Formerly the director of broadcasting at SUNY Oswego, Benoit has a broad background in radio, television, and public relations. He was executive officer of the American Forces Network in Europe and American Advisor to the Vietnamese Armed Forces Radio Network.

Contents

APPENDIX A

APPENDIX B

APPENDIX C

MODERN RADIO PRODUCTION

PART ONE

THE TOOLS

·1·

Production

---

in Modern Radio

A merica's radio broadcasting continues to thrive. Despite the forecasts of doom that grew out of television's emergence as the major entertainment medium in the 1950s, radio has adapted and grown. In fact, today there are more stations—with more listeners—than ever before.

Radio's beginnings in the early part of this century gave no hint of the role it would play in today's world of exciting media possibilities. The early radio experimenters such as Marconi and Fessenden never envisioned an era when their electronic toy would become a means of providing entertainment and information to audiences in their cars, in their boats, and in their homes, and even to audiences who are jogging.

Early radio programming gradually evolved from a novel attempt to bring the cultural offerings of major cities into the living rooms of all America; gradually, radio assumed its current status as a "companion." Early radio programming consisted of live symphony broadcasts, poetry readings, and live coverage of major news events, along with the kinds of drama, situation comedy, and other programming that form the bulk of today's television schedules.

Some radio historians put the time of radio's emergence into its present form at 1935, when Martin Block first aired his "Make-Believe Ballroom" show on New York City's WNEW. The idea for the program came from a West Coast station when a planned remote broadcast of a band performance at a local ballroom was canceled. To fill the time, the enterprising broadcaster obtained some of the band's recordings and played them over the air. He identified the program as coming from a "make-believe" ballroom, and the time was filled. When Block brought the idea to New York, it was the birth of the **disc jockey** (or DJ) era in radio.

Production in radio reached its zenith during what is generally referred to as the Golden Age of radio. Radio programs of that era (the 1930s and 1940s) often originated in large studios, where production people and performers created elaborate programs that depended for their effectiveness on sophisticated production techniques.

Music was provided by studio orchestras that performed live as the program aired. Sound effects were imaginatively created by production people present in the studio with actors and musicians. Coconut shells, for example, were used to recreate the sound of horses' hoofbeats; and the crackling of cellophane near the microphone recreated the sound of a fire.

The arrangement and orchestration of various sound sources combined to create the desired effect in the minds of the listening audience. Budgets were elaborate, large numbers of people were involved, and scripts were often complex. In fact, production is what made the so-called Golden Age golden.

Today, the mainstay of radio is recorded music, interspersed with news and information—and, of course, commercial messages, which pay for the whole operation of commercial stations. When television took over the living rooms of American homes and supplied, in a far more explicit way, the drama, variety, and other traditional program fare that had marked radio in its heyday, the DJ form became the dominant form of radio. Music and news and personality in a careful blend known as a **format** became the measure of radio's ability to attract listeners.*

The development of **solid-state** technology and later **microchip** electronics freed radio from bulky, stationary hardware. At the beach, in the car, and on city streets, radio can be the constant companion of even the most active of listeners. And freedom from the long program forms (half-hour and hour programs) that once characterized radio and still typify television programming means that information cycles quickly in radio. For example, when people want to find out about a breaking news event, they turn first to the radio.

All this has great significance for anyone who wishes to understand the techniques of radio production. **Production** in radio is basically the assembly of various sources of sound to achieve a purpose related to radio programming. You, as a production person in radio, are responsible for what is known as the "sound" of the station.

---

*Terms set in boldface type are defined in the glossary.

■ SOUND OF THE STATION ■

The sound of a station is created by using various sources of sound to create a specific result, a specific product that appeals to specific listeners. It's how these sources blend that makes one station different from the others that compete for the attention of the audience.

The unique sound of a station emerges out of a combination of the type of music programmed, the style and pace of vocal delivery used by the station's announcers, the techniques used in the production of commercials and public-service announcements, the sound effects used in the presentation of newscasts, and other special recording techniques and sound production methods.

■ FORMATS ■

Commercial radio stations make their money by targeting audiences for advertisers who buy time on the stations' airwaves. The audiences are "delivered" to the advertisers. They are measured by rating services, which use sampling techniques to provide a head count of the audience that includes data on such audience characteristics as age, sex, and level of income.

The programming goal of a commercial radio station is to provide on the air something that will attract audiences, which then can be "sold" to advertisers. If the programming doesn't achieve this, there will be few advertisers, and of course little money coming into the station's coffers. Without money, the station cannot operate. So, the name of the game is to attract and hold an audience that will appeal to advertisers. This crucial aspect of radio programming—that is, developing a format—becomes a highly specialized field of its own.

Just as commercial radio strives to attract and hold a specific audience to be successful in the marketplace, public radio stations must use the same fundamental techniques to design programming that will meet the needs of their audiences. Though public radio stations do not sell time to advertisers, they must successfully package their programming to obtain program underwriters and individual subscribers.

Reaching a Specific Audience

Unlike television, which tries to appeal to broader, more general segments of the public with its programs, radio has developed into a medium that focuses on smaller groups, the so-called *target audiences*. For example, a station may choose to program rock music to attract what's known as a young **demographic.** (Demographics are the statistical characteristics of human populations, and the word is commonly used in the singular form in the broadcasting industry to designate any given segment of the audience.) By appealing to one segment of the public (such as people of a certain age, sex, or income) that shares a preference for a certain type of music, a station can hope to attract advertisers wishing to sell products to people of that group.

How Target Audiences Affect Format

Much research and effort has gone into determining the types of programming that attract different types of audiences. The results of these efforts are identification of formats that appeal to specific audiences.

A format is essentially the arrangement of program elements, often musical recordings, into a sequence that will attract and hold the segment of the audience a station is seeking. For example, a format labeled "top 40" (or "CHR": contemporary hit radio) is constructed around records that are the most popular recordings sold to an audience mostly in its teens and early twenties. By programming these recordings successfully, a station will attract a number of these listeners in these age groups. The more teenagers and young adults who listen to the station, the more the station can charge the advertisers who want to use radio to reach this valuable target audience.

There are a great number of formats, including adult contemporary (which reaches adults with modern music), country, CHR (a newer and more inclusive version of the top-40 format), album-oriented rock or AOR (now a fixture on FM), beautiful music, and classical. There are other specialized formats, too, such as urban contemporary, ethnic, all-jazz, and news, which has developed several forms, including all-news, news-talk, and other hybrids.

An interesting phenomenon in recent times has been the decrease in differences between formats of AM and FM radio. The "screaming rocker" was once heard solely on AM; but now, in a surprising number of markets, the top-rated stations are FM rockers. Talk radio on FM is undergoing trial runs, too.

Format, remember, is more than music. The formula for constructing a format might be expressed as production, personality, and programming. How the production, personality, and programming are integrated into a format depends on a marketing decision by the station's management. This decision is usually based on a careful analysis of the competition in a given market and an ascertainment of which audience segments can realistically be expected to become listeners to a particular station. A format is then sought that will position the station to attract a large share of listeners in that market.

Stations switch formats frequently. This is usually done because of a decision to go after a more profitable demographic segment; in other instances, the tastes of audiences may shift. Perhaps there is too much competition in a particular format, and one station elects to go after a segment of the audience for which there is less competition.

How Formats Are Constructed

Stations assemble their formats in several different ways. Some simply obtain recordings and program them in some sort of sequence throughout the schedule. Other stations carry different formats for different parts of the day.

The different times of the broadcast day are called *dayparts*. Research has shown that different populations or demographics listen to different dayparts. We tune into one station because we want to hear traffic reports in the morning, but we may prefer another station in the afternoon because of the music that particular station plays. We tune into a third station at night because it carries a sports broadcast we're interested in hearing. (An extensive discussion of formats is presented in Appendix A.)

A very big industry that has grown up in recent years provides stations with "ready-to-use" formats. Firms known as **syndicators** will, for a fee, provide satellite feeds, music tapes, or program features ready for broadcast. The music has been carefully planned and produced in a pattern designed to attract maximum numbers of the desired audience segments. Some of these services have all the music and announcer segments included, with spaces for local commercials and newscasts. Others simply supply music tapes.

Automation in radio has made possible the use of tapes from syndicators by a minimum number of people at the station level to get the program on the air. Many stations whose programming appears to involve a number of people performing various functions over the air are in reality staffed by a sole operator, babysitting a large bank of automated equipment.

▪   NETWORKS   ▪

In the 1930s and 1940s, radio networks were major sources of programming for affiliated radio stations around the country. They supplied news, comedy, variety, and dramatic shows, along with music programs of all types. At one point, local origination on many stations merely filled the hole in the **network** schedules. In fact, rules were developed by the Federal Communications Commission to prevent the total domination of radio station schedules by network programming.

Figure 1.1   Satellite dish for a radio station.

Today's radio networks serve a function quite different from that of the networks of the earlier era. Stations today depend on their networks as ancillary sources of programming and use them to supplement locally originated programming. Many stations take news from networks, and this provides a national and international news service that usually is not available from a strictly local operation. In addition, radio networks often offer short feature programs to their affiliated stations; these programs may be carried directly from the network or used at a later date. Increasingly, networks are providing other forms of programming such as music or holiday specials; this programming is used by affiliates to supplement their local schedules. In return, networks expect their affiliates to carry the networks' advertising. Such advertising is the networks' basic source of revenue.

Networks also take advantage of modern technology to offer programs to their affiliates via satellite (Fig. 1.1), which provides excellent-quality sound reproduction—higher than that obtainable from "land lines." And while radio networks are certainly less a programming centerpiece than in pretelevision days, growth in services is occurring rapidly. The day is foreseen by many when network services will not differ greatly from those of format syndicators.

■ OTHER PROGRAMMING ■ DEVELOPMENTS IN RADIO

Format syndication, network programming, and locally produced elements form the bulk of programming sources in modern radio. Variations, such as syndicators specializing in short health features, food shows, business reports, and so on, emerge almost daily. And nonmusical formats such as all-news and all-talk also thrive.

It is important for the student of radio production to recognize that radio is a medium of great vitality, a medium that is still developing rapidly. It is exciting and full of career opportunities. Production—using sound elements to create an effect or deliver a message—has always been and always will be a key element in radio.

■ THE ROLE OF THE ■ PRODUCER IN MODERN RADIO

With all the excitement over automated radio and prerecorded formats, it may appear that little remains to be done in radio production at the local level. In fact, the opposite is true.

Production skills form the basis of producing a station's sound. Without those skills, the unique sound can't be created. But skills alone won't suffice, and that's why we've started this production book with a discussion of programming. Good production is an extension of the station's programming, and a producer—anyone who manipulates sound to create an effect or deliver a message—must tailor that production to reinforce the station's sound.

In this text we explore the nuts and bolts of radio broadcasting. By learning the elements of radio production, you will be exploring the essence of radio programming. Production, from a mechanical standpoint, can be seen as the method of combining various sources of sound into a product that accomplishes something specific. Anyone in a radio station can perform this function. The sales manager who records and assembles a commercial is a producer. So is the person who constructs a newscast. The staff announcer who runs the console (known as a **combo** operation) is a producer. In larger stations, the bulk of the production may be the responsibility of a production manager, who specializes in producing such items as commercials, public-service announcements (PSAs), or talk shows. Some very large stations and networks have full-time producers who exclusively handle specialized programming, such as concerts and sporting events.

Figure 1.2   Production studio of a major-market radio station.

Obviously, the particular responsibilities of a producer depend on the station where he or she is employed. Radio stations run a wide gamut in sophistication, from small daytime-only stations with minimal and aging equipment to high-tech powerhouses in major cities (Fig. 1.2). But regardless of the size of the station, the role and importance of production and the producer is the same.

The producer at any level may be called on to create and execute a commercial that sells a product for an advertiser, to put together a newscast introduction that arrests the attention of the listener, or to combine a number of previously recorded elements with live vocal delivery in a distinctive package known as an **airshift.** All these functions, and more, create the radio product in small, medium, and large markets.

By becoming proficient in these skills, you will be opening the door to a variety of opportunities in the radio field. And although our focus is radio broadcasting, the skills and knowledge in this text can be applied in a variety of other professional situations. Studio recording, sound production for multimedia presentations, audio for television, and specialized sound production for advertising agencies, production houses, and other commercial clients are only a few of the professional areas that require many of the skills covered in this text.

Overall, you will be exploring a field that requires a variety of skills, and you'll need to invest some time in learning them. But understanding the basics is just the beginning. Real proficiency in radio production requires professional commitment, experience, creativity, and a certain sense of adventure. A truly effective production bears the identifying mark of its producer. It is unique.

The skills involved are tools. The way you use the tools makes the difference. And while more than a small degree of frustration may be involved in trying to come up with a production that sounds the way you've heard it in your mind, a high degree of satisfaction results when the magic happens and you can hear the finished result of your efforts—and you say, "Yes! That's it!"

Many radio veterans feel that production is one of the most satisfying parts of their job. It's a chance to be an artist, a technician, and a performer, all at once. Production is one of the key jobs in any radio station. The people who do production well are the ones who form and shape the foundation of radio broadcasting. In addition, audio production opens up career opportunities in areas other than radio broadcasting alone. Film and television need competent audio producers, too; and business and industry also require the services of skilled in-house producers.

So enjoy yourself while you learn how to produce the magic. You'll work hard, but the rewards will be long-lasting. You will be acquiring not only skills that will last a lifetime, but perhaps an enduring passion for an exciting and rewarding activity in a profession that is a vital part of our world today.

SUMMARY

Radio has moved from a mass-audience medium to a more specific medium; that is, it reaches a specific target audience that is more narrowly defined than is the audience targeted by the modern mass medium of television.

Formats during the Golden Age featured imaginative and often lush production effects, including full symphony orchestras. The Golden Age also was the heyday of the theater of the mind—producers came to appreciate the full value of the medium's impact.

The sound of the station is the overall blending of music, vocal delivery, timing, pacing, and other production elements that combine to create a cohesive, identifiable signature.

The modern radio station carefully develops and fine-tunes its format to reach a quantifiable target audience—an audience that is, in turn, "sold" to buyers of radio-station advertising time.

The impact of networks declined considerably after the Golden Age, but satellite transmission capabilities and other technical advances have given new life to the network concept. Many stations now integrate network programming in a blend that complements their formats, allowing stations to localize the network feed.

Producers in modern radio still do their work in the theater of the mind. Today they use a wide variety of elements from traditional radio sources (as well as new digital computer-based equipment) to create effects. Despite technical advances, the skill of the producer is still paramount.

·2·

The Console

P robably nothing in radio production is more intimidating than one's first exposure to the **console**—a complex network of switches, knobs, and meters. However, operating the console, or **board,** soon becomes second nature. In fact, most radio professionals will tell you something like: "When I first started in radio, all I thought about was running the board, and what would happen when I changed jobs and had to learn a new board. But after a few months, I found out that running the board was really one of the simplest aspects of the job. And when I changed stations, I picked up the new board in an afternoon."

We think it's important to emphasize that one does acquire familiarity with the console, because many newcomers to radio production become discouraged with their first few experiences at the controls and never gain the confidence they need to experiment, to use the board as a versatile tool, and to "play it" like a musical instrument.

Remember, anyone can learn to run a console. You don't have to be an engineer or a technician; all you need is an understanding of what the console does and some practice in the necessary mechanical operating skills.

■ FUNCTION OF THE ■ CONSOLE

The console is simply a device for amplifying, routing, and mixing audio signals. *Audio* is the term used to refer to the electrical signals that are involved in the reproduction or transmission of sound. It's important to keep the distinction between audio and sound firmly in mind. **Sound** is a vibration through air or another medium; **audio** is the electrical signal used in reproducing or transmitting the original sound.

Amplification

Amplification is the boosting of a signal to a usable level. The tiny voltage produced by a phonograph is not strong enough to send to a loudspeaker or over the air. (This is precisely why the turntable on a home stereo is connected to an amplifier, whether built-in or a separate component.) The console gives the operator convenient control over the **volume** of various signal sources such as microphones, turntables (professional-quality record players), and tape playback units.

Routing

The console allows the producer to determine the path of the signal, or in other words to **route** it. As we'll see, the console can send a signal either over the air or into a **cue** channel, which lets the operator hear an audio source without having the signal go over the air. In addition to routing signals through the console, the operator can turn signals on and off.

Mixing

The console can put two signals out at once—the announcer's voice and music, for example. The console also allows the volume of both to be controlled separately, or **mixed**, so that the music doesn't drown out the announcer.

Through amplification, routing, and mixing, the console operator can produce a final product that will be sent out over the air (as in the case of a radio announcer doing an airshift) or routed to a tape recorder (as someone would do when producing a commercial to be played back over the air later).

▪ UNDERSTANDING CONSOLE ▪ FUNCTION: SOME HYPOTHETICAL EXAMPLES

The preceding discussion of amplification, routing, and mixing is fine as a theoretical explanation of how a console works, but how do they function in practice? To explain, we'll take an approach that is a bit unusual: We will present a series of hypothetical consoles used at equally hypothetical radio stations. We'll briefly touch on the use of turntables, microphones, and tape playback units, but detailed instruction about these devices comes in later chapters. So don't worry about anything except understanding what the console does and why it does it. The purpose of these examples is to demonstrate how a console carries out certain operations.

Hypothetical Console *A*

The radio station using console *A* plays only one sound, the same record, over and over. The only equipment owned by this station consists of a **turntable** and console *A* (Fig. 2.1). Here are the features on console *A*.

Preamplifier The signal from a turntable is very weak, so a device called a preamplifier (usually shortened to **preamp**) boosts it to a more usable level. Note that the preamplification process on turntables is different from that on some other sources; a turntable preamp can be outside the console, or "outboard." For purposes of explaining the console, though, it really makes no difference, so you'll find the preamp shown on the console diagram.

Potentiometer In engineering terms, a **potentiometer** is a variable resistor; in nonspecialist's terms, it's nothing more than a volume control. The potentiometer is almost always referred to as the **pot.** Usually, it is a knob that raises volume when twisted clockwise, just as a rheostat switch turns up the level of lights in a dining room. It raises the volume of the console's output; it is therefore an adjustment for the VU meter (discussed next) and not a control for the monitor. Some modern consoles have bars that perform the same function when raised vertically. Often, these are called **vertical** or **slide faders,** but for the sake of simplicity we'll refer to both kinds as *pots.*

Key This is an on–off switch that puts the signal out over the air when the key is pushed to **program.** The key is thrown into program when it is moved to the right. Other functions of this key are shown in later examples.

Volume-Unit Meter You know that the pot allows adjustment of the level of volume, but how do you know what level is correct? Volume is a pretty subjective judgment.

The volume-unit meter, usually called a **VU meter,** gives an objective visual representation of loudness. It's a very important component of the console, and the ability to read it properly is critical in every phase of radio production.

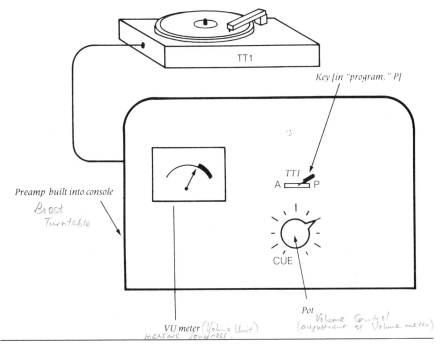

Key [in "program," P]

TT1

Preamp built into console

Boost
Turntable

TT1

A ⊏▭⊐ P

CUE

Pot

Volume Control
(adjustment of Volume meter)

VU meter (*Volume Unit*)
measure loudness.

Figure 2.1   Console at a station that uses only one turntable (TT1).

Essentially, the most important aspect of reading a VU meter is to know that zero on the top scale is the reference for proper volume. A close-up of the meter on console A (Fig. 2.2(a)) shows that the record is playing at proper volume or level of sound.

A reading of $+1$ volume unit (Fig. 2.2(b)) means that the signal is playing too loudly; if it goes much higher the signal will sound distorted. (A volume unit is a relative measurement of audio loudness and is similar to a **decibel,** ✗ a measurement discussed in Chapter 5.) A reading above zero is known as being "in the red," since the part of the scale above 0 is colored red. A reading of $+2$ indicates that matters are worse, and $+3$ will put the needle all the way to the right, known as "pinning the meter," and can cause severe distortion.

On the other hand, too low a reading will result in too little music level and too much noise. Noise is always present in these electrical components, and when there's not enough signal volume, the noise becomes much more apparent; this is known as an unacceptable **signal-to-noise ratio.** This is the ratio of signal in a **channel** to noise in a channel; the greater the signal-to-noise ratio, the better. A reading consistently lower than -3 or so (Fig. 2.2(c)) is known as running "in the mud."

Figure 2.2   VU meter readings.

(a) Proper-level reading.

(b) Reading "in the red." (Distortion)

(c) Reading "in the mud."

The operator of console *A* is responsible for keeping the peaks as close to zero as possible. This isn't particularly difficult because the VU meter is built to respond to averages. The needle tends to float around, seeking an average volume level. The operator should *not* crank up the pot each time the level drops below zero, or crank the pot down each time the needle goes into the red. Riding the pot too closely will result in an elimination of loud and soft passages in music, especially classical music.

By the way, you can also read the VU meter according to the bottom scale, which indicates the percentage of **modulation.** Modulation is the imprint of sound on a radio signal, and 100 percent is the ideal. Modulation is a measure in percentage of voltage passing through the console to a transmitter or to a recording device. If 100 percent represents the maximum voltage permissible, the fluctuating VU meter can compare the sound imprint of our source to that of the maximum desired level.

Note that 100 percent corresponds to 0 volume units, also the ideal reading. Too much modulation results in an overmodulated, distorted signal; too little causes problems with signal-to-noise ratio and makes the signal sound muddy. Regardless of which scale is used, the major task facing a console operator is to keep the needle on the VU meter hovering around

monitor ⎫ internal
Cue ⎬ listening Modes Only.

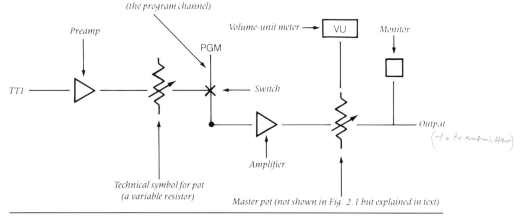

Figure 2.3 Engineering diagram of signal flow in console A.

the points marked 0 (top scale) and 100 (bottom scale). Occasional peaks into the red are acceptable–indeed, unavoidable—as are infrequent dips into the mud.

Monitor This is a loudspeaker that lets the operator hear what's going over the air. The **monitor** (or **air monitor**) is not really a part of the console, although it is connected to the console and operated by console controls. These **selection** controls allow the monitor to be used by the operator to listen to a number of sources other than what's going over the air. This is the operator's personal speaker; it has no impact on the sound going out over the air.

Amplifier Before the signal leaves the board, it must be amplified—boosted—again. The final step involves putting the signal through the **amplifier** for this purpose.

Review of Console A The signal from the turntable first passes through the preamp, an internal electrical function of the console. The volume of the preamplified signal is controlled by a pot. After the signal has run through the pot, a key functions as an on–off switch; in this case the on position is referred to as *program*. (You'll learn more about the need for this switch in the next console.) Finally, the signal is amplified again. In the case of a radio station that plays only one record, the **output** of the console is then sent to the hypothetical transmitter.

In Figure 2.3, we have diagrammed console A the way a broadcast engineer would do it.

Note

Console *A* is certainly simple to operate, and it ideally suits the needs of a station that plays just one record. But it has no flexibility. It allows only the constant repetition of a record played on the station's only turntable. You could, of course, change records, but doing so on-air would leave even larger gaps in the program than just picking up the tonearm at the end of the record and quickly placing it back at the beginning. So let's see how a more advanced console solves the problem.

Hypothetical Console *B*

The station using hypothetical console *B* has two turntables (Fig. 2.4). This allows the operator to make smooth transitions between records by having another record all set to go when one ends. This will eliminate gaps in the program, known in the trade as *dead air*.

But if the goal is to eliminate gaps, the operator must know where the starting point of the record is. There has to be a way to **cue** the record, to hear where the first sound in the piece of music starts and back the record up slightly so the sound can start immediately after the turntable is started. And as is common in many radio formats, the end of one song and the beginning of another can be overlapped for a second or two.

Console *B* is similar to console *A* but has several additions that allow the operator to eliminate gaps and overlap music.

Multiple Input Channels Having two pots allows the use of two turntables. There are two *input channels* on this console: channel 1 for turntable 1, and channel 2 for turntable 2. Turntable 1 and turntable 2 are both sources; that is, each provides an incoming signal. So, aside from the two pots, there will also be two preamps and two keys.

The Audition Channel Don't confuse the audition channel with the input channels on console *B*. The audition channel is a completely different animal.

Audition allows you to hear a record, tape, or other source without putting it over the air. The audition channel routes the signal from a source to a speaker in the control room. (And there's another specialized application, discussed in a moment.) Anything that can be put on program can be played over audition.

Do you notice, in Figure 2.4, the provision made for selecting the audition channel? The key in console *B* now has a left position for putting the signal through the **audition** channel, in addition to the program position, which was its only on position in console *A*.

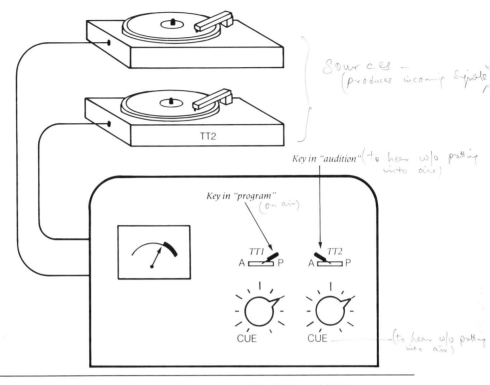

Sources –
(produces incoming signals)

Key in "audition" *(to hear w/o putting into air)*

Key in "program"
(On air)

(to hear w/o putting into air)

Figure 2.4   Console at a station that uses two turntables (TT1 and TT2).

The Cue Channel The cue channel serves one of the same purposes as the audition channel: It allows the operator to hear a source without putting it over the air. The operator of console *B* is able, using cue, to find the point at which the music begins on the records played over the station, and can therefore cue up the records to start immediately. Since cueing up a record involves some strange-sounding noise (the cueing technique is demonstrated in Chapter 3), the operator certainly doesn't want to do it over the air. The cue channel, sometimes called PFL (or Prefade Level) on newer boards, plays over a small speaker located within the console. To put the pot in cue, the operator generally turns the pot counterclockwise until the pot clicks into the cue position.

   Why, you might wonder, are there two provisions for hearing sources that are not on the air? Well, cue and audition have their separate advantages and disadvantages. Cue is very simple to use, since it takes only a flick of the wrist to put the pot in the cue channel. After cueing up a record, the operator of console *B* doesn't have to do anything until putting the

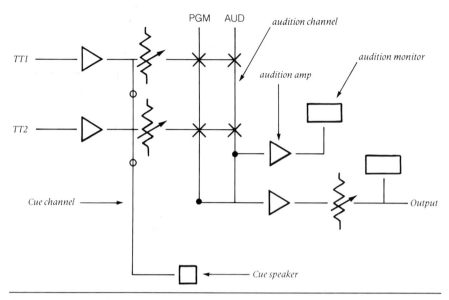

Figure 2.5   Signal flow in console *B*.

turntable on air—"potting it up," in radio lingo. But the cue speaker is often tinny and cheap, so if the operator wants to listen to a new piece of music to gauge its suitability for airplay, the cue system is a poor choice.

Audition, on the other hand, routes the signal through a high-quality loudspeaker. Sometimes it is a separate speaker in the control room, though often the audition channel is fed through the same speaker as the program. The operator uses a monitor selector switch to determine which channel— program or audition—goes to the speaker.

Audition has another very useful capability: At will, the operator can play a record over the air on the program channel while producing a commercial on the audition channel. The way this is done is explained later.

Adding the multiple-source channels, the audition channel, and the cue channel to the broadcast engineer's diagram, we have the signal flow of console *B* shown in Figure 2.5.

Review of Console *B* The outputs of two turntables are fed into console *B*; each turntable has its own source channel. Because of the two turntables, two source channels, and of course, two pots, the operator of console *B* is able to make smooth transitions between records, even overlapping the beginning of one with the end of another. More important, the operator of console *B* can use the audition or cue channel to listen to a source channel without putting it over the air.

As shown in Figure 2.5, the signal flow path for console *B* starts at the turntables, proceeds through the appropriate source channels, through the pots, and to the key. On this console, the key has the capability of putting the signal through the program channel or through the audition channel. Note, too, that the cue channel is activated by the pots, not by the key. The loudness of the signal is gauged by the VU meter, the output of the board is amplified, and the signal goes to the transmitter.

Hypothetical Console *C*

The operator of hypothetical console *C* has a microphone (Fig. 2.6) in the control room and, because of the expanded capabilities of console *B*, can put the microphone over the air and mix it with other sources. The **microphone** is on source channel 3. The abbreviation *mic,* which, of course, is pronounced "mike," is now used widely in the profession (in vendors' literature, in-station printed material, and audio and broadcasting publications). You will see newer consoles with labels "Mic 1," "Mic 2," and so on, and we have used *mic* both as noun and as adjective. However, the past and present participles, which are essential in many discussions of radio production, are spelled *miked* and *miking,* respectively. This small inconsistency represents an accommodation to ingrained habits of reading and pronunciation.

Aside from the microphone, there are some other additions on this console.

Muting System The **muting system** cuts the monitor (the loudspeaker that lets the operator know what's going over the air). The muting system is essential when a mic and a speaker are in the same room, because, without muting, the mic picks up the output of the speaker, feeds it through the amplification system, picks it up again as it exits the speaker, and so on. The result is known as **feedback,** the same unpleasant phenomenon that occurs when a rock singer gets careless with a microphone too near a speaker. So, every time the key switch on the mic channel is opened, the muting system built into the console will cut the speaker off. This, of course, makes necessary the use of the next item: headphones.

Headphones These form a close seal over the operator's ears, preventing any possibility of feedback. Because the headphones operate when the mic is open, they allow the operator to hear herself or himself speaking into the mic. There's an output for headphones on the console, and a pot that controls the headphone volume.

Note that console *C* also contains a headphone selection button. This allows the operator to hear, for example, the audition channel over the

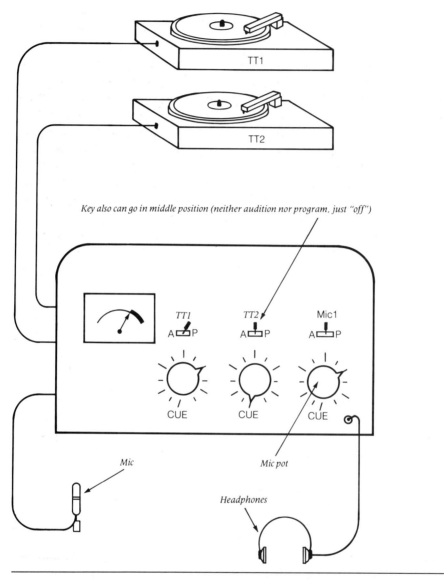

Figure 2.6   Console that could be used with two turntables and a microphone.

headphones, or the cue channel (very useful if the operator is talking over the air and finds that the next record hasn't been cued up yet).

Master Pot This pot controls the entire output of the board. Usually its proper setting is marked by the engineering staff and is not changed by the operator. The VU meter actually reads the output of the **master pot.**

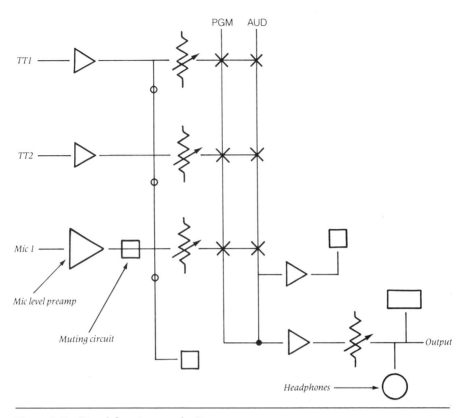

Figure 2.7   Signal flow in console C.

Review of Console C There are three paths from the equipment in the control room: the two turntables and the mic. In each path the source channel feeds through a preamp, a pot, a key, the console amplifier, and the master pot. Figure 2.7 is an engineering diagram of console C.

One bit of new information: Note that the preamp for the mic is different from the preamp for the turntables. Turntables commonly have preamps outside the console (those preamps are not shown in Fig. 2.7), and the turntable signal is brought into the board at what is known as *line level*. Other playback devices, such as tape machines, also come into the board at line level. Mics come to the board at a lower level than line-level sources, and the signal goes through a *mic-level* preamp. Because mic level is lower than line level, preamps on mic-level channels must raise the level of the signal higher than must preamps for line-level inputs. The goal of preamps, of course, is to bring both mic-level and line-level sources to the same level within the console. Turntable preamps also change the **equalization** of the audio signal; equalization is explained in connection with advanced radio production (Chapter 14).

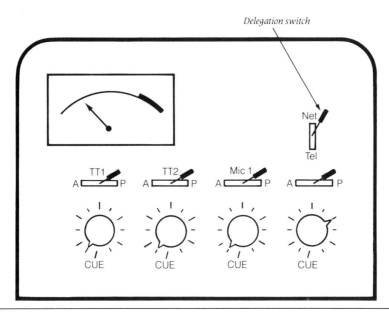

Figure 2.8   Console with a delegation switch.

Hypothetical Console *D*

The radio station using console *D* is linked up with a radio network that supplies a 5-minute newscast every hour on the hour. The network feed is brought in by a special telephone line, which the engineer has wired into the board. (These sources are often brought into the station via satellite, too.) Another program offered on the station using console *D* is a 10-minute telephone talk show, which starts at 30 minutes after the hour.

Now, it certainly doesn't make sense to have two separate pots for signals that are never used at the same time. Console *D* (Fig. 2.8) has an option that allows the operator to choose the network (Net) or the telephone (Tel). Many boards label theses signals "remote lines," because the sources are located outside the studio.

Delegation Switch   The operator has to be able to decide which signal will be chosen, or delegated, to go onto the source channel. Figure 2.9 shows how the delegation switch, which permits this, is drawn into the engineer's diagram of console *D*. The **delegation switch** is often, but not always, immediately above the pot.

Review of Console *D*   The only new addition to this console is the delegation switch, which brings a fourth input into the board. It allows the

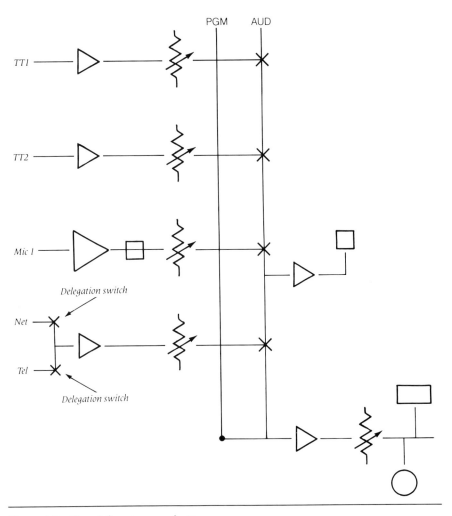

Figure 2.9   Signal flow in console D.

operator to select the signal that will go onto the source channel and be governed by the pot.

Summary of the Hypothetical Consoles

The consoles we've illustrated wouldn't be of much use in a modern radio station. Even the relatively sophisticated console D doesn't have the flexibility typically needed in a broadcast station, which may use two or more turntables, a compact disc player, three mics, two reel-to-reel tape units, and perhaps eight or nine **cartridge machines.** But the basic principles

Figure 2.10   Audio consoles.

(a) Broadcast audio console that uses slide faders. (Photo courtesy of Harris Corporation, Quincy, Ill.)

(b) Console that uses knob-style potentiometers. (Photo courtesy of Harris Corporation, Quincy, Ill.)

(c) Stereo console used at public radio station WRVO, FM 90, at State University of New York at Oswego.

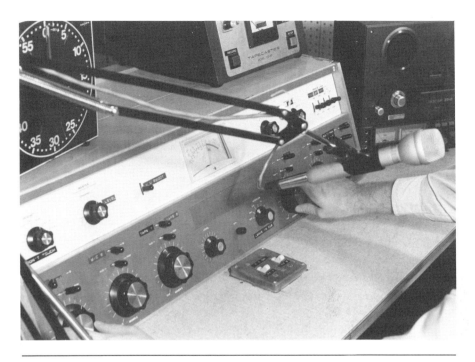

Figure 2.11   Board in use; note the labels.

illustrated are common to every console. If you understand the basic principles, you will be able to figure out the operation of any actual radio console.

▪   UNDERSTANDING   ▪
CONSOLE FUNCTION:
ACTUAL CONSOLES

The radio consoles shown and described in Figure 2.10(a), (b), and (c) allow the operator—who perhaps should now be called a producer—to choose from a large number of sources. The producer can mix the sources, route them, and put the combined product over the air or record it on tape.

Notice that the consoles pictured in Figures 2.10(b) and 2.11 have circular pots, while the consoles in Figure 2.10(a) and (c) have vertical or slide faders; both types accomplish the same purpose, utilizing the same basic principles demonstrated in the hypothetical consoles. As is apparent from the descriptions of the consoles, both units have the following elements:

‣ Preamps, which are built into the console and aren't visible.

‣ Input channels, which allow a number of signal sources to be used and, possibly, mixed together.

‣ A delegation switch, to determine which of several signals will go onto the source channel.

‣ Pots (either the traditional circular pot or the more modern vertical fader).

‣ A cue channel.

‣ A key to route the signal over either the audition channel or the program channel.

‣ A VU meter to give an objective reading on the loudness of the signal.

‣ An amplifier, which boosts the output of the console (and is not visible because it is built into the console).

‣ A master pot, which controls the output level of the console.

‣ Some miscellaneous controls, which allow the producer to adjust headset volume, choose the source feeding into the headset, or select other convenient functions. An important control is the monitor volume control, which should always be used (rather than the VU meter) when you are adjusting the level at which you choose to *listen*.

All consoles do essentially the same thing, using the principles shown with the hypothetical consoles. Think in terms of those principles, rather than using a learned-by-rote knowledge of console switches and knobs, and you'll be able to operate any board after a bit of mechanical practice.

Figure 2.11 shows a board in use at a radio station; you can see by the labels on the pots and delegation switches how many different sources are available to the operator.

There are many console types other than those pictured in Figures 2.8, 2.10, and 2.11. It is not practical to try and present a catalog of radio consoles, though. Don't get hung up on hardware. Rely on a thorough understanding of the principles of console function, and operation of almost any console will be a snap.

■ OPERATION OF THE ■
CONSOLE

The workings of your particular console will be explained to you by an instructor or an experienced operator at your radio station. Exercises at the end of this chapter will help you build your mechanical skills. Regardless of what equipment is hooked up to the console, and regardless of what kind of production is being done, you'll still be doing three basic operations through the board:

‣ Amplification
‣ Routing
‣ Mixing

All of these operations are used in the production techniques introduced in later chapters.

At this point you should primarily be concerned with finding the signals from input sources on the console, riding the **levels** properly (with the VU meter) to avoid distortion or muddiness, and understanding the signal path. The fine points of production will come later, and your performance will be enhanced with practice.

One other aspect of console operation involves the use of stereo consoles. A stereo signal, as you're probably aware, has been routed into two channels, and a stereo receiver decodes the signal and gives the impression of sound sources being located in certain positions. A station broadcasting a stereo signal uses a stereo console, as examined in Chapter 14 (Advanced Radio Production). For now, all you need to know is that, for all intents and purposes, operating a stereo console is exactly the same as operating the consoles described previously.

The next steps are to become familiar with the units that feed signals into the console: recording and playback units (Chapter 4), and microphones (Chapter 5). First, however, let's wrap up our discussion of console operation with a brief introduction to two options that extend the flexibility of the radio console: *submixing* and *patching*.

Submixing

A **submixer** is nothing more than a miniature console that combines or "gangs" a group of inputs; the output of the submixer is fed into the radio console.

An example will make it clear. Suppose you have in your studio four talk-show guests and one moderator, each with a separate mic. It might not be possible to use five separate pots, since your particular console might not have five mic-level inputs, or you might not be able to rearrange existing assignments. The solution? Plug the mics into a submixer (which has several pots and a VU meter so that each mic level can be adjusted), and run the output of the submixer (which is at line level) into your console, where it ties up only one pot.

Figure 2.12 shows a popular submixer. Submixers come in handy during remote recordings or broadcasts, as explained in later chapters.

Figure 2.12   The Electro-Voice ELX-1, a four-channel mixer that can be used to expand the capability of an audio console. (Photo courtesy of Electro-Voice, Inc., Buchanan, Mich.)

Patching

Patching allows you to route a signal in a way different from that envisaged when the board was wired together by the station's engineer.

Basically, the *patchbay* (explained in a moment) performs the same function as an old-time telephone switchboard, using connectors (plugs) to send a signal to a specific source. You, as a radio producer and console operator, will use the patchbay from time to time to make an operation easier or as a short-term emergency measure if something breaks down.

For example, let's assume that the output of a reel-to-reel tape recorder is normally connected to source channel 3 of a console. Suppose, though, that the tape recorder is broken. Suppose, too, that the only other tape recorder hooked up to the console can't be used because it's on the same pot with a turntable that is in constant use. (How? By using a delegation switch.)

The solution would be to patch the output of the working tape recorder into channel 3. This is done with a **patchcord** (Fig. 2.13(a)), which plugs into jacks on what's called the **patchbay** (Fig. 2.13(b)). Patchcords may be single- or double-pronged, depending on their intended use or configuration of the bay.

Generally, the outputs, or sources, are on the top row of the patch locations, with the inputs on the bottom. In other words, you will usually find what comes out of a unit (such as the working tape player) on the top row, labeled "Tape 2 Out" or something similar. The place where the signal can go in usually is on the bottom row, labeled something like "Channel 3 In."

Figure 2.13 Patching equipment.

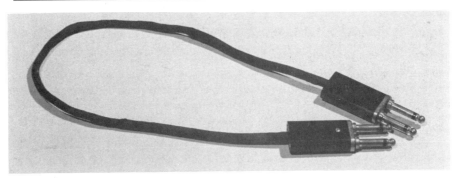

(a) Patchcord.

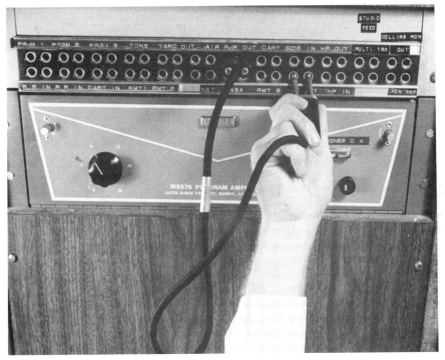

(b) Typical patchbay.

Close examination of a patchbay will reveal that the outputs and inputs that normally match up are in line vertically. Let's say that turntable 1 (TT1) normally goes into channel 2. The holes for TT1 will be directly above the holes for channel 2 on the patchbay. This, not surprisingly, is called a **normal connection.** The term is also used as a verb: TT1 *normals* *through* to channel 2. And when you change the arrangement with a patch-cord, you are *breaking normal*.

There's a special jack in the patch panel called a *multiple*. This allows you to patch one source into the multiple and plug in several patchcords that all carry the same output. That way, you can route one signal to several sources, a practice that is useful on rare occasions, such as when recording a network signal and sending it over the air simultaneously. Notice that in Figure 2.13(a), Programs 1, 2, and 3 (located on the left side of the patch-bay) feed different tape recorders.

It is a good idea always to normal a patchbay when you're finished with the studio, so that the next person doesn't inherit your special connections.

SUMMARY

All consoles perform essentially the same functions: amplification, routing, and mixing.

Among the most significant instruments and controls on the console are the potentiometers (pots), which are simply volume controls; the volume-unit (VU) meters, which give a visual representation of the strength of the signal; and the keys, which turn the pots on and off.

There are three main channels in the typical console: program, audition, and cue. Program goes over the air or to a recorder. Audition is used for private listening through a studio monitor. Cue feeds a signal through a small speaker and is used to find the beginning sounds on records and tapes.

A submixer is a miniature console that allows inputs to be ganged together before being fed into the console.

Patching allows you to reroute the normal signal flow in the console. It is useful for special operations or for emergency use of equipment not wired into the console.

All consoles, regardless of their configuration, operate in basically the same way. There is no need to be intimidated by a new console; if you learn the basics, you will able to run any board, regardless of how complex it may appear to be.

APPLICATIONS

■ **Situation 1** ■ *The Problem* A baseball game, fed from a network, was being aired, and would last until 11:30 P.M. At 10:00 P.M., a call came in from the station's general manager: A new commercial had to be made for a client, to go on the air first thing in the morning. Would the operator on duty produce the commercial?

One Possible Solution The operator on duty decided to produce the commercial, which consisted of an announcement read over a record, on the audition channel. To do so, she keyed the control-room mic and a turntable to the audition channel. She then found the audition output on the patchbay and patched Audition Out into Tape 1 In.

By producing the commercial on audition, she was able to use the same console that was sending the baseball game out on program. As an additional benefit, she was in the control room, not in a separate studio, and therefore was able to check on the game from time to time—not necessarily because she wanted to know the score, but because network feeds can and do run into technical problems, and an inattentive operator can put a half-hour of static over the air. Most boards have separate VU meters for audition and program.

■ **Situation 2** ■ *The Problem* The pot on channel 3 caused a crackling static noise every time it was adjusted. (This happens from time to time, often because the internal workings of the pot are shorted or badly in need of cleaning.) The pot on channel 3 controlled the turntable, and since the operator was in the midst of a record show, the problem was becoming critical.

One Possible Solution Before using the turntable, the operator simply patched the output of the turntable into a different channel, breaking the normal. Now, the turntable would be governed by a different pot and key until repairs could be made to the console. The operator also left a note for the next board operator, explaining the patch.

EXERCISES

1. Perform a combo operation (operate the console and announce) with two records and a mic. The goal is not clean production, just board operation. Start one record, and place the tonearm on the other record. (Don't worry about hitting a specific point in the music; that's cueing, discussed in the next chapter.) Start the second record after the first one ends, potting it up on the console. Try talking over the music, making what you think is a proper balance between voice and music. Do the typical disc jockey routine: Announce the name of the song just played, introduce the next song, start the turntable, and bring it up on the board.

2. Make out a slip of paper with the name of each piece of equipment hooked to the console in your radio production studio or lab—for example, Turntable 1, Mic 2, Cart 1, Turntable 2. Toss the slips of paper into a hat.

   Put records on the turntables and put tapes on the reel-to-reel and cartridge (cart) machines. Have someone standing by the mic(s). Your instructor or lab assistant will draw slips of paper out of the hat and announce the name of the piece of equipment.

   Your assignment is to quickly start the piece of equipment and pot it up on the board. There may be more than one source called up at the same time. When a mic is called out, you—the operator—are responsible for *throwing a cue* to the person stationed at the mic; that is, you point to him or her sharply. This is the standard instruction to begin speaking.

   When your instructor calls out "Lose it," you must pot down what's up on the board and then turn that piece of equipment off. Give the person at the mic a *cut signal* by drawing a finger across your throat. (Some of the more common visual signals used in radio are discussed in Chapter 7.)

   This drill may seem a little like boot camp; in fact, it is pretty much the same approach used to teach soldiers operation of equipment or assembly of weapons. You'll find, though, that trying to locate pots and equipment under this kind of pressure is a very effective way to learn the operation.

3. Draw a diagram, in the same form as the engineer's diagrams shown in this chapter, of the console in your studio or radio production lab. Don't worry about the details; just try to include the channels and label the sources and delegation switches.

·3·

Turntables

and CD Players

I n the preceding chapter, we spoke about the way an audio signal is routed through a console; we touched only briefly on the sources that produce that signal.

Chapters 3 and 4 describe all the sources you're likely to encounter in a modern radio station (except for microphones, which are dealt with in Chapter 5). Turntables and compact disc players are the subject of this chapter. Chapter 4 deals with tape recording and playback units. Learning specifics of the function and operation of record and playback units will prove to be of great value during actual production.

▪ STRUCTURE OF ▪ A TURNTABLE

A turntable operates in the same way as a record player, except that it's a heavier-duty device and uses a different type of mechanism to turn the record.

Now, to clear up some questions of terminology. In radio parlance, the turntable is never referred to as a "record player." And a phonograph record, more often than not, is called a **disc.** From now on, we'll use the terms *turntable* and *disc.*

The broadcast turntable pictured in Figure 3.1(a) has several components. And although some minor operational and cosmetic differences exist among various turntable models, all work in basically the same fashion.

Figure 3.1   Turntable and components.

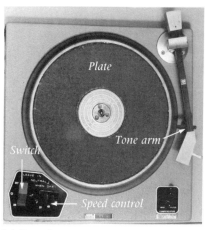

(a) Overview.

(b) Switch and speed control for Technics SP-15 turntable.

(d) Tonearm.

The Plate

The disc is placed on the **plate;** this is the part of the turntable that actually turns around.

(c) Drive mechanism. The rubber wheel
    (with pencil pointing toward it)
    turns on the inside rim of the plate.

(e) Cartridge and stylus.

The Switch

The *switch*, also known as the *start switch*, is a smooth-action, noiseless switch (Fig. 3.1(b)) that turns the turntable on and off. It's noiseless because you don't want a click while the mic is open.

The Speed Control

The speed control on some turntables resembles the gear shift in a manual transmission auto. On the unit shown in Figure 3.1(b), the operator can select from among speeds of $33\frac{1}{3}$, 45, and 78 rpm (revolutions per minute) by merely pressing one of three buttons. The 12-inch discs play at $33\frac{1}{3}$ (sometimes shortened to read "33" on turntable settings), while the smaller discs with the large holes play at 45 rpm. Although 78-rpm records aren't made any more, many turntable units retain the option of playing that speed. On some models (particularly older models), there is a neutral position, too, which allows the motor to idle out of gear.

The Drive Mechanism

What the gear shift controls (in the illustrated unit—some are driven by other means) is a rubber **drive wheel,** which makes contact with a rim on the inside of the plate. We've removed the plate (Fig. 3.1(c)) to show you the rubber drive wheel. If your turntable operates with a drive wheel like the one pictured, it's important that you leave the turntable speed control in the neutral position when the unit won't be in operation for a long time; otherwise, the drive wheel can be flattened.

Some newer broadcast turntables are known as direct-drive turntables; that is, the motor drives the plate directly. With these turntables there is no neutral position, and speed change is accomplished electronically.

The Tonearm

The **tonearm** (Fig. 3.1(d)) is the movable device that is put onto the disc. At the end of the tonearm are the **stylus** and the **cartridge.** The stylus (Fig. 3.1(e)) is usually a pointed piece of diamond; some people call it a needle, but it really isn't one. The stylus is attached to a strip of metal called a *cantilever,* which in turn is attached to the cartridge (Fig. 3.1(e)). The cartridge translates the physical vibration of the stylus into an electrical signal. The process of changing one form of energy into another is called *transduction. Transducing* is a very important concept, and we'll refer to it many times in this text.

▪   THE DISC   ▪

Where do the vibrations picked up by the stylus come from? They're impressed into the grooves on the disc. The vibrations cut into the grooves correspond to variations in the sound that was recorded.

Actually, the vibration patterns are pressed into the **grooves** of the disc. At the beginning of the manufacturing process, the master disc is cut with a stylus, which is connected to the output of a tape machine. When the master disc is cut, an electrical signal is transduced into a physical vibration.

You'll notice that there are gaps between the *cuts,* or individual pieces of music, on the disc; these separating grooves (and the groove at the beginning of the disc) carry no sound. They are called *lead grooves.*

During operation of the turntable, you will want to place a disc on the plate, place the stylus at the beginning of the cut you select, and position the disc so that the beginning of the music will start immediately, or at least within a second or so of your starting the turntable. Positioning the disc, as noted earlier, is called *cueing.* Handling discs and cueing them up are very common tasks in radio production, and there's a proper way to do both.

Handling Discs

Putting your fingers on the grooves of the disc will coat the grooves with oil; worse, the stylus may pick up that oil, causing the sound quality of the playback to deteriorate. You can avoid this problem by handling the disc as shown in Figure 3.2(a). To turn the disc over, hold the edges of the disc with the palms of your hands and flip it, as shown in Figure 3.2(b) and (c).

These ways of handling discs may seem awkward at first, but with practice you'll find that they become second nature. Unfortunately, you will see some pretty careless handling of discs at many radio stations. But although you can sometimes get away with handling a disc by the grooves, it's just as easy to do things right from the beginning. Incidentally, another good habit to get into is to use commercially available disc-washing machines and hand-held dust and static removers frequently. Clean, static-free discs produce much better audio quality.

Cueing a Disc

The first step in cueing a disc is to select the cut you wish to play and place the stylus in the lead groove (the gap preceding the cut). If the cut you wish to play is the first on the disc, place the stylus at the beginning groove.

All cueing operations involve a **backtracking** of the disc. You will spin the record (and/or the plate, as explained in a moment) backward and forward until you've pinpointed the spot where the sound starts. Don't be squeamish about backtracking a disc; the stylus of a broadcast turntable won't damage the grooves.

There are three methods of cueing a disc: spinning the plate, spinning the disc, and slipcueing.

Figure 3.2 Handling discs.

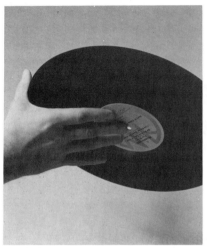

(a) Holding the disc in this manner prevents the oil on your hands from contaminating the grooves.

(b) You can observe both sides of the disc by holding the edges with your palms . . .

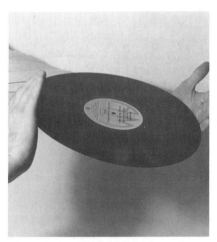

(c) . . . and turning it in the manner shown. This way you won't touch the grooves.

Spinning the Plate Put the turntable speed control into neutral. This will enable the heavy metal plate to spin freely. Start the plate spinning with your hand (Fig. 3.3(a)); you should try to spin it at approximately the same speed at which it normally runs. The plate is heavy and will keep up to speed for a surprising amount of time.

Drop the stylus in the beginning or separating grooves, and let the disc turn until the sound begins. (Remember to use the cue or audition channel of the console; you don't want the cueing noises to go out over the air.) Then stop the motion of the disc with your hand, and move the plate in the opposite direction, backtracking the disc. By rocking the disc clockwise and counterclockwise, you'll be able to pinpoint the exact spot where the sound begins. Be careful not to nudge the tonearm.

With the stylus over the exact point where the sound begins, move the plate counterclockwise one-eighth to one-fourth of a turn. Backtracking the plate and the disc will give the turntable time to get up to speed before the cut begins. If the turntable can't get up to speed before the sound starts, there will be an objectionable noise known as a **wow**.

Figure 3.3(b) and (c) review the sequence of cueing a record. For the sake of illustration, we've placed an arrow (the large white one) on a disc to show the point at which the sound begins. (Be careful to keep your hand away from the tonearm while backtracking, or you may accidentally bump the arm and knock the stylus out of the groove.)

Keep in mind that the amount of backtracking you'll have to do to allow the turntable to get up to speed varies with the turntable. Some older models may need a full quarter-turn to get up to speed, while modern models usually need only an eighth of a turn. The correct amount of backtracking depends on how quickly a particular turntable gets up to speed. Some models require as much as a third of a turn.

In any event, after you've pinpointed the sound and backtracked the disc by spinning the plate, make sure the motor is off and put the speed selector in the proper gear. Now you're all set to start the disc by turning on the switch and potting the proper channel up on the board.

Spinning the Disc The piece of hard rubber or (on very old turntables) felt covering the turntable plate provides just the right amount of friction. This material holds the disc in place as the plate spins, but also allows the operator to spin the disc separately from the plate.

To cue up by spinning the disc, leave the speed selector in gear; this way, the plate won't spin freely. Drop the stylus into the groove preceding the cut you want to play. Then, placing your finger on the label as shown in

Figure 3.3   Cueing by spinning the plate.

(a) Set the plate spinning with
    your hand.

(b) Rock back and forth until you
    locate the first sound
    (indicated by the white arrow).

(c) Then backtrack the plate a
    quarter-turn, and put the speed
    selector into gear.

Figure 3.5 Slipcueing.

(a) The plate is spinning, but the disc is being held in place.

(b) The disc is released.

▪ REVIEW OF ▪
TURNTABLE
OPERATION

The turntable is a heavy-duty version of a record player. It's almost always called a *turntable* (rather than a *record player*), and records are more commonly called *discs*. The parts of the turntable are the plate, the switch, the drive mechanism, the tonearm, the stylus, and the cartridge.

Figure 3.6   EMT 948 turntable. (Photo courtesy of Gotham
                 Audio Corporation, New York City.)

All turntables have the same basic components, and although various
models are manufactured (such as those pictured in Figures 3.6 and 3.7,
they all have the same basic principles of operation.

Turntable cartridges operate on the principle of transduction, whereby
one form of energy is changed into another. In this case, vibrational energy
picked up by the stylus vibrating in the grooves is changed—in the cartridge—to electrical energy. The principle of transduction surfaces again
and again in radio production, so it's a good idea to be familiar with it.

The discs themselves require some care in handling, to avoid getting skin
oil on the grooves. There are three methods of cueing: spinning the plate,
spinning the disc, and slipcueing.

Figure 3.7 Technics Turntable System SL-B210. (Photo
courtesy of Panasonic Company, Secaucus, N.J.)

■   COMPACT DISCS   ■

Compact discs, virtually a novelty item when the first edition of this book
was published in 1986, have become standard in radio. Indeed, a station
without one or two compact disc (CD) players is the exception, not the
rule, in today's radio marketplace.

The compact disc (Figure 3.8(a)) comes in two sizes (both less than 5
inches in diameter) and is made of plastic; the CD resembles a traditional
vinyl disc. The information on the CD is read by a laser beam contained
in a special CD player (Figure 3.8(b)).

Unlike a vinyl record, a CD does not have grooves. And because the disc
itself is not touched physically by a stylus, it is less subject to wear than a
standard phonograph record.

But there is another, more profound difference between the conventional
phonograph record and the CD. The phonograph record is an **analog** recording, whereas the CD is a **digital** recording.

The word *analog* means something that shows a resemblance or simi-
larity to something else; it is the root of the words *analogy* and *analogous.*
In the case of analog recording, it means to produce a series of sound waves
that closely resemble the sound waves of the original signal. We use the
term *analog recording* to refer to any of the conventional transduction
techniques involving audio tape or vinyl records.

Digital recording means using samples of sound to produce a recording
that is stored in computer language—the on-or-off binary code of digital
technology. The exact method by which sounds are transduced into digital

Figure 3.8   Elements of a compact disc system.

(a) Compact disc.   (b) Compact disc player.

information is not particularly relevant to radio production work (nor is it readily understandable), but the following basic points are important:

1. Digital recordings are actually composed of numerically transcribed samples of the original sounds, so in engineering terms the digital recording is a collection of samples of sound and not an analog of sound. Hence the difference in word usage (although a case could be made that the digital version is obviously a representation of a sound, too).

   These samples are taken with great rapidity. In most cases, digitally processed information is sampled at ranges in the vicinity of 40,000 samples per second; this is the **sampling frequency** and is expressed in units called *hertz* (cycles per second, abbreviated *Hz*). One of the sampling frequencies typically used, then, would be expressed as 44.1 kHz. (*kHz* stands for *kiloHertz*, which is a unit of 1,000 cycles per second). Samples are then coded into the binary digits that give digital recording its name.

2. Digital recording produces a cleaner-sounding signal. Very little (if any) extraneous noise is introduced into the system during digital recording and playback—no tape hiss, no scratching of a stylus in worn grooves.

3. The cleaner technology produces a different sound than does analog; many listeners characterize it as "clearer," and unquestionably noise is reduced. Some listeners, however, claim not to like the digital sound as much as (or better than) analog. Many maintain that it is too harsh, too mechanical, or too unnatural.

   In any event, the entire concept of a natural sound is difficult to define. The natural sound of a concert hall, for example, almost always involves some peculiarities of room acoustics, unintended echoes, and various background noises of seat shuffling and coughing. A recording that

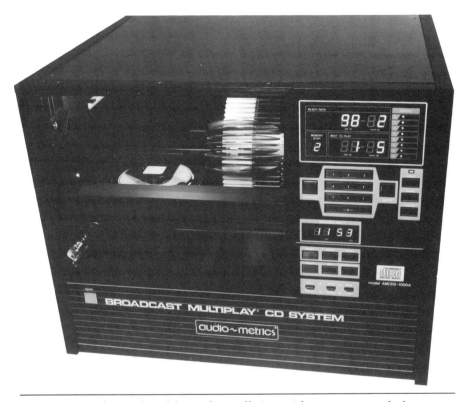

Figure 3.9   Professional model CD player offering quick access to any of a large
number of recordings. (Photo courtesy of Allied Broadcast Equipment,
Richmond, Ind.)

omits these sounds can hardly be faulted for being unnatural, so we can
assume that the goal of audio is not always to reproduce with total
realism whatever sounds were originally made.

The preceding factors have contributed to an explosion of compact disc
use in radio. Despite the fact that the CD is only one link in the audio
chain (since the signal still must pass through many analog devices), listeners feel that the CD sound is superior, and many radio stations have
converted entirely to CD playing.

At their present stage of development, CDs seem well suited, but perhaps
not perfectly suited, to broadcast operations. On the plus side, they do not
wear out or suffer damage as easily as does standard vinyl. They can also
be convenient to use and to automate. Professional-quality compact disc
players, such as the model pictured in Figure 3.9, can store many discs with

virtually instantaneous access to any cut on any disc. This makes CDs an excellent choice for automation applications or in situations where partial automation is used to assist the on-air operator.

Moreover, CDs provide what listeners seem to want in audio quality. Many stations advertise themselves as being "all-CD," and ratings reflect the all-CD format's initial success in the so-called fidelity wars.

Ironically, that advantage can also work against a station using CDs. Many program directors feel that airing a portion of the station's music from CDs causes the remaining analog fare to suffer badly by comparison. This was a more vexing problem when CD offerings were limited; today, full music libraries are available on CD.

Another problem with CD technology is that the discs can be used for playback only. While efforts are underway to develop a simple, inexpensive, and commercially practical method to record on CD, such a development does not appear imminent at the time of this writing (mid-1989).

Difficulty in handling CDs was initially viewed as a drawback to the advancing technology, but that perception is changing as the hardware becomes more thoroughly established and refined, and as production and air staff become more accustomed to handling the CDs. Most experts maintain that the majority of CD "crashes" have been due to poor handling by production personnel. Despite initial claims to the contrary, CDs are not immune to damage; surface scratches can badly impair playback, and damage to the disc can result in poor audio quality, skipping, or shutdown of the playback.

CD playback is generally quite simple. You insert the disc into a mechanized drawer, which closes automatically and brings the disc into position for playback. The laser-reader works in reverse of a typical stylus, reading the disc from the inside out toward the edge. CDs, like standard LPs, have several cuts, and a selector on the machine allows you to pick the cut you want to play (selection number 3, for example). Unlike standard records, CDs have information only on one side, but that one side can hold up to an hour of program material.

When CDs are automated, the cut numbers are programmed into the computer. Methods of programming range from a simple computer instruction to play at random without repeating any cuts for a certain time, to complete program control, cut by cut and hour by hour.

Many knowledgeable observers expect that compact disc players will eventually replace the turntable in all or almost all radio-station control rooms. Alternatives to using a control-room CD player are emerging, however, and one of these options is to use digital audiotape (discussed at the end of the next chapter).

SUMMARY

A broadcast turntable consists of the plate, switch, speed control, drive mechanism, and tonearm. The tonearm has a stylus and a cartridge on the end. The stylus picks up vibrations from the grooves in the disc, and the vibrations are transduced into audio.

A compact disc employs a laser beam in place of a mechanical stylus. The laser reads sound information encoded digitally on the compact disc.

Cueing is the procedure by which a standard vinyl disc is positioned so that the recording starts precisely on time. There are three basic methods of cueing: spinning the plate, spinning the disc, and slipcueing (slipstarting).

Compact discs are cued electronically, often by computer. Computerized control units can be programmed to play a long sequence of CD cuts; the CD player is capable of locating a particular selection almost instantaneously.

Compact discs offer more nearly distortion-free sound reproduction than do standard discs, and they are less subject to wear. CDs, though, are not indestructible; they do wear eventually.

APPLICATIONS

▪ **Situation 1** ▪ *The Problem* A producer at a rock station was putting together a commercial that called for very tight meshing of musical elements. The station format involved fast-paced, extremely closely packed sound elements. Backtracking the disc and potting it up on the board resulted in a tiny, but noticeable gap in the sound.

One Possible Solution The producer decided to slipcue the musical elements. By identifying the first sound of the music selection desired, backtracking ever so slightly, and hot-potting the cut, she was able to make a very tight production.

▪ **Situation 2** ▪ *The Problem* The producer of a spot wanted to use a lyric from a popular song. Unfortunately, there was an instrumental introduction leading directly into the beginning of the lyric. The spot really needed that lyric, but the 10-second instrumental before the lyric wasn't appropriate.

One Possible Solution The producer elected to use a combination of slipcueing and potting up. She made a very tight backtrack before the beginning of the vocal and kept the turntable motor running. She did not, however, choose to hot-pot. Instead, she released the disc and very quickly potted up. By using this method, she avoided the slight wow that can be heard when slipcueing (starting) a record if there is audio in the grooves.

After a few practice runs, she was able to coordinate the slipcue and the quick pot-up so that the vocal seemed to start cold, with no wow and only the briefest (almost unnoticeable) portion of the instrumental lead-in.

EXERCISES

1. This exercise is strictly a matter of practicing some mechanical movements. It may seem a bit tedious, but practicing some of the basic movements will make the more complex operations much easier.

    The movements to practice are:

    ‣ Dropping the stylus into the lead grooves on a disc. Keep trying until you can hit all the grooves on an entire side without picking up any of the music.

    ‣ Handling discs as shown in Figure 3.2.

2. Using three discs, go from one piece of music to another, and then to another. (With two turntables, obviously, you'll have to change one disc.) Play each disc for 10 or 20 seconds; then fade it down and bring up another.

    The trick to the exercise is this: Cue each disc by a different means (if, of course, your equipment allows). Cue up the first disc by spinning the plate. After you start the first disc (and put the output of that turntable in program) cue up the second disc by spinning the disc. While that's playing, cue up the third disc and slipcue it.

3. **Cross-fade** from a vocal to an instrumental; choose an instrumental cut that has a definite ending (rather than just a fade-out). Make the resulting segment exactly 5 minutes long. To do this, of course, you will have to backtime and dead-pot the instrumental.

$\cdot 4 \cdot$

Tape Recording
and Playback
Units

Most material in radio today is prerecorded. Discs, obviously, provide the vast majority of music. A disc, though, can't be used to record material during production. It might interest you to know, however, that, as late as the 1950s, many radio stations had disc-cutting machines just for this purpose.

Cutting discs was impractical because discs are useful primarily for permanent storage of sound. The need for a convenient way to record material that might be used only once or a few times, with further changes possible after recording, led to the development of *audiotape*.

Audiotape is often called **magnetic tape** because its magnetic properties allow the storage of sound. Actually, sound isn't stored on the tape. Sound energy is first transduced into electrical energy, and that electrical energy is then transduced into magnetic form. To understand this process, let's start by examining how the tape itself works. Then we'll discuss the machines that record and play back the tape.

■ MAGNETIC TAPE ■

Audiotape is a strip of material with a thin coating of **iron oxide** (a fancy name for rust) on one surface. The iron oxide particles line up when they are exposed to an **electromagnetic field** (more on that in a moment) and are the elements that hold the magnetic information.

The backing of the tape—the material over which the coating is applied—is made of **acetate** or **mylar.** Acetate is similar in composition to Scotch

Figure 4.1   Reels in $10\frac{1}{2}$-, 7-, and 5-inch sizes.

tape. It is somewhat brittle and can be snapped easily. Mylar is a resilient, extremely tough substance that will stretch before it breaks. This isn't necessarily an advantage, because a snapped tape can be repaired, whereas a stretched tape can't.

The most commonly used tape in radio is $\frac{1}{4}$ inch wide, although there are different sizes for specialized applications. The most common sizes of reels for broadcast use are 5, 7 and $10\frac{1}{2}$ inches (Fig. 4.1). The larger reels need a special kind of hub arrangement to hold them on the tape machine.

■   WORKINGS OF THE   ■
REEL-TO-REEL TAPE
MACHINE

The process of magnetic tape recording happens when a tape passes by an electromagnet, which arranges the pattern of magnetism in the particles to correspond to that of the sound message being fed into the recorder.

A device called a **head** is the electromagnet in the tape machine. The heads in a typical tape recorder perform three functions, but before describing them, let's see where the heads are and how the tape is brought into contact with them.

Figure 4.2 is a simplified diagram of a reel-to-reel tape machine. All reel-to-reel tape machines, regardless of their design differences, operate in pretty much the same way. Notice how the units pictured in Figure 4.3(a) and (b) have the same basic anatomy.

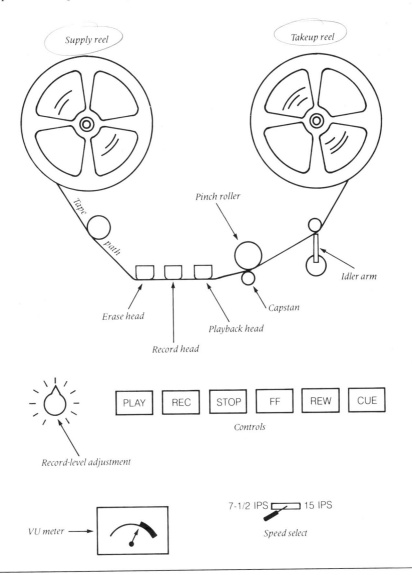

Figure 4.2 The tape path in a typical tape recorder. The control buttons are identified on pages 58–59.

Basically, the tape machine draws the tape from the left reel to the right reel. The technical names of the left and right components, respectively, are **supply reel** and **takeup reel**. As tape passes from the supply reel to the takeup reel, it is drawn across the heads, where a signal is implanted on the tape or played back from the tape. We'll start with an explanation of the heads, and then move on to the tape transport system.

Figure 4.3   Two varieties of reel-to-reel tape recorder.

(a) Reel-to-reel tape recorder that will accept up to $10\frac{1}{2}$-inch reels. (Photo courtesy of TASCAM, TEAC Professional Division, Montebello, Calif.)

(b) This tape recorder is frequently used in broadcast operations.

The Heads

Figure 4.4 shows the heads on a tape machine. The heads perform three distinct functions: *erase, record,* and *play*. They work as follows:

▸ The **erase head** produces a magnetic field, called a **flux,** that scrambles the pattern of the iron oxide particles and obliterates any information previously stored on them.

▸ The **record head** produces a magnetic field that arranges the iron oxide particles in a particular order, storing the information on the tape.

▸ The **playback head** reads the patterns formed by the arrangement of the iron oxide particles and produces an electrical signal carrying the sound information.

The heads are always arranged in this order (from left to right): erase, record, playback. If you're ever stumped when trying to identify a head (you'll need to know the location of the heads during tape editing), try to think the problem out logically. Erase *must* come first; if the erase head were second in line, you'd erase whatever had just been recorded on the tape. And it makes sense to have the record head in the second position because this allows the tape to pass over the playback head, which is in the third position. Since the tape passes the record head immediately before

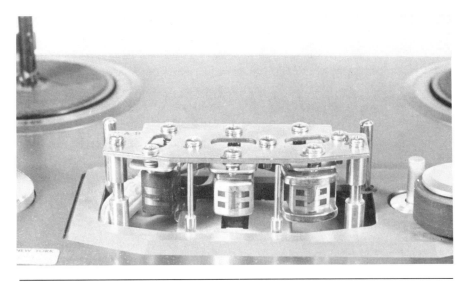

Figure 4.4 Heads of a typical tape recorder. Left to right: the
erase head, the record head, and the playback head.

the playback head, the operator of the tape machine can play back what
was just recorded to make sure that there is, indeed, a recording on the
tape. You wouldn't have this option if the positions of the record and
playback heads were reversed.

Remember: erase, record, playback. And if you can't recall the logical
explanation of their order, just remember that they spell *ERP*.

Now, to throw you a curve: In some machines, there are only two heads:
an erase head and a combination record/playback head. For purposes of
radio production, all you have to remember is that erase comes before
record/playback. Cartridge machines, as you'll see in a moment, have only
record and play heads; that's why the cartridge must be bulk-erased, as
shown on page 66.

The Tape Transport Mechanism

Regardless of the difference among models, the goal of all tape machines
is the same: to pass a tape across the heads at a constant rate of speed. For
the layout of the tape transport mechanism, refer to Figure 4.2. Here's what
the components of the drive mechanism do:

▸ The supply reel contains the tape that will be drawn across the heads.

▸ The takeup reel draws the tape up after it passes across the heads.

‣ The **tape guides** are precision-designed to keep the tape exactly in position.

‣ The **capstan** is a revolving metal post that determines the speed of the tape's movement. It turns the next piece of equipment—the pinch roller.

‣ The tape passes between the **pinch roller,** which is made of rubber, and the capstan, and is pulled along at the proper speed. The capstan and the pinch roller keep the tape moving at a constant speed; they are connected to the feed and takeup reels through a series of clutches.

‣ The tape idler arm (a feature on most larger tape machines) drops down if the tape breaks; when the idler drops, it shuts down the tape machine's drive mechanism. This prevents tape from spilling out onto the floor if there's a break, and it also shuts down the drive mechanism when the tape runs completely off either reel.

Tape Machine Controls and Indicators

Although the style of levers and buttons differs from machine to machine, the controls and indicators perform typical functions (see Fig. 4.2).

Play Depressing the Play button (or, in some units, flicking a lever) will cause the machine to play back the recording on the tape. The tape moves from the supply reel, across the heads, to the pickup reel. The erase and record heads don't operate when the machine is in play.

Record (Rec) Usually, Record is a button that is pushed along with the Play control. When Record is activated, the record head impresses a signal on the iron oxide particles on the tape; this is the signal that can be read back by the play head. When the machine is in Record mode, the erase head is also activated; there would be no point in recording if the previous information (if any) on the tape were not removed.

Volume-Unit (VU) Meter Like the meter on the console, the tape machine's VU meter monitors the signal coming into the tape machine so that proper levels can be maintained when recording. There are also separate controls on the tape machine to govern the level of the incoming signal. It is very important to maintain a proper level on this meter.

Fast-forward (FF) The FF control moves the tape forward (in the same direction as Play) at a high rate of speed. In some units, the Fast-forward control brings the tape into contact with the heads, and you'll hear the chattering of the fast-moving tape. Other machines, though, lift the tape away from the heads, so you have to use Cue if you want to hear the sounds of the tape.

Cue The Cue control brings the tape into contact with the heads by defeating the tape lifter; it allows you to cue the tape when it's moving in Fast-forward or in Rewind. On some machines, the Cue control is also used if the operator wants to hear the sounds on the tape when moving the reels by hand (as when editing tape).

Rewind (Rew) Activating the Rewind control causes the tape to move backward—that is, from the takeup reel to the supply reel.

Stop Pressing Stop brings the motion of the reels to a halt.

Speed Select This control governs how quickly the tape moves past the heads. The most frequently used speeds on broadcast reel-to-reel tape machines are $7\frac{1}{2}$ and 15 inches per second (IPS); that is, $7\frac{1}{2}$ (or 15) inches of tape is driven past a given point per second. A seldom-used but sometimes available speed is $3\frac{3}{4}$ IPS. Note that each speed is exactly double or half the previous speed.

▪   CUEING A TAPE   ▪

Just as in the case of discs and turntables, you'll need to know where the sound information on a tape begins so that you can put it out over the air or use it in studio production. Say, for instance, that you have a recording of an interview show. You might thread the tape and fast-forward it with the Cue control on (although some machines play sound in Fast-forward without using a Cue control) until you hear the chattering of sound on the tape—over the console's cue speaker, of course! Then, you would rewind it to the approximate point at which the sound started, stop the tape machine, and rock the reels by hand until you hear the beginning in cue.

Usually, there'll be a countdown or cue tone on prerecorded tapes to help the operator in cueing. For instance, the interview show might start with the host saying: "Meet the Community Program for air Sunday, March 17, rolling in five, four, three, two, one, Good afternoon, welcome to . . . ."

With experience, you'll learn to listen to the countdown on cue, stop the tape machine after "one," and be set to put the program on air.

You can also use leader tape to cue. Leader tape, which is described fully in Chapter 6, can be inserted within the tape and used as a visual cue to make the cueing job easier.

▪   HEADS AND TRACKS   ▪

Now that we've covered the manner in which the heads impress a signal on the audio tape, let's look at a technical detail that can be confusing.

A tape machine's heads place the signal on a specific location on the tape, a strip called a **track**. It is a function of recorder/player configuration, not a property of the tape itself. Many tape machines place the signal across the entire width of the tape; sensibly, this is called a **full-track** recording (Fig. 4.5(a)).

Some machines, however, record on only half the track, as pictured in Figure 4.5(b). This allows a stereo signal to be recorded on the tape, as explained in later chapters. A **half-track** recording is also known as **two-track**. Another type of recording is **quarter-track** (Fig. 4.5(c)). The quarter-track reel-to-reel system can be used to record stereo. Two of the stereo tracks would be recorded with the tape moving in one direction (tracks 1 and 3), and two would be recorded going in the other direction (tracks 2 and 4). This track system is not commonly used in radio. Cassettes have a four-track configuration that allows for either mono or stereo playback of a cassette tape.

How Tracks Work

Each track is placed onto the tape by means of a separate head. However, multiple heads can be situated on the same structure. The element that actually puts the signal on the tape is a tiny rectangle on the structure that holds the head. When there's more than one head, the structure holding them is called a **headstack**.

Machines may contain up to thirty-two heads on a stack, but these are not commonly used for general radio production. Applications for multi-track recording in radio are considered in Chapter 14.

Why There Are Different Head Mechanisms

The varied types of track arrangement give different options to the producer. In the case of half-track, the producer has the ability to record a **stereo** signal or a **monaural** signal on both tracks. (As you probably know, a monaural signal is not separated into components. For now, don't worry about the fine points of monaural and stereo.)

The version of quarter-track recording shown in Figure 4.5(d) is generally used on cassette machines (Fig. 4.6). **Cassettes** have some use in radio broadcasting, and are briefly discussed later in this chapter.

Machines using more than four tracks operate with tape wider than $\frac{1}{4}$ inch; they generally are used for recording original music.

Figure 4.5   Tape recording track configurations.

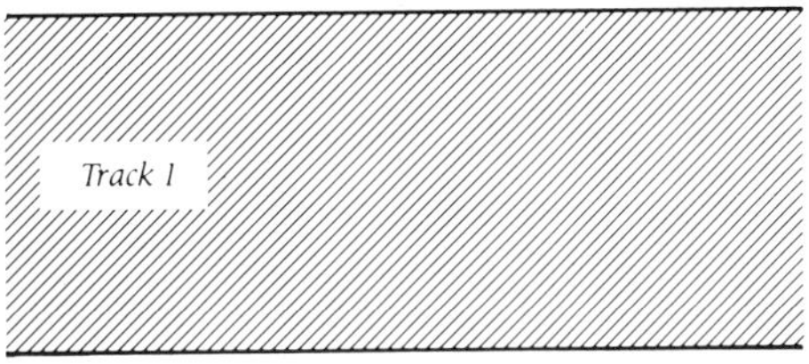

(a) Full-track recording.

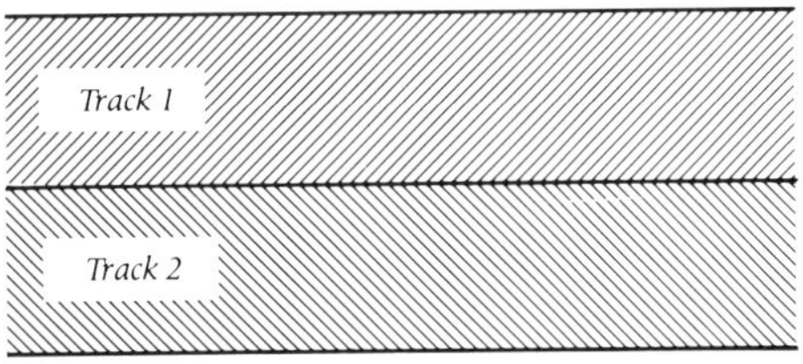

Track 1

(b) Half-track (or two-track) recording.

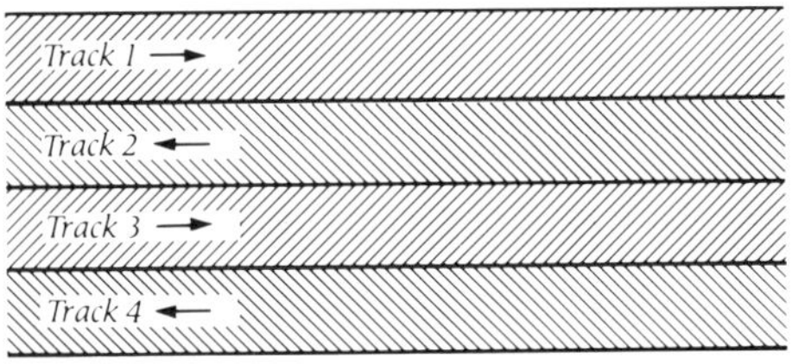

Track 1

Track 2

(c) Quarter-track reel-to-reel recording.

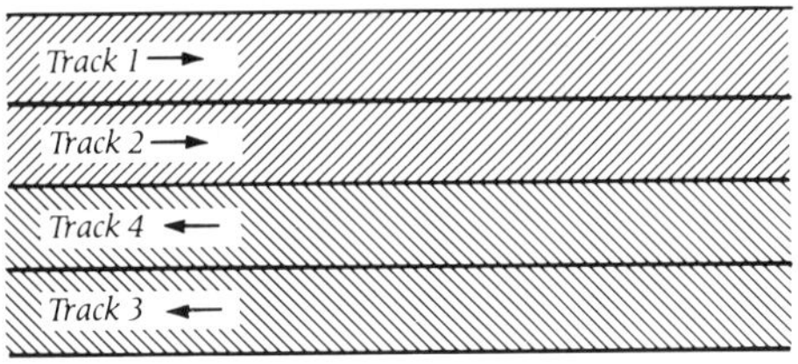

Track 1 ⟶
Track 2 ⟵
Track 3 ⟶
Track 4 ⟵

(d) Quarter-track cassette recording.

Track 1 ⟶
Track 2 ⟶
Track 4 ⟵
Track 3 ⟵

Regardless of the track system, the basic operating principles remain the same, so the difference in track formats shouldn't present a problem. The only point that can foul you up is this: A tape recorded on only one track of a two-track format will lose quality when played back on a full-track machine, because the full-track head will be playing back half a track that contains nothing except hiss and other electrical noise. Likewise, a quarter-track tape cannot be played back on a half-track machine without the audience's hearing information played forward and backward simultaneously. So always strive to play back tapes on a machine that has the same track arrangement as the machine on which they were recorded.

Figure 4.6   Broadcast-quality cassette recorder. (Photo courtesy of
TASCAM, TEAC Professional Division, Montebello, Calif.)

Review of Reel-to-Reel Tape Machines

The purpose of a reel-to-reel tape machine is to pass audiotape, also known
as magnetic tape, over the heads. The heads are tiny electromagnets that
erase, record, and play. Erasing, recording, and playing are always performed by the heads in that order, although the record and play heads are
sometimes combined.

   The erase head scrambles the alignment of iron oxide particles on the
audiotape. Those particles are realigned by the record head.

▪   CASSETTE MACHINES   ▪

Cassette record and playback units are highly portable, which is why such
devices have come into such common use in radio newsrooms. The size of
the tape, however, limits its usefulness in other areas of radio production.
Smaller tape size (and therefore a smaller area of the track) yields a recording of lower quality. A slower recording speed ($1\frac{7}{8}$ IPS) also detracts
from sound quality. Noise reduction devices such as Dolby are used to
counteract these problems, as discussed in Chapter 14. Another problem
with cassette machines, at least from the standpoint of radio production,
is that the tape is difficult to edit mechanically. Most news operations dub
cassettes up to $\frac{1}{4}$ inch for editing.

   Some newer units operate differently from the standard cassette machine
and are, in some cases, used for playback of music over the air.

■   CARTRIDGE MACHINES   ■

While reel-to-reel tape provides high quality, it has some drawbacks. For one thing, it's time-consuming to thread up a reel of tape and find the cue. Reels of tape are somewhat cumbersome to handle. Cartridge machines were developed as a solution to this problem. They utilize a cartridge—usually called a *cart*—which is an endless loop of tape (Fig. 4.7).

The advantage of using carts is that the units designed to play them (Fig. 4.8) are able to sense a **cue tone** on the tape that will stop the tape automatically after it has played through full cycle. This means, too, that the tape will be all set to start again from the beginning. In essence, the tape cues itself up. This is why cart machines are so useful in radio production. There are two tracks on a mono cart machine; one track contains only the cue tone.

A 60-second commercial often is put on a 70-second cart. The commercial, for reasons to be explained in a moment, is all set to go when it's put into the machine. To play the spot, the operator on air hits the cart machine's play button. The tape, an endless reel, is pulled past the heads; when the commercial ends, the producer lets the cart play until it reaches the cue tone and stops automatically. The cart is then said to be *recued*.

Carts can also be loaded with a number of different spots—for instance, six or seven 10-second station identifications on a 70-second cart. This is a convenient way to play such cuts, and it ensures that they will be rotated throughout the broadcast day.

Now, let's see exactly how the cart machine works. The cart is an endless loop of tape; that is, the start of the tape is spliced to the end of the **cartridge tape,** a special heavily lubricated tape that feeds out from the middle of the reel. A rubber drive wheel snaps into place when the cart is locked into its location. This is done differently in various models; sometimes a level is used to swing the drive wheel into the proper spot.

A cart machine also has a Stop control and a Record control. The Record controls puts the unit in Record mode; this also activates the function of the machine that places the cue tone on the tape. Some cart machines are **playback only** and do not record.

The cue tone (which you can't hear) is placed on the tape when the cart machine is in Record and the Start button is pushed. A stop tone cannot be put on in the Play mode. Newer cart machines have a Fast-forward control that allows the cartridge tape to be rapidly advanced to the next cue tone. This spares the operator from the inconvenience of having to wait until the cartridge plays through at normal speed before reaching the start of the tape or the next recorded item. As on a reel-to-reel tape machine,

Figure 4.7 Broadcast cartridge.

there is a VU meter to gauge the level of the recording. And again as on reel-to-reel machines, cartridge units have a record head and a playback head. What they don't have is an erase head. This is because an erase head would erase the cue tone before the cue tone reached the play head, where it would be sensed and the recording stopped. As a result, the erasing would continue in an endless loop until someone intervened manually.

Like reel-to-reel tape recorders, monaural and stereo cartridge machines have different track configurations. As a result, carts recorded on a stereo machine cannot be played back properly on a mono machine, and vice versa. This is often an important consideration in AM-FM operations, where the carts may be recorded in stereo for the FM and in mono for the AM.

Because of the cart machine's lack of an erase head, you'll have to use what's called a *bulk eraser* to wipe a cart clean. The bulk eraser, often called a *bulker,* is a large electromagnet that scrambles the impulses on the iron oxide coating of the tape. The bulk eraser also works with reel-to-reel tapes and cassettes, should you desire to erase them completely.

There's a technique to using a bulk eraser properly (Fig. 4.9(a), (b), and (c)). If you practice it, you can save yourself a great deal of trouble. Essentially, you must move the bulker slowly, in a circular motion, across the flat side of the cart; then wipe it across the front of the cart (the head area

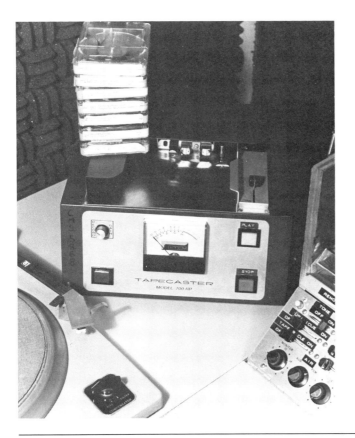

Figure 4.8   Cart machine.

of the tape), to ensure that that section is erased. Finally, move the bulker slowly away from the cart before turning it off; suddenly collapsing the magnetic field will impart a noise to the tape. Follow the same procedure for bulking a cassette or reel-to-reel tape—although, with the reel-to-reel tape, you obviously won't have to erase the head area. Note that we've described the procedure as one of moving the bulker; of course, you can also move the tape, and on some style bulkers this is easier.

Any strong magnetic field can erase a tape, so be cautious and never place tapes or carts near strong magnetic fields such as those generated by transformers, amplifiers, or speakers, which could damage or erase your production. By the same token, magnetism from the bulking operation can damage your wristwatch, so be sure to remove your watch before you begin to erase tapes.

Figure 4.9 Operating a bulk eraser.

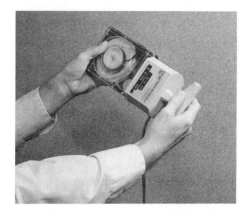

(a) Using a swirling motion, erase the cart across the flat side.

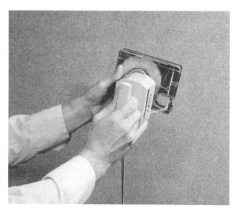

(b) Swirl the bulker in front of the head area of the cart.

(c) Move the bulker away from the cart gradually before turning off the switch.

■ SPECIAL PROBLEMS ■ ASSOCIATED WITH CARTRIDGE MACHINES

Improper erasure is one problem involved in working with carts. As handy as they are, it's important to point out that a good share of the errors heard on live radio and made in studio production can be traced to faulty use of carts. Let's consider some special problems we face when working with carts.

Sound over Sound

If you don't erase the cart before recording over it, you'll get **double audio.** If you don't do a good job of bulking, you'll get the residual sounds of a "dirty" cart in the background; those residual noises often sound something like a heartbeat. And if you don't erase the front of the cart (the opening where the tape is), an extra cue tone may be left on the tape.

Recueing

A cart must be given the opportunity to cycle through the full length of tape, in order to return to where the recording started (the cue tone). For various reasons, carts sometimes get taken off the machine without being recued. Punching up an uncued cart can be inconvenient and, in some cases, embarrassing.

Wowing

A wow (the noise made by a sound source that is picking up speed) can occur on a cart machine if the Start button is pressed too soon after the cart was locked in place. On some cart machines, the motor doesn't start until the cart is locked into place, so if you quickly jam the cart into the machine and smack the Start button, you'll get a wow for the first few moments of the tape. The solution is to plan ahead: Don't hit the Start button until the cart machine has had a chance to sit for a second or two after the cart is locked in place.

Other Features of Cart Machines

Eliminating the Cue Tone on a Cart Machine With some machines, such as the one pictured in Figure 4.10, you can pull out the wire that places the cue tone on the tape, producing a cart without a cue tone—that is, a cart that will run endlessly. This maneuver is called disabling the cue tone,

Figure 4.10 To prevent the cue tone from being recorded on the cart, remove the
green wire from the connecting point on the machine.

and it can come in handy in certain applications. For example, you can
elect to use such arrangement for a **sound effect** (discussed in the Applications section of this chapter). Just remember to plug the green wire back
in when you're done. (Be sure you ask permission of the studio supervisor
before doing this.)

Intentional Sound-on-Sound on Carts Earlier, we mentioned that, since a
cart doesn't erase itself, sound can be recorded over previous sound. If that
happens by accident, it's a problem. But the feature can be turned to your
advantage in some production situations.

Several layers of sound can be recorded onto a cart. If, for instance, you
are recording a production that calls for a sound effect and a narration,
the sound effect could conceivably be layered directly onto the cart that
contains the narration. You'll save a step, since you won't have to do another
dub and mix; but sound layering on carts can add quite a bit of noise to
the production, and it reduces the high-frequency response on the first
recording. Keep these factors in mind when planning sound layering.

Review of Cartridge Machines

A cart is an endless loop of tape in a plastic case. The case is locked into a
cartridge machine, which has a Start button, a Stop button, and a Record
control (except units that are designed for playback only, which just have
Stop and Start buttons).

When you record a cart, put the Record control on and hit the Start button. This will automatically put a cue tone on the lower half of the tape. The cue tone, which is inaudible, will be sensed by the play head. It allows the tape to play through its entire length and then stop automatically, ready to be played again.

Cart machines don't have an erase head, so carts must be wiped clean with a bulk eraser.

Although carts are convenient, problems can accompany them, including sound inadvertently being recorded over sound, failure of an operator to recue the cart, and wowing (if the cart is started too soon after being put into the machine).

■ RELATION OF RECORD ■
UNITS TO THE CONSOLE

Throughout this chapter, we've avoided calling reel-to-reel, cassette, and cart machines *recorders*. The reason for this is that they are used both for recording and for playback; the term *machine* (or *unit*) is more accurate and less confusing. **Deck** is another commonly used and accurate term. We take this approach because it's especially important for the producer to distinguish mentally between playback and record, and to translate these functions to console operations.

Nothing seems to cause more confusion to newcomers in radio production than what to do with the console when recording in one unit and playing back in another. Suppose, for example, you are mixing the output of a tape machine and a microphone, and you want to record the product on a cart machine. What happens on the console?

You put the mic and the tape machine in program. You want to play back these units, and therefore you want the signal to go through the console, where it will be amplified, mixed, and routed.

When you switch a tape or cart machine to Record, the signal from the board will in most cases be routed directly to the tape or cart. (Sometimes you'll have to patch the signal to the record unit.) The important thing to remember is that, when you are recording on a particular unit, you do not want to pot that unit up on the board.

You are not playing the output of that particular machine, so there is no reason to bring it up on the console. You will, in fact, cause feedback by potting up a unit when that unit is in Record mode. (For now, don't be concerned about the reason, just be aware of this source of feedback.)

In summary, always remember: When you want to play back the output of a tape or cart machine, bring the unit up on the console. (Most tape devices are hot-potted, by the way.) When you want to record on a tape or cart machine, do not bring the unit up on the console. In almost all production work, you are recording the output of the console.

■ DIGITAL AUDIOTAPE ■

While not currently in widespread radio use, **digital audiotape** promises to be a valuable tool in modern radio production. Digital audiotape is the tape correlary of the compact disc: It is recorded using the same sampling and coding methods described in Chapter 3. However, digital audiotape (known as DAT) has the advantage of being suitable for recording as well as for playback.

Digital audiotape is essentially the same type of substance as analog audiotape, although it is thinner. The thinness of the tape arises from the fact that digital recorders play at a faster rate than do analog machines, and hence more tape must be packed on a reel or cassette.

Configurations of the tape recorder used to imprint the digital signal on tape vary widely. Head configurations, number of tracks, and even speed of the tape vary from manufacturer to manufacturer. For radio purposes, however, it appears as if a standard is emerging: the rotating-head digital audiotape recorder, usually referred to as an *R-DAT machine.*

R-DAT uses two tracks of digital audiotape on a cassette that is approximately the size of a cigarette pack. The cassette is loaded into a machine that resembles a tiny videotape deck. For an example, see the R-DAT machine pictured in Figure 4.11.

Most machines have a variety of sampling rates (the number of times per second that a sound is digitally sampled, as explained in the section on compact discs in Chapter 3). R-DAT units typically offer sampling rates of 44.1 kHz, 48 kHz, and (for digital inputs only) 32 kHz.

The rotating head spins at a slant, crosswise over the tape, as the tape is moved past the head; thus its action resembles that of the mechanism in a videotape recorder. A digital audiotape recorder can produce audio of roughly the same quality as audio from a compact disc. This allows the user to make copies that are virtually as good as the master.

Remember that, with digital recording, generation loss is not as significant a problem as it is with analog recording. The best example for understanding this might be to consider that producing multiple generations of analog tape are like making a copy of a Xerox copy and then making a copy of the second copy, and so on. But digital recording essentially retransmits series of on and off pulses, and the pulses are either on or off, so there are no shades of gray; consequently, the on-and-off pulses reproduce with great accuracy.

Figure 4.11 Sony PCM-2500 DAT Recorder. (Photo courtesy of Sony Corporation of America, Teaneck, N.J.)

This is not to say that digital audiotapes (or compact discs, for that matter) are immune from wear. It appears that the thin tape can wear and break. But the point is that, as long as the tape itself retains its integrity, copies of copies of copies, ad infinitum, will not suffer appreciable loss of audio quality.

Many industry observers feel that a primary use of digital audiotape in the future will be in recording field events, such as concerts or even news audio, and then dumping the results into a digital editing station, a concept explained in Chapter 15. Digital audiotape is also sure to meet with widespread acceptance in radio studio operations (it is already used widely by recording studios) in various production applications. Digital editing promises to increase the producer's flexibility, creativity, and control over the final product.

As of mid-1989, development of sophisticated and practical editing systems for R-DAT had already begun, but there remained concern over the legal future of the technology. Music industry executives, fearing wholesale violation of copyright laws if digital recording comes into widespread use (enabling anyone to obtain a perfect copy of an original work), have sought legislation to stop the production of consumer-available digital audiotape cassette units. At this writing, Congress is still considering the pros and cons of such legislation.

An interesting relationship of digital to analog has developed at many radio stations, incidentally. Many stations dub compact discs onto standard broadcast cartridges. While this may seem self-defeating, it is generally accepted that analog tape recorded from a digital source gives better fidelity than analog tape recorded from an analog source (tape recorded from a standard LP). Thus, stations often prefer to dub their CDs onto carts and then to use the carts for actual airplay. A cart is generally easier to handle—ostensibly because radio people are more accustomed to it—and many users feel that carts provide better performance reliability than CDs.

SUMMARY

Audiotape is a thin strip of material coated with iron oxide. The oxide particles align to conform with the signal generated by a magnetic head. In this way, sound information is transduced and stored for later playback.

Typically, there are three heads on a tape deck. Each has a specific function: to erase, to record, or to play back.

The reel on the left (as you face the machine) is the supply reel. The reel on the right is the takeup reel.

If there are multiple heads on the machine, more than one track can be laid down on the tape. Multiple tracks are useful for stereo recording and for recording music when multiple inputs need to be recorded and controlled separately.

Cassettes, which are small enclosed reels, are useful for portable operations and are increasingly used in studio operations. Cartridges (carts) use a continuous loop of tape in a plastic case.

Digital audiotape (DAT), while not yet commonly used in radio operations, may be widely adopted in the near future, pending the outcome of technical and legal complications. DAT, like a compact disc, stores and plays back a digital signal, rather than an analog signal.

APPLICATIONS

■ **Situation 1** ■ *The Problem* The producer of an hour-long news program wants the sound of a teletype in the background. He has a sound-effects record with the teletype sound, but the cut runs for only 3 minutes, and it would be impractical to keep dropping the stylus back at the beginning of the cut.

One Possible Solution The producer pulled the green wire (see Fig. 4.10) on the cart machine, placed a 70-second cart in the machine, and recorded exactly 70 seconds of the teletype effect on the cart. Now, the cart plays endlessly throughout the newscast.

▪ **Situation 2** ▪ *The Problem* A community bulletin-board segment airs twice every hour at 15 minutes and 45 minutes after the hour. The producer has found a perfect piece of music to introduce the segment, but she notices how inconvenient it is to tie up a turntable twice an hour for 10 seconds of music.

One Possible Solution The producer simply records, or *dubs*, the first 10 seconds of music from the disc onto a cart. The cart is labeled and placed in a rack; it's now very convenient for the console operator to grab the cart and plug it in.

EXERCISES

1. Using a reel-to-reel tape machine, record someone counting from 1 to 20. Then have someone call out a number between 1 and 20; your assignment is to cue the tape up, as quickly as possible, to start at that number. For example, if the number 16 is called out, you'll want to find the part of the tape on which the announcer is reading 13 . . . 14 . . . 15 . . . and stop it there. (You will, of course, do this in cue or in audition.) Then, bring the tape recorder up on program and start it. You should hear the tape cleanly start with the number 16. Have several numbers called out until you're proficient at cueing up the tape.

2. Decide which type of machine (turntable, cassette, reel-to-reel tape, or cart) would be best for the following applications, and explain your reasons:

   ▸ The musical opening to a news program.

   ▸ An interview a news reporter will be doing at the site of a demonstration.

   ▸ A 60-second commercial.

   ▸ A half-hour radio drama.

   ▸ A 10-minute interview segment done in the studio.

   ▸ Multiple station identifications. (You might want to try producing sample station IDs on the type of machine you decide is most appropriate.)

·5·

Microphones

and Sound

I n many cases you don't need to know all the details of microphone use to do your job in a radio station. A person doing production duties in a small radio station will generally use the mic that happens to be hooked up to the console. A reporter will use whatever mic is handed out before going out on assignment. And in many production situations, the simplest of miking techniques and arrangements will be used time and time again.

However, you'll be able to do even a basic production job better with a good working knowledge of microphones. In some cases a detailed knowledge of microphone use will help you solve a thorny problem. And in the more advanced areas of radio production, such as recording live music, you *must* know mic use inside and out.

We're offering a realistic explanation of the situation because many newcomers to radio production become somewhat cynical after plowing through explicit details of microphone use and selection but never using the knowledge during the class or in their first few jobs. Even though this knowledge might not seem essential right now, it just might prove invaluable down the road.

■ THE BASICS OF ■ SOUND

The microphone, like many other pieces of equipment discussed earlier, is a **transducer.** It changes the energy of the motion of sound into electrical energy. The microphone is the instrument that transforms sound into something usable by the record and playback units hooked up to a radio console.

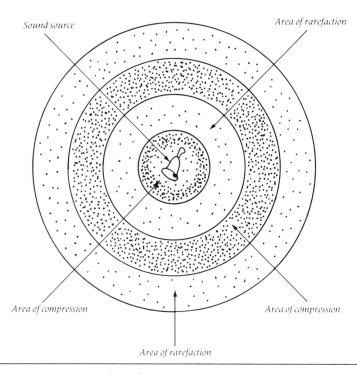

Sound source

Area of rarefaction

Area of compression

Area of compression

Area of rarefaction

Figure 5.1 Compressions and rarefactions.

Sound itself is a vibration—a specific motion—of air molecules. What happens is this: A sound source (a cymbal, perhaps) creates changes in air pressure. When molecules are pushed together, they are said to be in **compression.** Areas of low pressure, where molecules are pulled apart from each other, are called **rarefactions.** To visualize the situation, look at Figure 5.1. A sound source causes alternating waves of compression (dense dots) and rarefaction (sparse dots) through the air.

Now, the vibration traveling through the air carries information. The way that the cymbal sounds to our ears is determined by the pattern of vibration. As a matter of fact, the eardrum is a transducer, too. It performs the first step in converting motional energy of vibration into electrical energy in the brain.

The microphone also transduces the motional energy into electrical energy. That energy then might be transduced into electromechanical energy (storage on audio tape), or it might be transduced back into **motional energy** by a **loudspeaker.**

How does a mic do this, and why are certain mics better than others at reproducing certain sounds? To understand these things, let's first explore

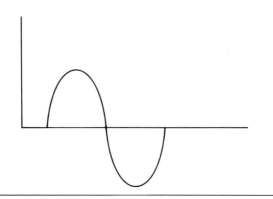

Figure 5.2 Sine wave.

a bit further the nature of sound itself. The information will come in handy when we try to understand the behavior of sound and the way mics affect its reproduction.

The Elements of Sound

A pure-tone sound is represented by a **sine wave** (Fig. 5.2), one of the most frequently used symbols in the world of sound, microphones, and radio, and one of the most frequently misunderstood. A sine wave is a graphic representation of the rarefactions and compressions of air molecules. If we were to sample the density of the molecules of a **wave** (pictured in Fig. 5.3), we'd find a thick area, then an area becoming thinner, then a very thin area, then an area somewhat thicker, and then a thick area again. A graph of this pattern would look like the one in Figure 5.4(a), which is a plot of the sound pattern, not a picture of it. Thus, the sine wave only represents sound; no sine waves emanate from a sound source. The sine wave can be used to analyze several elements of sound.

Cycle Each time a wave goes through its pattern and returns to its starting point, it has completed one **cycle.** A cycle passes through a complete rotation every 360 degrees. The time it takes for a wave to make a complete cycle is called an *interval.*

A cycle can be measured from any starting point. The plot of a cycle is illustrated in Figure 5.4(b). Note that, though a sine wave has 360 degrees in a complete rotation, this representation is composed of two equal intervals, called *positive* and *negative intervals,* and that each interval is 180 degrees long.

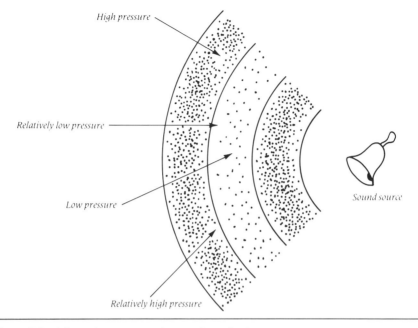

Figure 5.3   Measuring compressions and rarefactions.

Frequency This is a measure of how often a cycle is repeated in a given period of time. Formerly, **frequency** was measured in cycles per second. In recent years, the term *cycles per second* has been replaced by the term **hertz** (Hz), named in honor of the mathematician Heinrich Hertz, who first demonstrated the existence of radio waves. We'll see how frequency plays a role in the nature of sound shortly.

Amplitude In technical terms, the **amplitude** is the height of the sine wave. Amplitude indicates the volume of the sound. The higher the amplitude, the louder the sound.

These elements determine the characteristics of sound, and the sine wave is a visual representation of those characteristics. If nothing else, remember that any sound can be described by one or more sine waves.

The Nature of Sound: Frequency

Why one or more sine waves? Essentially, because sounds consist of combinations of wave patterns or **waveforms**. While a device called a *tone generator* will produce, by electronic circuitry, a pure wave (when represented on an oscilloscope), most sounds are a combination of many waves of different shapes and frequencies and are called *complex waveforms*.

Figure 5.4 Characteristics of a sine wave.

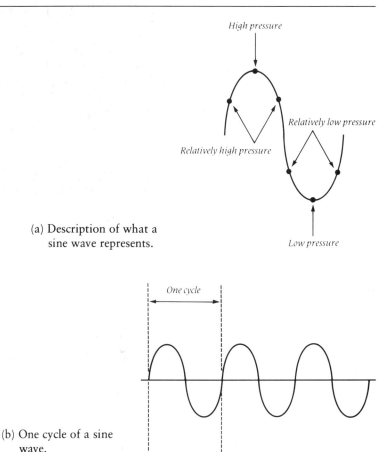

(a) Description of what a
sine wave represents.

(b) One cycle of a sine
wave.

Frequencies and Your Ears The human ear can hear frequencies from about 35 to 20,000 Hz. This, of course, depends on the age and health of the ear's owner. Older people generally don't hear high frequencies as well as young people do. The low end of the scale is a deep bass rumbling; the high end is a thin whine that's barely audible to people.

How Frequency Shapes Sound A sound is a combination of various waves—some higher, some lower. The fundamental (basic, most important) frequency of an average male voice, for example, is typically around 300 Hz. But consonant sounds such as *t* and *d* are much higher, perhaps in the 1,000-Hz range. Very high, hissy consonants, such as *s* can be well into the

4,000-Hz range, while the *th* in *thin* can approach 6,000 Hz. Other components of the sounds of human speech can range as high as 9,000 Hz.

The higher-frequency sounds, the consonant sounds, lend intelligibility to speech. If high consonant sounds are not reproduced by any of the transducers in the radio production chain, human speech becomes less intelligible. Music from which the high frequencies are absent sounds muddy and dull; the high frequencies add clarity and vibrance.

Limiting the range of transduced frequencies affects the tone of speech, too. The telephone reproduces frequencies from about 300 to 3,000 Hz. The difference between speech over a telephone and speech over a high-quality mic is readily apparent. Various mics reproduce frequencies with varying degrees of effectiveness.

The Nature of Sound: Amplitude

The amplitude of the sine wave represents the volume of the sound. Another way to measure sound volume is in *decibels*. A decibel (dB) is a very complex measurement. Two points about decibels are essential:

1. The higher the decibel reading, the louder the sound. Thus, 20 dB is a whisper; 55 dB is loud conversational speech; 75 dB is city traffic; 110 dB is a loud, amplified rock band; and 140 dB is a jet engine at takeoff. (These measurements are expressed in a particular form called *dB SPL—decibel sound pressure level.*)

2. It is considered that an increase or decrease of 1–2 dB SPL is the smallest change in sound level a human ear can perceive. An increase of 6 dB SPL is what the human ear perceives as a doubling of the sound's volume.

A more detailed explanation is this: The ear does not hear in a linear fashion. That is, if you were playing a radio at a level that was equal to 10 watts of power and you turned it up to a level equal to an output of 15 watts (an addition of 5 watts), you would not perceive the increase as being 1.5 times the original volume. Because it is difficult to measure apparent volume by talking about watts, we use a system that measures sound in a geometric fashion and corresponds to the way the ear appears to hear sound. Hence, the decibel is a very useful tool to measure significant increases or decreases in apparent volume.

Remember the VU meter, and the readings on the top scale? Those volume units correspond to decibels. People often wonder why the VU meter uses 0 dB as the loudest modulation of sound we would wish to transmit, when common sense suggests that the louder the sound, the higher the dB reading. Actually, though it would be very confusing to have a VU meter scale that read, say, from 60 to 120 dB. Therefore, in broadcasting we have standardized 0 VU to equal a relative sound level that will power our transmitter of recording devices to their maximum permissible outputs. This way, we don't have to work with such large dB numbers. Remember, the 0 dB reading is relative. A reading of − 1 means that your input is 1 dB lower than the optimum level.

Other Characteristics of Sound

We've pretty well covered the physical properties that make up the nature of sound. Some other areas are also worth considering. **Pitch,** a term commonly used to describe sound, is not the same thing as frequency. Frequency is a physical measurement; pitch is the ear's and mind's subjective interpretation of frequency and loudness, signifying the way we hear a frequency. The human ear just doesn't hear the same way a scientific instrument does.

Duration is a characteristic of sound, too. It refers to the amount of time a sound exists, and to the amount of time individual harmonics exist within a complex waveform.

Velocity and distance also play a role in the way we hear sound. Sound is not very fast; it travels through air at only a little more than 1,100 feet per second, or 750 miles per hour. Sound travels at different rates through different media; it travels about four times faster through water, for example. But it has to vibrate through a medium; there's no sound in a vacuum.

The relative slowness of sound in air can be illustrated by a familiar example. When sitting in the bleachers during a baseball game, you will see the batter complete his swing before you hear the crack of the bat hitting the ball. Because of the slowness of sound, you can perceive echoes (the immediate bounceback of sound) and reverberation (the continued bouncing of sound) in an enclosure with reflective walls. A large room with reflective walls will cause the reverberations to take longer to *decay,* or die out.

Distance also makes a difference in how loud the sound is when it reaches us. When sound travels two times a specified distance, it arrives at only one-quarter of its original intensity. This behavior is said to comply with the inverse square law.

A final characteristic is the sound's quality or timbre. This, again, is a factor in how our ears and mind perceive sound. It has to do with the way harmonics are combined, and with the relative intensities of those harmonics. Those combinations make us perceive a difference between the middle C played on a piano and the same note played on a harpsichord.

Summary of the Basics of Sound

Understanding how sound behaves is a prerequisite to learning about microphones, and much of what you need to know concerns how a mic reproduces sound.

Sound is a vibration of molecules in the air, and it consists of rarefactions and compressions. A sine wave is a graphic representation of a sound wave; it is not supposed to be a picture of the wave.

Sound is measured in terms of frequency and amplitude. Frequency, which tells how often in a given period of time the sound wave makes a complete cycle, is measured in cycles per second, now called *hertz*. Amplitude is the height of the sine wave. It refers to the loudness of the sound and is measured in decibels. Sound travels through air at about 1,100 feet per second.

Characteristics of sound include pitch (the way we perceive frequency), loudness (the way we perceive volume), and quality or timbre (the way we interpret the complex waveforms).

Now that we've prefaced this chapter with an explanation of sound, let's move on to the ways mics work, the various types of mics and their uses.

▪   THE MICROPHONE: ▪
HOW IT WORKS

One of the ways in which a producer selects a microphone and decides on its use is by determining how the microphone reproduces sound and how it *colors* that sound. (The meaning of this term should become clear shortly.)

Electronics of the Microphone

Sound reproduction is affected by the mechanical and electronic means used within the mic to change the **acoustic** or motional energy of sound—a vibration of molecules in the air—to electrical energy. Certain varieties of microphones are much better adapted to some tasks than are other types. That's why it's important to understand the workings of the three types of microphone most common in radio broadcasting: the **moving-coil,** the **ribbon,** and the **condenser.**

Moving-Coil Electricity is formed by moving a conductor through a magnetic field. That's exactly what happens in a generator: Coils of wire are moved through a magnetic field, and electrical current results.

And that's also what happens in a moving-coil microphone. The diaphragm in a moving-coil mic (Fig. 5.5(a)) is attached to a coil of wire. The **diaphragm,** a thin membrane, vibrates as it is driven by the sound waves. The coil attached to the diaphragm vibrates, too, and the vibration of this moving coil cuts through the magnetic lines of force produced by the magnets within the microphone. The electrical wave produced now carries the imprint of the sound wave by mirroring both the frequency of the acoustical energy and the amplitude of that energy. Moving-coil mics are sometimes referred to as **dynamic mics.**

Ribbon This type of mic has a thin (usually corrugated) metal ribbon suspended between the poles of a magnet (Fig. 5.5(b)). The ribbon vibrates in harmony with the sound waves. Technically, the ribbon mic responds to a difference in pressure between the front and back of the ribbon; that's why some people refer to this type of instrument as a **pressure-gradient mic.** Ribbon mics are gradually becoming less common in radio.

Condenser A condenser mic operates through the use of an electrical element called a **capacitor.** *Condenser* is actually an old-fashioned name for a capacitor, and it stuck as the name for this type of mic. A capacitor stores an electrical charge. In a condenser mic (Fig. 5.5(c)), a charge is applied to the side of the condenser known as the *back plate;* as the diaphragm vibrates, it changes the distance between itself and the back plate and changes the amount of charge held by the back plate.

Condenser microphones often need a separate power supply to place a charge on the back plate; thus, batteries are used. Some more modern condenser mics draw a charge from the console, a "phantom" power supply.

Pickup (Polar) Patterns of the Microphone

The electronics of a mic also affect the pattern in which it picks up sounds. These patterns, called **pickup patterns** or **polar patterns,** have a major effect on how a particular mic is used. Some mics pick up sounds from all directions, or from the front and back but not the sides, or from the front only. The basic pickup patterns are **omnidirectional, bidirectional,** and **cardioid.** (*Cardioid* is sometimes called *unidirectional,* meaning "one-directional.")

Omnidirectional An omnidirectional mic picks up sounds equally well from all sides, as pictured in part (a) of Figure 5.6, the complete display of pickup patterns on pp. 86–87. To visualize what a pickup pattern is, it's helpful to know how one can be drawn. The mic is placed on a stand, pointed toward a speaker, and twisted in a circle (kept parallel to the floor).

Figure 5.5 The three types of microphone elements.

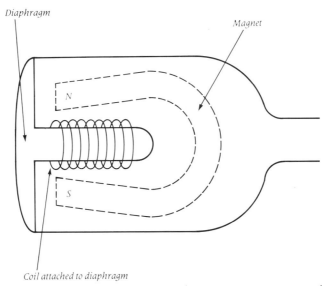

(a) In a moving-coil mic, the thin diaphragm vibrates in response to sound energy. The attached coil moves through a magnetic field, generating an electrical current with a pattern that corresponds to the pattern of the original sound.

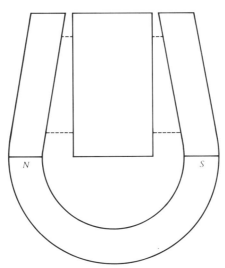

(b) In a ribbon mic, sound energy causes vibrations of a metallic ribbon, which moves through a magnetic field to produce an electrical current.

(continued)

Figure 5.5   *(continued)*

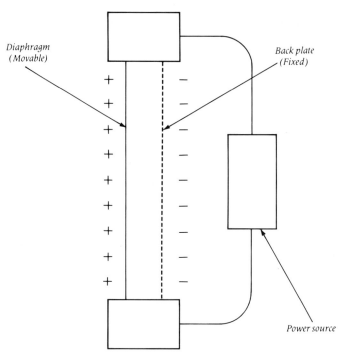

Diaphragm
(Movable)

Back plate
(Fixed)

Power source

(c) In a condenser mic, sound vibrates the diaphragm. Movement of the diaphragm
   varies the electrical pattern on the back plate.

Then the amplitude of the wave it picked up at various poles is measured.
As shown in Figure 5.6(a), the amplitude is as great at 90 degrees as at 0
degrees (0 being where the mic faces dead-on to the speaker). Remember,
the pickup pattern is a *three-dimensional* representation, so mics hear sound
from above and below, too. Although we generally assume that the omnidirectional mic picks up sound equally well from all directions, there is a
small glitch at 180 degrees, simply because the mass of the microphone
gets in the way of the sound waves.

   The reason, incidentally, that an omnidirectional mic can be equally
sensitive to sounds from all directions is related to the fact that sound is a
series of rarefactions and compressions of air molecules. Since the back of
the microphone is closed to air, the diaphragm is pulled out by the rarefactions and pushed in by the compressions, regardless of the direction of
the sound. The importance of this concept, illustrated in Figure 5.7, will
become apparent shortly.

Bidirectional The bidirectional mic accepts sound from the front and rear and rejects it from the sides. Its pickup pattern is shown in Figure 5.6(b). Notice, too, that the concentric rings indicate sound level in decibels; when the pickup pattern dips toward the center of the circle, it's declining by the number of decibels indicated on the concentric rings. The bidirectional pattern is typical of ribbon mics that have the ribbon open to air on both sides.

Cardioid *Cardioid* means "heart-shaped," as in Figure 5.6(c). You can visualize this pattern in three dimensions by imagining that the mic is the stem of a gigantic apple. Often, the cardioid pattern is called **unidirectional,** meaning that it only picks up sound from one (*uni-* means "one") direction. Sometimes, the term *directional* is used to indicate the same concept. (For three-dimensional representations of microphone pickup patterns, see Figure 5.8(a) and (b)).

A microphone with a cardioid pattern achieves this directionality by means of holes or ports in the back of the mic. Sound entering these ports is routed through an acoustic network (Fig. 5.9(a)) that causes the mic to cancel sound coming from the rear. In physics terms, the sound waves entering from the rear are *out of phase* with sound waves entering the front of the mic (Fig. 5.9(b)). That is, when the waves are combined, the high points will combine with the low points and the low points will combine with the high, thus canceling each other out. The concept of **phase** is important in advanced radio production.

The cardioid pattern is a function of sound wave cancellation due to porting in the mic and is not a result of the particular electronic element in the mic. Mics with a cardioid pattern can have moving coil, ribbon, or condenser elements. Mics with an omnidirectional pattern usually have a moving-coil element, but occasionally have a condenser.

A special version of the cardioid pattern is the **supercardioid** pattern (Fig. 5.6(d)), which has a tighter curve in front and a lobe in back. The **hypercardioid** pattern (Fig. 5.6(e)) has an even narrower front angle and a bigger rear lobe. Supercardioid and hypercardioid patterns, also called *unidirectional,* are generally used for highly directional applications on booms, such as in television studio work, when it is important to reject unwanted noises.

Frequency Response of Microphones

Different mics respond differently to sound frequencies. There are two components of **frequency response:** *range* and *shape.*

Figure 5.6   Microphone pickup patterns. Shaded areas represent the shapes of each
                mic's coverage areas.

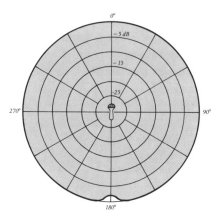

(a) Omnidirectional pickup pattern.

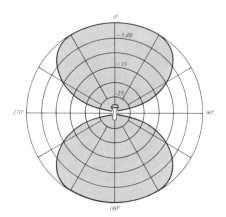

(b) Bidirectional pickup pattern.

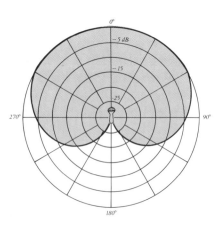

(c) Cardioid pickup pattern.

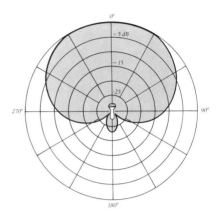

(d) Supercardioid pickup pattern.

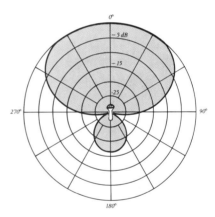

(e) Hypercardioid pickup pattern.

Range Range simply means the amount of the frequency spectrum a mic can hear. Good mics can hear frequencies all the way up to 20,000 Hz, which is beyond the range of most normal adult ears. A good mic can also hear all sounds equally well, plus or minus about 5 dB (Fig. 5.10). Figure 5.11 is a graph of frequency response. How far such a graph extends to the right shows how high a frequency the mic can pick up. The graph also indicates how well the mic reproduces frequencies. The higher the line, the better the mic reproduces the frequency indicated on the bottom line of the graph. This characteristic of the response curve is known as *shape*.

Shape See how the **shape** of the mic response pattern in Figure 5.11 has a bump in the upper frequencies? This is because the mic, by its nature, gives a boost to those frequencies; a mic like this would be useful for speech,

Figure 5.7   Reaction of a mic's diaphragm to sound. Notice that it makes little difference to the diaphragm which direction the sound is coming from.

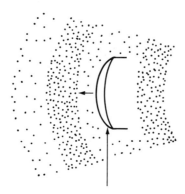

(a) Diaphragm pulled out by rarefactions (low pressure).

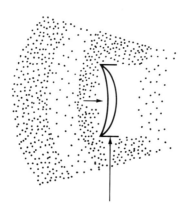

(b) Diaphragm pushed in by compressions (high pressure).

Figure 5.8   Three-dimensional representations of pickup patterns.

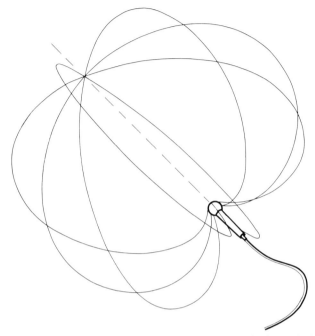

(a) Approximation of how the cardioid pickup pattern extends through three
     dimensions. If you think of the pickup pattern as forming a huge apple, the mic is
     like the stem.

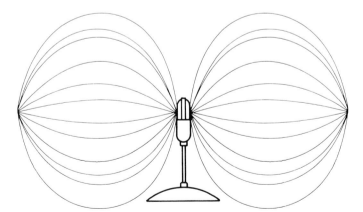

(b) Approximation of how the bidirectional pickup pattern extends through three
     dimensions. It consists of two giant pickup spheres on either side of the mic.

Figure 5.9   Mic ports and phase cancellation.

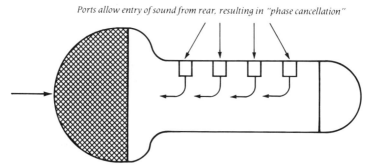

Ports allow entry of sound from rear, resulting in "phase cancellation"

(a) Simplified diagram of ports in a mic. The ports let sound enter from
     the rear and, in effect, cancel itself out.

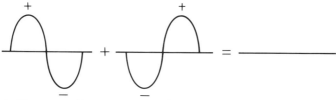

(b) Phase cancellation as a sum of sine waves of opposite amplitudes.

since it powerfully reproduces the frequencies that lend intelligibility to
speech. Such modifications of frequencies also add to the coloration of
sound, just as a mic lends a sound a certain quality or timbre.

Often, recording engineers miking music setups will want a mic with a
flat response—a mic that is capable of responding equally well to all frequencies in the whole audio spectrum. The term **high fidelity** applies well
to this characteristic, since it means "high accuracy." A mic that responds
equally well to all frequencies is high in fidelity, and the term also applies
to speakers, amplifiers, and so forth.

Cardioid mics tend to boost bass (lower) frequencies as the sound source
moves closer to the mic; this is known as a **proximity effect.** That's why
some announcers who want a deeper sound move in very close to mics
with a cardioid pickup pattern.

What does all this mean to you? By understanding the polar patterns of
mics, you'll be able to avoid various problems. For example, a cardioid mic
will reject sounds from the rear and will be useful for console operations,
where you do not want to broadcast the clicking of switches and rustling
of papers. An omnidirectional mic might be the proper choice for on-the-
street news interviews, where you want to pick up surrounding noise to
lend authenticity to the situation.

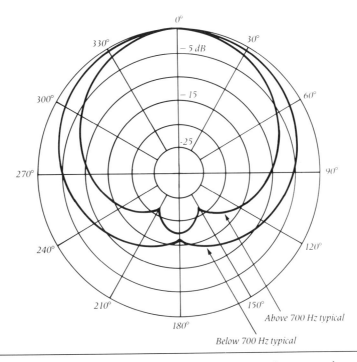

Figure 5.10 Graph of a pickup pattern supplied by a microphone manufacturer. Scale: 5 dB per division. (Reproduced with permission of Electro-Voice, Inc., Buchanan, Mich.)

In some cases, a producer might opt for a mic that boosts specific frequencies because, for instance, the high frequencies in speech need a boost for intelligibility. Some mics, such as the RCA 77DX and some Neumanns, have variable frequency responses and polar patterns; the varying responses are achieved by adjusting switches on the body of the mic.

Review of Microphone Workings

Microphones are transducers that change the motional energy of sound in the air into electrical energy by means of an electronic element. There are three elements common in radio use: moving coil, ribbon, and condenser.

Some microphones are more sensitive than others to sounds coming from certain directions. A visual indication of this property is called a *pickup pattern*. The most common pickup patterns in mics designed for radio use are omnidirectional, bidirectional, and cardioid.

Frequency response varies from mic to mic. Because some mics have a broader range than others, they can reproduce a wider range of frequencies. Some mics also tend to boost certain frequency ranges.

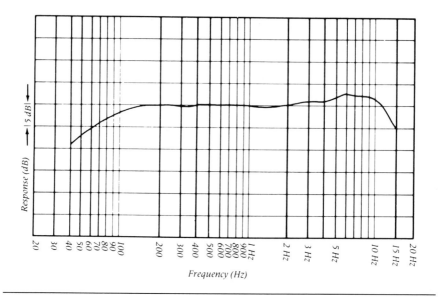

Figure 5.11   Graph of a mic response. (Reproduced with permission of Electro-Voice, Inc., Buchanan, Mich.)

■   PHYSICAL TYPES   ■
OF MICROPHONES

Examples

We're using a somewhat imprecise phrase when we speak of "microphone physical type"; it's not a standard term in the industry. It is, however, a good way to classify mics by their intended use. Some of these uses may not usually apply to radio, but we'll show some examples anyway.

Hand-held   Mics meant for hand-held use are, of course, small enough to be easily handled. Other characteristics of a mic that can be held in one hand include durability and the ability to reject handling noise. The Electro-Voice 635A (Fig. 5.12(a)) is one of the most commonly used hand-held mics in broadcasting.

Studio, Mounted   Mics intended for studio use are usually mounted on a stand or boom. They are generally larger than hand-held mics, and more sensitive. The Neumann U-87 (Fig. 5.12(b)) would be very difficult to use in a hand-held situation not only because of its shape but because this fine mic is so sensitive that it would pick up every bit of handling noise. Some mics, which are small enough and provide high-quality sound reproduction, can be used in both studio and hand-held situations.

Headset These mics (Fig. 5.12(c)) offer hands-free operation and are useful in radio for such tasks as sports play-by-play. **Headset mics** also work well for rejecting noise surrounding the announcer.

Lavalier The lavalier mic hangs from a string or is clipped to a performer's clothing (Fig. 5.12(d)). Lavaliers have little application to radio, but are very common in television.

Shotgun These mics are used for long-range pickup (Fig. 5.12(e)) in television and film; **shotguns** have very little use in radio.

We can conclude this discussion of mic type by saying that in radio production you will be using studio and hand-held mics primarily. The way in which you'll choose mics depends not only on type, but on all the factors discussed so far in this chapter.

Some condenser mics allow you to change the pickup capsules. These are called *system mics* because you can change the capsule opening and change the use of the mic from a shotgun to a studio type, or even to hand-held. This allows a small station to buy one very good microphone system and adapt it to various applications. Unfortunately, most of these condenser mic systems require external or phantom power supplies, and this can detract from their usefulness in certain situations.

Review of Physical Types

The most common mics found in radio are hand-held and studio; sometimes headset mics are used for sports applications. There is some overlap: Some mics can be used for studio or hand-held use, and condenser mics of the type called *system mics* allow you to change the pickup capsule.

▪   MICROPHONE SELECTION   ▪
AND USE

As mentioned earlier, you may not always have much choice when it comes to selecting mics. You'll use what's available. Even then, however, you'll benefit from a knowledge of mics because you'll better understand how to use the one you're given. When you do have a voice in selection, you'll want to make your choice based on these five factors:

1. Type
2. Pickup pattern
3. Element
4. Frequency response
5. Personality

Figure 5.12 Physical types of microphones.

(a) The Electro-Voice 635A, an excellent hand-held mic.

(b) Neumann U-87 (left) U-89 (right) studio mics. (Photo courtesy of Gotham Audio Corporation, New York City.)

(c) Headset mic commonly used for sports broadcasts and other occasions when mic stands would clutter the workspace. (Photo courtesy of Telex Communications, Inc., Minneapolis, Minn.)

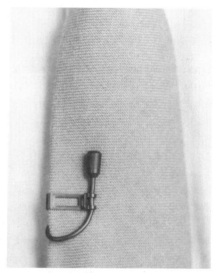

(d) Sennheiser MKE 2 lavalier mic, which has few applications for radio. (Photo courtesy of Sennheiser Electronic Corporation, New York City.)

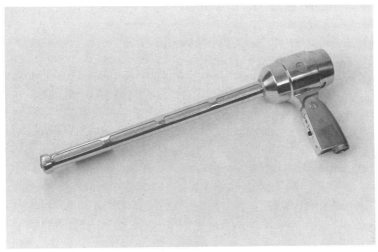

(e) Commonly used shotgun microphone.

Selection by Mic Type

This is a pretty self-limiting category, since you'll generally be using hand-held or studio mics, and the choices are obvious. As mentioned, some high-quality mics can be used in either application, but beware of using a cardioid mic with many ports in the stem and back in hand-held situations. You'll be changing the pickup pattern of the mic by covering the ports with your hand.

Changing the pickup pattern in this manner sometimes happens when pop singers cup a mic too tightly and inadvertently cause feedback: Cutting off the ports changes the cardioid pattern to an omnidirectional pattern and thus picks up the sound from the loudspeakers. Feedback, in this case, happens when sound comes out of a speaker, is picked up by the mic and amplified by the console, is fed through the speaker, is picked up and amplified again, and so on—until the sound is amplified into a loud squeal.

Selection by Pickup Pattern

A news reporter doing a great deal of hand-held interviewing will probably find an omnidirectional pattern more convenient than other patterns, since the mic won't have to be moved around so much to keep more than one speaker within the pickup pattern (referred to as being *on mic*). In studio applications, mics with a cardioid pattern are usually favored because they cancel out extraneous noise. A two-person interview, with guest and moderator facing each other, can be accomplished quite nicely with a bidirectional mic, although using two unidirectional mics allows for greater control if one voice is much more power than the other; the volume on one channel can simply be lowered to compensate.

Selection by Element

Certain **elements** do various tasks better than others (Table 5.1).

Selection by Frequency Response

There's usually neither the opportunity nor the need to consult a frequency response chart for the intimate details of a mic's sound reproduction. Should you wish to examine a frequency response chart, though, you'll generally find one packed in the box the mic came in. In fact, quality mics come with a chart individually prepared for the buyer. You don't have to read a chart every time you want to pick out a mic. What you do want is some general knowledge about range and curve shape.

Range   An extremely high-quality mic, with response as high as 20,000 Hz, is useful in music recording because of its "wide" response.

Curve Shape   A mic with a bump in the response curve up around the consonant frequencies makes speech more understandable. But you don't need that speech bump in a mic intended purely for music recording.

Also, some mics have what's called a *bass roll-off* to compensate for the proximity effect. In other words, they deemphasize the bass. A producer who knows that the mic will be used for close-in speech work and wants to negate the proximity effect can activate the bass roll-off control on the mic.

More advanced production may call for a detailed examination of frequency response, but for most purposes it's enough to know whether a mic has a wide—or very wide—frequency response, whether it emphasizes certain frequencies or has a flat curve, and whether it has adjustable responses.

Selection by Personality

The personality of a mic is a quality that can be difficult to define, but it's a factor nonetheless.

Most announcers develop a fondness for a particular mic whose characteristics appeal to the individual. Some announcers like ribbon mics because

Table 5.1 | ▶ Microphone Element Chart

Element	Advantages	Disadvantages
Moving-coil	Relatively inexpensive. Performs well in difficult sound conditions, such as wind. Usually very durable.	Since the diaphragm has to move a lot of mass, it can't vibrate as quickly as diaphragms on many condenser models or as some ribbons. This translates into less response to high frequencies.
Ribbon	Very good high-frequency response in many cases. Coloration of sound perceived by many announcers as warm and rich tones. Excellent sensitivity.	Delicate and easily damaged, especially by wind and severe noise overload. Sensitive to **popping** of such speech sounds as *b* and *p*.
Condenser	The very high-quality condensers have extended high-frequency response, along with what are perceived as bright and crisp highs. Versatility, including, in some cases, the ability to undergo extensive changes in pickup patterns and frequency responses; in some condenser mics, the entire element can be unscrewed and replaced with another. Reasonable durability to mechanical shock (certainly better than ribbon mics).	Susceptible to moisture-related damage. Expensive. Somewhat inconvenient at times because of the need for a separate power supply.

they add warmth and richness. News reporters often favor a particular moving-coil mic because of its ruggedness and dependability. Recording engineers frequently have high praise for a particular condenser mic that delivers crisp highs when used to record piano music. On the other hand, certain mics may seem temperamental and therefore fall into an announcer's disfavor. Some announcers don't like ribbon mics because of problems with popping *p*'s and *b*'s. When it comes right down to it, choosing a mic because of its personality (if indeed you have the option at choosing a mic) is just as valid as selecting one for any other reason.

Adding up Selection Factors

Once again, you might not be in a position to choose mics for particular tasks. But we emphasize that knowing the selection factors may be very valuable in proper use of the mic and may someday pay off when you need a mic to deal with a particularly difficult situation.

Although we've tried to avoid the catalog approach to presenting information on microphones, Table 5.2 assembles some of the mics most commonly used in radio production and includes some comments on microphone type, pickup pattern, element, frequency response, and personality.

Notes on Microphone Use

Mic use can be an extremely simple or an extraordinarily complex category, depending on the situation. Preparing to speak into a studio mic is no more complicated than being sure that you're within the pickup pattern (which will be obvious from listening through the headphones) and not being too close or too far away. It is extremely important that you monitor your voice through headphones whenever possible. Simply monitoring your levels on a VU meter will not tell you if you're popping or speaking off the mic's axis. Make it a rule: Whenever you're ready to switch on the mic, put your headphones on first.

The proper distance for speaking into a studio or hand-held mic ranges from about 6 to 12 inches, although there's no set rule. Actually, the only hard and fast guideline is: Work at a reasonable distance, based on what sounds correct for a particular speaker and a particular mic.

Setting up several mics in a studio is more complicated. The first thing a producer has to know in this case is how to plug the mics in. Figure 5.13 shows the connectors you will use to feed the mic cable into a studio wall outlet, which in turn will be fed (through existing wiring) into a console. The plugs shown, XLRs, are the most common. Incidentally, there is a trick to connecting and disconnecting XLRs. The push-lever mounted on the female wall connector (Fig. 5.13) locks the connectors in place. (You'll feel it snap when you make the connection.) To remove, press the lever and remove the male end by the connector; don't ever pull on the wire.

You'll encounter other connectors on occasion—most often the phone plug connector, a prong about $1\frac{1}{4}$ inch long, and the miniphone plug, a prong about $\frac{1}{2}$ inch long. In some cases, you will need adaptors to make one source compatible with another. Should you wish to plug a mic directly into the record input of a videotape recorder, for example, you'll need a female-XLR-to-male-phone-plug adaptor.

Table 5.2 | ▶ **Microphone Model Chart**

Microphone	Element	Description	
Neumann U-47	Condenser	Cardioid pickup pattern; excellent voice mic; flat response; warm sound; **blast filter;** bass roll-off	Gotham Audio Corp.
Sony C-37P	Condenser	Omnidirectional/cardioid; four adjustments for bass roll-off; good for voice pickup and musical instruments	Sony Corp. of Am.
Sennheiser 416 (middle), with 417 and 418	Condenser	Supercardioid; usually boom-mounted; flat response; eliminates unwanted ambient sound; excellent for remotes, where directionality is desired	Sennheiser Electronic Corp.
Electro-Voice RE-30, RE-34	Condenser	RE-30 is omnidirectional, RE-34 is cardioid; power supplied by 9-volt battery or phantom power supply; feeds line-level or mic-level signal; graphite in handle improves comfort in cold conditions	Electro-Voice, Inc.
Electro-Voice RE-18	Moving coil	Supercardioid; excellent shock protection makes this a good choice for hand-held use; blast filter; bass boost with close use	Electro-Voice, Inc.
Electro-Voice RE-20	Moving coil	A high-quality mic, rapidly becoming one of the most popular announcing mics in radio; bass boost with close use; good frequency response; durable	Electro-Voice, Inc.

(continued)

Table 5.2 | ▶ (*continued*)

Microphone	Element	Description	
Electro-Voice RE-50	Moving coil	Omnidirectional; similar to popular 635A; shock resistant; excellent all-purpose mic; internal wind screen; blast filter; rugged	Electro-Voice, Inc.
Shure SM-58	Moving coil	Cardioid; good studio mic; rugged; **pop filter**	Shure Brothers, Inc.
Shure 300	Ribbon	Bidirectional; warm sound; pop prone; very good voice mic	Shure Brothers, Inc.
Shure SM 33	Ribbon	Cardioid; mellow sound, bass enhanced with proximity; excellent voice mic; favorite of many announcers	Shure Brothers, Inc.
RCA 77DX	Ribbon	Omni-, bi-, or unidirectional (switch selector); classic mic of radio's golden age; switchable bass response; delicate; very fine mic for voice and many musical instruments	

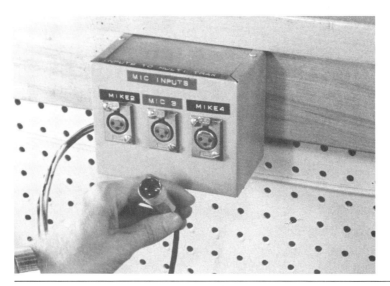

Figure 5.13   XLR connectors. The type being held in the hand is a male.
The receptacle is a female. They snap together easily.

It's generally best to check with engineering staff about connectors you'll need; the specifications can become quite technical, and a certain level of audio engineering sophistication may be needed to make the connection properly.

Usually mics are placed on floor stands or table stands. After the mics have been mounted, the next responsibility of the producer in the studio is to place them properly. This task, of course, will vary with the situation. A news interview program may require placement of only one or two mics; a music-recording session could require the placement of 20 mics—with three of them placed on the drums alone!

Because of the wide variety of situations, we're going to address mic placement separately in appropriate chapters. Placement of mics for news interview shows is dealt with in Chapter 12; the section on music recording in Chapter 14 explains mic placement for music; and so on.

SUMMARY

Sound is produced by the vibration of air molecules. Sound is a combination of wave patterns consisting of higher and lower frequencies. The intensity of a sound is measured in decibels (dB). Microphones transduce the sound vibrations into electrical current, which can then be fed to a recording device or, through a console, to a broadcast transmitter.

Three basic types of microphones are used in broadcasting: moving-coil, also known as *dynamic,* in which sound vibrations cause a coil to move through a magnetic field, thus producing an electric current; ribbon, which features a thin metallic strip suspended between the poles of an electromagnet; and condenser, which discharges current in response to the vibrations of a moving diaphragm.

Microphones have various pickup patterns. Omnidirectional mics pick up sound uniformly from any direction; bidirectional mics pick up sound from the front and rear of the mic but not from the sides; unidirectional or cardioid mics (also known as *directional* mics) pick up sound in front of the mic but not from the sides or rear.

Mics vary in their ability to reproduce sound. The frequency response of a particular mic determines how well it will reproduce a given range of frequencies. Some mics can be adjusted to vary their frequency response. Selecting a mic depends on finding a mic that has the right pickup pattern, physical characteristics, and personality for the particular job.

APPLICATIONS

▪ **Situation 1** ▪ *The Problem* The producer of a 5 o'clock radio program has a touchy problem: The newscaster, Paul Prince, pops his *p*'s badly. What's worse, the station is WPPG (a hypothetical station name) in Pittsburgh, and the name of the show is Public Radio Profiles. Paul sounds terrible when he gives the station identification and introduces himself and the show.

One Possible Solution Short of speech therapy for Paul, the best solution is to exchange the ribbon microphone for a good-quality moving-coil mic, which is exactly what the producer did.

▪ **Situation 2** ▪ *The Problem* The sports director of a small station started to do basketball play-by-play from the gym of the local high school. But listeners complained that at times they had trouble understanding him because of the crowd noise and the related fact that his voice sounded muddy. The sports director surmised that the omnidirectional mic he had mounted on a table stand just wasn't the right unit for the job.

One Possible Solution Although he didn't have a specialized headset mic, the sports director did have access to a microphone with a cardioid pickup pattern, a durable moving-coil element, and a nice speech bump in the response curve. He replaced the omnidirectional mic with this more suitable unit.

EXERCISES

1. Put a microphone on a stand, and set up the console to record its output. Have someone walk around the mic in a circle, while counting or talking. Do this with three different mics: one with an omnidirectional pattern, one with a bidirectional pattern, and one with a cardioid pattern. Play back the tape, and notice the differences in sound pickup.

   Now, using the mic with the cardioid pickup pattern, record some copy read 16 inches from the mic (speaking directly into it) and then 6 inches from the mic. Notice the proximity effect. If the mic has a bass roll-off switch, experiment with using it and gauge the effect on the sound.

2. Set up as many different mics as you have available. Have someone read 30 seconds or so of copy into each mic and record it. (Make sure that person identifies each mic: "I'm reading into the RCA 77DX, 'Four score and seven years ago. . . .' "

   Play back the tape and write down (or discuss) your impressions of each. Give details on why you like or don't like each mic, and what characteristics each has. Make a diligent effort to come up with details. Characteristics of mics aren't always blatantly obvious, and it takes close attention to recognize them.

3. Choose mics for the following applications. You can choose mics from those illustrated in this chapter, or just list the selection factors you'd want for the particular application. For example, a speaker who tends to work very close to the mic and has a bassy, overpowering voice probably should not work with a ribbon mic. A moving-coil or condenser mic would be a better choice. The mic should have a bass roll-off control, and it should have a personality that emphasizes brightness and clarity.

   Now, try the same reasoning with the following situations. (There really aren't any right or wrong answers; most are judgment calls):

   ‣ A speaker with a weak, high, breathy voice
   ‣ Locker room interviews
   ‣ Amateur speakers (guests on an interview show)
   ‣ An announcer who's doing a commercial for a classy restaurant
   ‣ A screaming disc jockey

PART TWO

THE TECHNIQUES

·6·

Splicing and Dubbing

T he next three chapters deal with the mechanics of operating radio production equipment and with the art known as *editing*—the process of rearranging, correcting, and assembling the product into a finished whole.

Production as we've noticed, is something of a nebulous term. Many of us tend to think of radio production as the process of putting together a commercial or assembling a news show. But in truth, any manipulation of sound constitutes production:

‣ Cutting a small piece out of a long interview for airplay during a newscast is production.

‣ Making a 60-second commercial is production.

‣ Running a board while doing a combo operation is production, too— and a very important type of production at that, since the combo operator reflects the overall sound of the station.

We're going to divide the basic production chapters along the lines of the three examples above. This chapter spells out the basic mechanics of manipulating sound physically and electronically, and it shows some of the patterns this manipulation takes. Chapter 7 focuses on some of the techniques specific to working in the studio and producing segments to be played back on air at a later date, such as commercials and public-service announcements. Chapter 8 deals with the techniques used in on-air work.

There is, of course, quite a bit of overlap among the techniques, but we think you'll find this a logical way to go about exploring the nuts and bolts of radio production. Chapter 8 expands on the foregoing ideas and moves on into the subtleties of using radio production techniques to reinforce a message and to create a particular effect, which is the real goal of sitting down at the console in the first place.

▪   THE BASICS OF SPLICING   ▪
AND DUBBING

The processes of splicing, dubbing, and editing are the most basic ways in which a radio producer manipulates sound. In **splicing** the tape is physically cut apart and taped back together again. **Dubbing** means transferring sound from source to source electronically, instead of snipping and cutting. **Editing** is a combination of the two, and more: It is the process of rearranging, correcting, and assembling a finished product. *Editing* is a general term, and the process is something you'll pick up in the course of doing different kinds of production.

Some people use the words *splicing* and *dubbing* in a slightly different way, considering splicing to be a simple, physical repair, whereas dubbing involves making a copy of a tape. To acknowledge this distinction, they use the terms *physical editing* and *electronic editing* to express the functions discussed above. We'll stick to *splicing* and *dubbing* as defined at the opening of this section, but be aware that the terminology can vary.

Splicing and dubbing require the mastery of some specific techniques before those physical skills can be used in the editing process.

▪   SPLICING   ▪

The most common reason for cutting a tape and sticking it back together again is to eliminate a portion of what was recorded. Alternatively a producer may splice to rearrange portions of a tape into a more logical sequence, or simply to shorten what has been recorded. Proficiency at splicing is helpful because it allows you to fix broken tapes quickly. Tape breaks occur quite frequently, and if you're pulling an airshift you may have to put a tape back together in a hurry.

The steps in splicing are as follows: marking the first edit point, marking the second edit point, cutting the tape, and making the splice. Let's take them in order.

Marking the First Edit Point

Suppose you have just completed an interview with the mayor, who has told you about an important development. You want to use a brief segment of the interview for an upcoming newscast. The recorded interview goes like this:

> MAYOR: We have decided to go ahead with construction of a new cross-town expressway from the junction of Interstate 440 to, as you can see right here on the map, Commercial Street, where there will be a major interchange.

Because the reference to the map is lost on a radio audience, we don't want to include the mayor's mention of the map. The task at hand, then, is to cut out the portion of the reel-to-reel tape where the mayor says, "as you can see right here on the map."

Since the statement would make much better sense if the reference were eradicated, the logical place to make the first edit point would be:

> MAYOR: We have decided to go ahead with construction of a new cross-town expressway from the junction of Interstate 440 to, as you can see right here on the map—   ∧
> **First edit**
> **point**

The first edit point is where we want to physically cut the tape. To do so, we have to find that point exactly on the tape, which means that we have to mark it as it passes over the play head.

Play the tape until you reach the approximate first edit point, then stop it quickly. Now, rocking the reels as shown in Figure 6.1(a), manipulate the tape until you've got the play head directly between *to* and *as*. With practice, you'll be able to recognize both words, forward and backward. Remember, if the tape runs at $7\frac{1}{2}$ IPS, a second's pause between the two words will be $7\frac{1}{2}$ inches long—quite enough tape to make cutting in the gap easy.

Next, with a grease pencil, mark the spot where you plan to make the cut, as shown in Figure 6.1(b). Be very careful not to smear the grease pencil on the head. Just put a precise dot on the back of the tape at the edit point. Grease pencils (also called *china markers*) come in a variety of colors, and for editing purposes you'll want a light color, such as white or yellow.

Marking the Second Edit Point

Since you want to cut out the part where the mayor refers to the map, you will play the tape past the first edit point (which you've already marked) and find the second edit point:

Figure 6.1   Preparing a tape for splicing.

(a) Rocking the reels of the tape
   recorder.

(b) Marking an edit point. Be careful
   not to get grease pencil on the head.

Second edit point

∨

MAYOR: —right here on the map, Commercial Street, where there
will be a major interchange.

Repeat the process of rocking the reels until you isolate the gap between
the words *map* and *Commercial.* Mark the second edit point. At this point,
you have two marks on tape: at the beginning of the mayor's visual reference, and at the end. Now that you've marked the tape, you can cut out
and throw away the italicized segment of the interview:

MAYOR: We have decided to go ahead with construction of a new
cross-town expressway from the junction of Interstate 440 to, *as
you can see right here on the map,* Commercial Street, where there
will be a major interchange.

Cutting the Tape

You're ready to cut the offending section (marked in italics) out. To do
this, you will use an **editing block** (Fig. 6.2(a)), which has a lip that holds
the tape lightly but securely in the channel, and two grooves for guiding
the razor blade. To prepare to make the cut, rewind the tape to the first
edit point. Then, using your hands to turn the reels, spool out the tape
until you have a good length to work with. Remove the marked tape from
the heads (Fig. 6.2(b)), bring the tape down, and place it into the channel

Figure 6.2   Cutting a tape at the edit points.

(a) Editing block. The pencil indicates the groove in the editing block. The groove has a lip that holds the tape down.

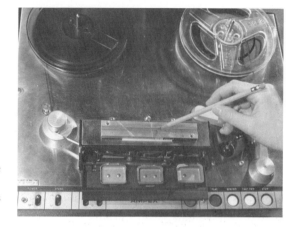

(b) Removing marked tape from the heads.

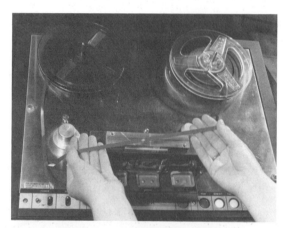

(c) Positioning the tape in the channel, with the first edit point over the groove.

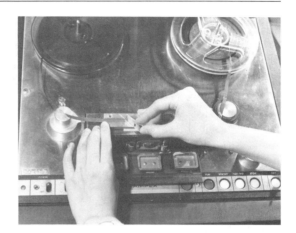

(d) Making the cut.

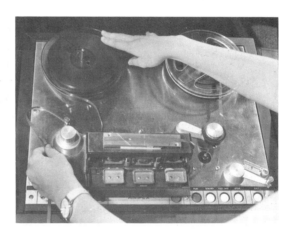

(e) Spilling off tape after making the cut.

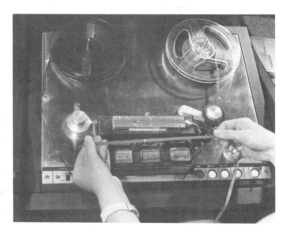

(f) Finding the second mark.

of the editing block (Fig. 6.2(c)). Position the first edit point in line with the 45-degree groove. You'll want to use the 45-degree groove in almost all editing applications, because the angled cut eliminates much of the magnetic popping noise that can result from vertical cutting and joining. The vertical groove is useful primarily for extremely tight edits.

Sweep the razor blade through the groove (Fig. 6.2(d)). Don't chop down, or all you'll get is a mangled tape. Remove the unwanted tape from the channel of the edit block, and then thread the tape from the supply reel back through the tape guides and between the capstan and drive wheel. Spill off the tape until it reaches the second edit point. You can either place the tape recorder in play or simply pull the tape by hand (Fig. 6.2(e)), until you locate the second edit point (Fig. 6.2(f)). Beware of stretching the tape as you pull.

Once you've located the second edit point, repeat the cutting procedure. You can discard the piece of tape that's been cut off, but it's wise to save it at least momentarily, in case you've made a mistake in the cutting process and have to try to patch things up.

Making the Splice

The final step is to stick the two ends of the tape together. This can be done with splicing tape, as shown in Figure 6.3(a), or with specially made editing **tabs**. Try to keep pieces of splicing tape about $\frac{1}{2}$ to $\frac{3}{4}$ inch long. Too long a piece may result in a noisy edit; too short a piece may not hold. Try not to touch the sticky portion of the tape; if you do, you'll weaken the adhesive.

Now place the first end of the tape (the end you want to join to the piece you've just cut) in the channel (Fig. 6.3(b)). It's wise to move the joint away from the groove where the cut was made, to avoid having a piece of tape stick down in the groove and cause trouble with the splice. This isn't done by most editors, but it can't hurt and could possibly save a splice.

Butt the ends of the tape together, but don't overlap them. Then cut off $\frac{1}{2}$ inch or so of editing tape, place the tape or tab over the joint, as shown in Figure 6.3(c), and burnish the tape with your fingernail (Fig. 6.3(d)) to secure the edit tab to the tape. It's very important to secure the splice at this point, because you don't want to take the chance of having the tape come apart during fast-forwarding or rewinding. Finally, grasp the tape at both sides of the editing block, as shown in Figure 6.3(e). Gently snap the tape out of the channel, and give it a little tug to test the security of the splice (Fig. 6.3(f)).

Figure 6.3   Making a splice.

(a) Splicing tape.

(b) Butting the two ends
together in the channel of
the editing block.

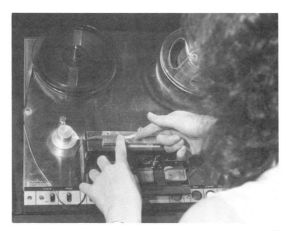

(c) Placing the splicing
tape over the butt.

(continued)

Figure 6.3   *(continued)*

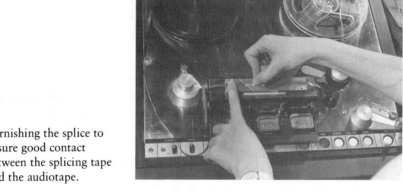

(d) Burnishing the splice to ensure good contact between the splicing tape and the audiotape.

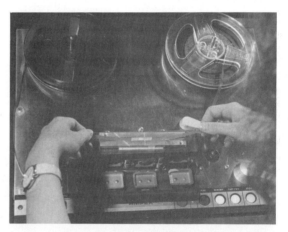

(e) Removing the tape from the channel.

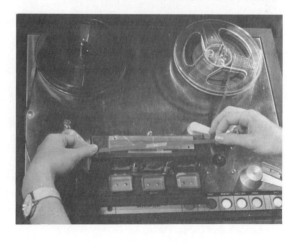

(f) The completed splice.

After the splice has been completed, the reels of the tape machine can be manipulated so that the tape is spooled back on the reels. Play the tape back to check the edit. It should sound like this:

MAYOR: We have decided to go ahead with construction of a new cross-town expressway from the junction of Interstate 440 to Commercial Street, where there will be a major interchange.

Playing back the tape will also show whether you've timed the splice correctly. In other words, you will find out whether you left the right amount of space—not too much and not too little—between the words, so that the edit sounds natural. With practice you will gain expertise in the proper pacing of words as you edit.

Two brief cautions: First, razor blades can become magnetized, so it is a good idea to demagnetize them with the bulk eraser before each editing session. Second, always remember that clean heads are essential. Use a swab dipped in alcohol to wipe the heads clean, and be especially careful to remove any marking pencil residue.

Leader Tape

Another reason for splicing is to attach **leader and timing tape** (Fig. 6.4). Leader tape doesn't record or play back any information. It's used because it's visible. Leader tape is often used to separate cuts. The tape allows the operator to see where the next cut starts, rather than having to search for it and cue it by ear.

Leader tape is also very useful for the start of a tape. For one thing, the start of a tape suffers a lot of wear and tear because it typically spools off the takeup reel and flips around when the tape is rewound. Leader tape protects the recorded portion of the tape from damage. By the way, the technical term for the start of the tape is the *head;* the end of the tape is the *tail.* Tape boxes are often marked "head" or "tail" out, to indicate whether the reel has been rewound or not after recording or playback.

A handy feature of leader tape is that most varieties are timed; that is, they have a pattern that visually shows $7\frac{1}{2}$ inches of tape, allowing the producer to tell by looking how much time the leader represents. One other point: You can write on leader tape, so the head of the tape can be labeled.

Review of Splicing

Splicing is the process of cutting a tape and sticking it back together again. Splicing is useful for eliminating unwanted portions of a tape, shortening program material, or rearranging material.

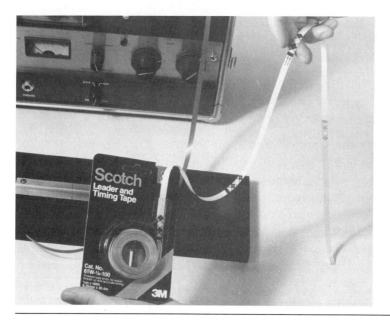

Figure 6.4   Leader and timing tape.

The cut is made at a 45-degree angle in an editing block, with a razor blade. A very convenient way to make the splice is with edit tabs. Leader tape is often spliced to regular audiotape. Leader tape is used to separate segments and protect the head and tail of the tape; it can be written on.

▪   DUBBING   ▪

Dubbing is often used in what's called **electronic splicing** or **electronic editing,** and those are pretty good descriptions of what happens.

A producer could, for example, accomplish the same goal with the mayor's interview by dubbing portions of the tape onto another tape or onto a cart. For example, the producer might mount the mayor's interview tape on tape 1 and record the output of the board on tape 2. To do this, the producer puts tape 1 in Play and tape 2 in Record, and dubs:

MAYOR: We have decided to go ahead with construction of a new crosstown expressway from the junction of Interstate 440 to—

After the word *to* tape 2 is quickly stopped and tape 1 is allowed to play until the extraneous material ["as you can see right here on the map"] is over.

Rocking the reels, the producer cues tape 1 up exactly between the words *map* and *Commercial,* and then puts tape 1 in Play and tape 2 in Record simultaneously, dubbing over the last portion of the quote ["—Commercial Street, where there will be a major interchange."].

Incidentally, if you can disable the cue tone on the cart machine model you're using, the same result can be accomplished by dubbing the cuts onto a cart. Be sure to ask your instructor or studio supervisor if doing this is permissible, and be certain to arm the cue tone again when you're done, or the next user of the cart machine will encounter problems.

Many newer tape machines have a synchronization feature for locating the exact recording spot on the tape by using the record head as a temporary playback head. These machines also have the ability to punch in and out of Record mode without putting pops and clicks on the tape. If your machine has this feature, you can easily delete a word or a sentence and punch in a new one without physically cutting the tape.

Problems Associated with Dubbing

The same goal is accomplished by using electronic editing in dubbing, as by splicing. Playing back the tape, though, will probably reveal that the edit is not as clean as the splice; there may be some electronic noise at the edit point, and the rhythm of the pause may not be perfect. That's one of the main difficulties with dubbing: It's just not as precise as cutting and splicing the tape.

Also, dubbing from one source to another too many times can cause the quality of the recording to deteriorate. Every new dub of a recording is known as another **generation.** Generating the tape too often can result in a loss of quality, including the introduction of additional noises into the recording.

Advantages of Dubbing

Dubbing allows you to overlap elements. If, for example, you want to edit in a piece of music and talk over it, fading the music out, you will have to use dubbing. Another plus of dubbing is that it's much, much faster and simpler than cutting the tape. Production by dubbing will probably account for the vast majority of the editing work you'll do.

You will often use the dubbing technique when editing a cassette tape. To edit a cassette, either dub the whole tape onto a reel-to-reel and splice the reel-to-reel, or make electronic edits while playing the cassette and recording on reel-to-reel or cart.

Review of Dubbing

Dubbing involves recording program material from one source to another. It is very useful in editing, because it's less work than splicing; but dubbing isn't quite as accurate when it comes to locating editing points. Dubbing is almost always used when elements are overlapped, especially in music.

▪   EDITING   ▪

Both splicing and dubbing can be used in the editing process. But what, exactly, are you trying to accomplish during an editing session? Of course, a radio producer undertakes a great number of tasks—from running a live air show to producing a commercial to assembling a newscast. This book devotes separate chapters to the content and production techniques used in each of those categories.

Some of the basic editing structures, however, are common to live shows, commercials, newscasts, public-affairs programming, and so on. By "editing structure," we mean particular patterns of construction that appear frequently in radio production.

For example, notice how many commercials start with music: The music **fades** down as the announcer starts reading, and the music comes back up when the announcer has finished the spiel. This technique—a structure used in editing and production—is pretty common in radio today. You'll be able to apply it in many situations.

Let's look at some of the basic **editing/production structures**; in later chapters, we will apply these structures to the production of specific pieces.

Establish Music, Music Under, Voice Up

Establish music, music under, voice up is a sequence frequently used as an introduction to certain types of radio programs. In this procedure, you **establish** the music—allow a second or two so that the listener gets a chance to recognize that a piece of music is being played—and then pot the music under, to a low but still audible level. As soon as the music is under (potting the music under should take just a second or so), the voice comes in.

The trick here is to strike a good balance between voice and music. Ideally, the establishing music should peak the VU at 0, and when the voice is brought in, the voice should also peak the VU at 0. The music under the voice should not be loud enough to make the voice difficult to understand, but the listener should be able to hear it.

As you've certainly guessed, there's no standard formula for how loud the music should be. It's a judgment call that must be made by ear. But one advantage of working in radio is that there's plenty of opportunity for hearing how your colleagues do the same job.

Cross-fade

The technique of **cross-fading** is used in all sorts of production, including airshifts. You simply pot one source down while potting the other up. The result should be a smooth transition between the two, usually with a moment of overlap. The sound from the second source is established before the first source is (quickly) dropped.

A cross-fade is the technique used to move gracefully from one source to another, to **segue.** *Segue* means transition, and a cross-fade is one type of transition. Not all segues, or transitions, are cross-fades, however.

Sometimes, cross-fades are used to camouflage the need to shorten a piece of music that is used as background, or **bed,** for a commercial. For example, a producer who wants to use a 3-minute music cut for a 1-minute commercial may record the final 30 seconds of the music on a cart. By playing the first 30 seconds of the cut off the disk and then cross-fading into the final 30 seconds on cart, the producer creates a bed that has a definite beginning and end. This spot will involve use of the next editing structure: voice out, music up.

Voice Out, Music Up

Commonly used at the end of a spot, voice out, music up is particularly effective when used with music that ends with a definite climax. In this case, dead-potting the cut is often used. (Dead-potting, as you remember, involves starting and playing a cut when it is not up on the board; the cut is backtimed to end at a specific predetermined point.)

Voice out, music up is also, of course, used by radio announcers who talk over the beginning of a cut and then bring up the music—usually at the start of the vocal.

Music Wrap

The **music wrap** is a combination of the three editing structures discussed so far. It is the structure we described in the example of a 1-minute commercial that featured music at the beginning, voice in the middle, and music at the end.

Voice Wrap

In a **voice wrap,** one voice starts, another voice is edited in, and the first voice returns to close out the segment. This structure is used extensively in news production. Here's an example:

ANNOUNCER: Mayor Louis Hazzard today ended weeks of speculation about the new highway that has been proposed for Centerville.

MAYOR: We have decided to go ahead with construction of a new crosstown expressway from the junction of Interstate 440 to Commercial Street, where there will be a major interchange.

ANNOUNCER: The crosstown expressway is expected to be the first leg of a major transportation network designed to link Centerville with the neighboring communities of Leftville and Rightville. This is Bob Robertson reporting from City Hall.

Using Editing and Production Structures

There are, of course, countless variations of editing structures, but the ones presented here are among the most basic and frequently repeated. By recognizing the basic editing structures, and by practicing the mechanics necessary to manufacture them using the console and equipment, you can develop habits that will greatly simplify production in the future. For example, *establish music, music under, voice up* is a very common component of radio production. After you have executed this structure a few times, it will become second nature. Every time it's called for, you'll be able to do it as a reflex.

Review of Editing

Editing is the process of rearranging, correcting, and assembling the product into a finished whole. Splicing and dubbing are the mechanics; editing is the art.

One way to look at editing is to examine some of the basic editing structures: *establish music, music under, voice up; cross-fade; voice out, music up; music wrap;* and *voice wrap.* Other structures exist, and there are many variations on the basic editing structures, but a good grasp of the basics will make production much easier because constructing the common patterns will become automatic.

SUMMARY

Taped segments are separated and joined in two ways: by mechanical splic-ing (the cutting and pasting of the tape), and by dubbing (the electronic copying and reinsertion of the taped material). Splicing is usually accom-plished by using a grease pencil to mark the edit points; a razor blade is then used to remove the extraneous material, and the ends are butted together and joined with splicing tape. Dubbing is usually done by copying the audio onto cartridge or onto another reel-to-reel tape.

The purpose of splicing is usually to eliminate words on a tape, although it can serve other purposes. Dubbing can accomplish the same process, but is also useful for combining many production elements in the least com-plicated fashion (for example, adding music under voice and sound effects over voice). One great advantage to dubbing is that it is nondestructive; if you blow it the first time, you can always try again.

The goal of splicing and dubbing is editing, the process of picking and arranging program elements. Editing structures include *establish music, music under, voice up; cross-fade; voice-out, music up; music wrap; and voice wrap*.

APPLICATIONS

▪ **Situation 1** ▪ *The Problem* A production manager at a local radio station was given the job of producing a commercial for a local political candidate. As part of the commercial, the candidate discussed his views for 40 seconds. However, the candidate had an unfortunate speech pattern: He interjected "uhhhh" many times during his presentation.

One Possible Solution Since it was the producer's job—in this case—to present the candidate in a positive light, the producer took out the editing block and razor blade and sliced all the "uhhhhs" from the politician's remarks. The job took 20 minutes, but the resulting tape sounded smooth and clean.

▪ **Situation 2** ▪ *The Problem* The producer of an entertainment show did an interview (on location, using a cassette) with the head of a local theater group. The producer wanted to weave three cuts of the interview into her script.

The script went along the following lines: "And what does Pat Wilbur, head of the Starlight Theater Group, have planned for this season?" . . .

(Cut of interview) . . . "But will attendance be better this year than last year's dismal totals?" . . . (Second cut of interview) . . . "So how does Pat Wilbur intend to get those attendance figures up?" . . . (Third cut of interview).
What would be the best way to weave those cuts into the script?

One Possible Solution The producer listened to the entire interview several times and made precise notes on where she wanted to cut in and out of the interview. Because time was short, she decided to dub the three cuts directly onto cart, which would be used to play the cuts over the air (the show was done live). She put the cart machine on Record, rolled the cassette tape, and started the cart as soon as the appropriate section of the interview began, stopping the cart as soon as the desired section of the interview ended. This was repeated for the other two cuts. The cue tones were left on, of course. Thus there were three cuts on the cart. Every time the producer wanted to play a cut of the interview, she simply hit the start button on the cart machine. The cart cued up the next cut automatically.

EXERCISES

1. If you have two or more cart machines available, dub a piece of audio from cart to cart. For example, start with a 10-second music cut dubbed onto a cart; take that cart and dub from Cart 1 to Cart 2. Now dub from Cart 2 back to Cart 1 (put a clean cart in Cart 1) or to Cart 3, if you have a Cart 3.

   This exercise will accomplish two goals: letting you hear what impact successive generations of tape have, and understanding the relationship of cart machines (in terms of record and playback) to the console.

2. Interview a classmate or colleague, take three cuts from the interview, and weave them into a script similar to the one described in Situation 2 of this chapter. (What you're doing is assembling a series of voice wraps.) Don't be too concerned about the content of the interview or the script; this is just a vehicle for practicing editing techniques. The whole program need not be longer than a minute or so.

   In this exercise you will assemble the show first by using dubbing techniques; you can dub onto cart or onto reel-to-reel tape, whichever seems easier.

3. Now, edit the same show together, using splicing.

4. Listen to a half-hour of radio, and identify as many editing structures as you can. Write down, for example: "Introduction to the 4 o'clock news on WAAA: An *establish music, music under, voice up.* This was followed by a *voice wrap* during the first news report. . . ."

·7·

Recorded Program
Production

Recorded program production is a term we use to refer loosely to any radio production work that is not done live over the air. In most cases, the recording is done in preparation for use over the air at a later date.

The basic difference between recorded production and live, on-air production (covered in the next chapter) is that on-air production is a one-shot affair; there's only one opportunity to get it right. In recorded studio work, the producer has the freedom to do several retakes of the same production element, to try different blends and mixes, and to scrap the whole project and start over again if it's not working out.

Because of these luxuries, much more complex productions are attempted in recorded work. Whereas mixing a narration, multiple sound effects, and a musical bed would be next to impossible all in one take, it becomes a simple matter in the recording studio, since the tasks can be attempted one at a time, with the various elements divided into logical steps.

■ RECORDED VERSUS LIVE,
ON-AIR PRODUCTION ■

How does a radio producer decide whether a production will be done live or put together in advance? There are three elements to consider.

Complexity

As mentioned above, a production containing many elements must be done in advance. Many commercials are read live, but these are almost always one-voice affairs, with the announcer simply reading copy or **ad-libbing** from a fact sheet.

Scheduled Airtime

A talk show that airs at 5:30 A.M. Sunday will be prerecorded in the studio, usually during normal weekday working hours. Obviously, it is not practical to try to get guests to appear live on a predawn show.

On the other hand, newscasts generally are not recorded (and when they are, it's done as close to airtime as possible), because they become outdated quickly, as the news changes.

Convenience

If a production calls for the voice of a specific announcer, is it more convenient to record the announcer or to have her or him come in every time that production is aired? The same rationale applies to the need for repetition of a production. While the use of music and narration for the introduction of a show might be done live if the program is a one-time affair, prerecording the introduction will be far more convenient if it is to be repeated weekly or daily.

Along the same lines, preproducing a piece reduces the chance that an error will be made over the air.

■   LAYOUT OF A   ■
PRODUCTION STUDIO

In a small radio station, the production studio is usually located wherever it fits; often, it is in the record library or in an engineering area, or even in a corner of the manager's office. In a somewhat larger station, the basic production studio often looks like the one shown in Figure 7.1.

On the other end of the spectrum is the fully equipped, high-tech production studio (see Fig. 1.2, p. 9). Another variation of the top-of-the-line studio is a setup with **multitrack** mixing capabilities for recording and remixing original music. Recording and mixing music are discussed later in this chapter.

Figure 7.1   Basic production studio.

Most large studio setups feature a glassed-in area between the main control room and the studio; in large music production studios, the glass divides the performance area of the studio from the control area. The glass is typically double-layered, and the panes are not set parallel to each other or to the studio wall (Fig. 7.2), to prevent internal and external reflections of sound.

The more typical radio-station production studio is a one-room setup, with the equipment usually intended for combo use. Although the studio is intended for off-air production, there generally will be a **hard-wired** link to the main control room so that the output of the production studio can be put live over the air. This arrangement comes in handy when the main control room is out of commission during repairs or other emergencies. The studio may also double as an announce booth, used especially by the news department. The news department may also have its own production area (Fig. 7.3).

Equipment in the Production Studio

In most cases, the production studio's equipment will virtually duplicate what's in an on-air studio, although there may not be as much of it, and in some stations the production equipment may be hand-me-downs from

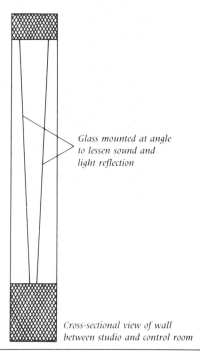

*Glass mounted at angle
to lessen sound and
light reflection*

*Cross-sectional view of wall
between studio and control room*

Figure 7.2   Double layer of glass used to separate control room from production
studio. Air space between the panes of glass provides sound insulation
from adjacent areas.

the on-air control room. The minimum equipment usually includes some
sort of console, a mic, two cart machines, two tape recorders, and two
turntables. The console may be a portable mixer or the portable console
the station uses for **remotes.**

A patchbay is almost always a fixture of the production studio. In many
cases, the patchbay allows interconnection of the production studio with
other studios, with the network, or even directly with the transmitter.
There is often some sort of talkback system between studios.

Sound Treatment in the Production Studio

A commercially available sound-deading material (Fig. 7.4) is commonly
used to dampen sound reflection in the production studio. Sometimes, egg
cartons are cut up and attached to the walls, serving the same effect.

A carpet is very helpful for deadening sound reflection. On occasion,
the carpet is applied to walls to help create a dead environment. Studios

Figure 7.3   News production area.

Figure 7.4   Sound-deadening material attached to
studio walls to reduce unwanted sound
reflection.

designed for music recording often have curtains, which can be spread to deaden sound or pulled back to expose the bare walls when a livelier sound is desired.

As mentioned earlier, the production studio in a small station may serve double duty, and a combined record library–production studio is common; in fact, stacks of records do a good job of sound baffling.

■ WORKING IN A ■
PRODUCTION STUDIO

Who works in the production studio environment? In some stations, a production manager is in charge of the studio and has the responsibility of overseeing all the station's off-air production. Staff announcers also use production facilities for such duties as commercial production. In smaller stations, sales people often produce their own commercials. Basically, the studio is used by anyone who has to construct a production for later airplay. In this sense all staff members assigned such duties are producers.

Anyone who undertakes the duties of a producer is responsible for knowing much more about the process of radio than someone who acts simply as an announcer or as a technician. A producer must understand the methods of constructing a **spot** or program. For example, it may be more efficient to break the production down into a number of discrete tasks, such as doing all the music work first and all the narration next, even though that is not the sequence in which the components will appear in the final product.

An analogy from the movie production business is illustrative. Perhaps a certain restaurant is the setting of the last sequence of a movie, and the film begins in the same restaurant. From the standpoint of the producer, who has to move around crew, actors, extras, and sets, it makes sense to shoot the beginning and ending scenes on the same day. (It's not unheard of for the ending of a movie to be shot on the first day of production.) In other words, the pieces or sequences of a movie can be filmed in any order and then edited together in accordance with the script.

You'll find that the same strategy often proves useful in the radio production studio. And, since time demands on a studio are usually high, you'll be able to get in and out much faster if you learn to plan work in **task-oriented sequence**. If, for instance, you have three similar commercials to produce, it may prove useful to do the announcing for all three first—on the same tape—and add the music beds to all three next.

Working in task-oriented sequence will become second nature as long as you make an effort to break old thought patterns that require you to work in real-time sequence (doing the beginning first, the middle next, and the ending last). Always structure your tasks according to the most convenient and efficient method for the best use of the production studio available. Understanding this principle is what separates a producer from someone who just puts sound on tape.

Another factor that will help you develop skill and recognition as a radio producer is an understanding of the basic building blocks of radio and how they relate to studio production. We're talking about music, voice, and sound effects.

▪ MUSIC ▪

Music is a very important element in radio production; indeed, it can be argued that music is what radio is all about. In any event, it's important for a producer to have an understanding of music. Good producers have the ability to use music to their advantage, to manipulate music to create an effect. Good producers also understand the kinds and varieties of music, and thus can fit productions into the station's overall format. In a production studio setting, you will generally be using segments of music, rather than entire cuts.

Sources of Music

The music you will use will almost always be prerecorded on disc or CDs, or downlinked from a satellite. The use of music is licensed to a radio station by means of a fee paid to music licensing organizations, the largest of which are the American Society of Composers, Authors and Publishers (**ASCAP**) and Broadcast Music Incorporated (**BMI**). Licensing fees also cover the use of music in production work. Popular music (the kind played over the air as entertainment) is commonly used in all sorts of studio production.

Sometimes, though, specific requirements are not filled very well by the popular music available. Specialized musical selections have been developed to meet these needs. Various companies sell what are usually called **production libraries**: recorded original music that fits the most common production and time requirements in typical stations. For example, **music beds** run exactly 60 or 30 seconds.

Generic vocal selections are available that can be adapted to fit the needs of commercial production for local merchants. Thus a 30-second cut might start with a group of vocalists singing: "Downtown is the greatest place to shop." The instrumental background would continue, serving as a bed for

the local announcer to fill with copy advertising a local downtown merchant. The vocal would return, 25 seconds into the cut, to close out the
piece with: "Do your shopping downtown, where you'll find everything
you need!"

Advertising agencies, which commission the composition of original music
for clients, are another source of music. Such music usually takes the form
of a jingle, which is incorporated into the client's radio (and sometimes
TV) advertising. The beds supplied by ad agencies are very similar to the
works furnished by the production library companies, except that the ad
agency's musical jingle is specific to one client. Some large companies provide their franchises with standardized commercial beds that can be "local-
ized" at the different radio stations.

Specialized productions generally are easier to work with (you don't have
to do as much adaptation of the music, such as telescoping the beginning
and end together for one 30-second spot). However, the station has to pay
for prepackaged production music, and some of it is pretty hokey.

It's safe to assume that most of your production work will be done with
popular music whose main purpose is airplay. But you can adapt it for
production purposes.

Choosing Music for Production Work

Music can make or break a production. A commercial, for example, can
gain significant impact through the selection of background music that
reinforces the message. A poor selection, though, can detract from the
message or even be at odds with it. For instance, copy that touts the benefits
of a relaxing vacation through the Acme Travel Agency won't be reinforced
by blaring rock music. No copy will be helped by an overly familiar vocal
selection that draws attention away from the message. The selection of
music, incidentally, can be a formidable task. Even the smallest radio station may have thousands of records in the station library.

In many cases, radio stations categorize music held in their libraries by
type (rock, country, jazz, and so on). Still others utilize a color code, or a
numerical or alphabetical listing for their music libraries. It is important
to understand the broad classifications that stations use so that you can
locate music by type quickly and easily. We'll be discussing some broad
classifications later in this chapter.

Many stations segregate music libraries into vocal and instrumental
selections, and since most production music is instrumental, your choice
will be narrowed somewhat. Some stations designate a shelf for good production music, which is handy but may entail the risk of causing a few

pieces of music to become overused. And there is a danger of overusing popular music. As indicated above, a catchy, popular tune might attract more attention than the message of the commercial; the listener will be hearing the music, not the message.

Many production pieces are chosen by someone who—after years of studio production experience—notices that a certain **cut** on the air would be a particularly good piece for production work. Perhaps it is an instrumental section that conveys excitement, or enjoyment, or some other mood. A great many air people develop their own particular favorites for commercial production, although this, too, entails a risk that the music will be used too often.

In any case, the music must reinforce the message, not distract or detract from it. The style has to fit both the message and the station's format.

Styles of Music

A broad knowledge of music is critical to the radio professional. First of all, even if your intention is to pursue a career in rock radio, circumstances may dictate a two-year stint at a station with a country format, or a beautiful-music format. Stations with a broad-ranging format may use a variety of music styles in production, and it's incumbent on you to understand the styles and be able to utilize them effectively. In addition, modern music produces many **crossovers** from one style into another. Some country music, for example, almost sounds like jazz. Being able to recognize elements of various styles will help you categorize music and better utilize it to achieve effects. Trade magazines can help you learn more about music and music categories.

Here are the characteristics of some of the major styles of music.

Rock In most cases, rock features drums and electric guitars. There's generally a distinctive rhythm, which is maintained by bass drum and bass guitar. More avant-garde types of rock music include elaborate electronic effects. The milder rock music selections are probably the most commonly used pieces in radio production.

Country The twang of country music is its most recognizable attribute, although much of the country music repertoire is orchestrated and virtually indistinguishable from general popular music. The steel guitar was once the cornerstone of country music, although nowadays almost any combination of instruments can be used.

Country music is used in production to achieve special effects (as a musical bed for a rodeo commercial, perhaps) and, of course, is used extensively in production on country-format stations.

Jazz This style of music can run the gamut from traditional big-band dance music to bizarre and highly experimental compositions. Jazz generally uses a syncopated rhythm.

Jazz has many uses in production and is particularly helpful because so much of it is instrumental. The more experimental types of jazz are less useful, although they can sometimes be selected for effect.

Classical The term *classical music* is something of a misnomer, because the word *classical* really refers to one type of music in the spectrum popularly understood as "classical." The classical period is typified by the music of Mozart. The baroque period, which preceded the classical, is most commonly associated with Bach, who created multiple melodies that interact contrapuntally. (This type of music is referred to as *polyphonic;* its sound can be approximated by the familiar round "Row, Row, Row Your Boat.") The romantic period of music followed the classical period and is characterized by the works of Tchaikovsky and by the later works of Beethoven.

For lack of a better term, *classical* will suffice, although some people refer to this style as *concert music* or good music. Classical music occasionally is useful in production, generally to achieve a special effect.

General Popular Music This broad category can encompass many others. Essentially, though, general popular music tends to be more melodic and orchestral than rock. Violins and other bowed strings are used, as are woodwinds. Piano is a typical feature of general popular music. Many of the lower-key rock music selections certainly fit into this category. At the other end of the spectrum are the beautiful-music selections of Henry Mancini or the Hollywood Strings. This style of music is especially useful in general production duties, since much of it is instrumental.

Specialty Music This category includes polkas, waltzes, and marches, which are used in production work when a specific effect is called for.

▪ RECORDED VOICE ▪

Voice, the second major element of production, can be recorded by an announcer running a combo operation, or by a producer running the console while others speak into a mic or mics.

One common studio production task is the miking of several speakers, sometimes in a roundtable type of discussion. Here, the microphone techniques discussed in Chapter 5 come into play, along with some other considerations we'll discuss shortly. The most important goal of recording voice in a studio production setting, though, is to get a clean recording that accentuates the announcer's voice and delivery. Achieving this goal may involve such considerations as:

▸ Selecting a mic that deemphasizes peculiarities of a performer's speech, such as *p*-popping or excessive **sibilance.**

▸ Replacing a highly sensitive mic with a less sensitive model to cut down on noise from air conditioning or from the clicking of the speaker's dentures.

▸ Eliminating table noises (nonprofessional speakers are notorious for table-tapping or clicking pens) by hanging the microphone from a boom rather than having it attached to a table stand.

▸ Instructing speakers, both professional and nonprofessional, on positioning and use of the mic. Nonprofessional speakers frequently need to be cautioned about speaking too close to the mic.

Duties of these types are common in all production setups. While in some instances recording voice in the production studio is a very simple affair, other situations are complex. Two of the most common difficulties encountered in production work are the problem of miking multiple speakers and the problem of communicating with speakers when the mics are open.

Miking Multiple Speakers

One typical function of the radio station's production specialist is to set up and record panel discussion shows. With a number of interviewees in the studio, it is tempting to string up mics for everyone who is likely to open her or his mouth. Most experts agree, however, that the fewer mics you can get away with, the better. An overabundance of mics can cause difficulties in engineering the show (trying to find the right pot to adjust, for example, when you're dealing with six or seven) and phasing difficulties.

It is, however, practical to use two mics when there are two speakers. Perhaps the most common type of interview program involves a single host and a single guest, and recording of the show can be pulled off quite nicely with two cardioid mics, with little overlap of the pickup pattern (Fig. 7.5).

The advantage of this setup is that the operator is free to control the individual volumes and to maintain a comfortable balance. A bidirectional

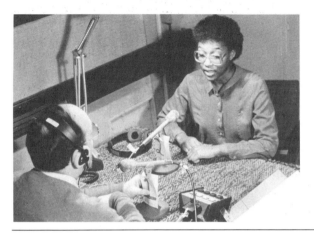

Figure 7.5 Simple two-person interview, using
cardioid mics.

or omnidirectional mic can be used instead, but the loss in flexibility usually
isn't worth the convenience gained from a simpler setup. But when there
are several speakers, simplicity of mic setup is indeed a virtue. One mic
suspended from the ceiling may give better results than an individual mic
for each speaker. As we mentioned, phasing problems plague the multiple-
mic setup. Moreover, every time you open a mic, the *room tone*, or noise
present in the studio, increases.

To understand phasing problems, let's first recall our discussion of directional mics in Chapter 5. Remember that a **directional mic** cancels sound
by means of an acoustic network inside the mic; that is, sounds reach the
diaphragm at different times and therefore cancel themselves out. The same
effect occurs in the studio: Sound arrives at different mics at different times,
with just enough difference to throw the phasing off.

This will seem less abstract when you consider that sound does not travel
very quickly; while 1,100 feet per second may seem like a pretty fast clip,
note how sound lags behind vision. From the top row of the bleachers, you
can easily discern the gap between when the basketball hits the floor during
a dribble and when you *hear* it hit the floor. Track runners start when they
see the smoke from the starter's pistol, rather than waiting for the noise,
which they hear a split second later. Now, with sound waves making, let's
say, 5,000 cycles per second (5,000 Hz), it's easy to see how a small delay
can cause the cycles to be out of phase.

The solution to phasing problems is to avoid, as much as possible, any
overlap among the mic pickup patterns. Sometimes this entails putting
more than one speaker on a mic, to avoid overlapping pickup patterns. For

Figure 7.6   Layout enabling six speakers to be positioned around three mics. Separation and proper orientation of the mics could, if cardioids were used, prevent overlap of their pickup patterns.

example, miking six speakers could be accomplished with three mics, each trained on two speakers in such a way that there's little or no overlap of their pickup patterns (Fig. 7.6).

The concept of phase problems will become crystal clear when you hear an out-of-phase broadcast. In many cases, all that's needed to overcome the problem is some additional separation of the pickup patterns. Moving the mic around and playing the situation by ear will usually solve the problem. Remember, phase problems are nothing more than the effects of sounds reaching mics at different times and cancelling each other out. Remember, too, that even a tiny difference in the times at which sounds reach a mic can cause phasing problems.

One other difficulty of miking multiple talkers is, of course, the matter of sound levels. A speaker who has an overpowering voice generally does not belong on the same mic with someone who habitually whispers. This situation, too, will call for some trial-and-error maneuvering.

Working with nonprofessional speakers creates a secondary problem with setting the level. While a professional announcer will (usually) know enough to give you several sentences of speech to let you set the pot at the proper level, amateurs will not. The typical scenario before a panel discussion goes something like this:

PRODUCER *(Whoever happens to be running the board):* Mr. Smith, could I have a level, please?

SMITH: What?

PRODUCER: A voice level . . . Could you just talk for me, so I can set your mic?

SMITH: What do you want me to say?

PRODUCER: Anything.

SMITH: Hello, hello. Is that enough?

PRODUCER *(Who hasn't even found the pot yet):* No, no, just talk until I tell you to stop.

SMITH: But what am I supposed to say now?

To make matters worse, the level Mr. Smith finally gives the producer has absolutely no relation to the booming voice he will use when the tape starts rolling. While there's no perfect solution to this problem, one of the least objectionable ways of getting a level from amateur talent is to ask each person to count to 20. Granted, the voice a person uses to count aloud is different from the one used in conversation, but the voice level used by a self-conscious speaker to give a snippet of conversation for the level-taker isn't necessarily what's going to come out during the program, either. Asking the talent to count does, at least, eliminate the "What am I going to say?" routine and guarantees several seconds of speech. If there's a rehearsal of the program before airtime, use the rehearsal to set levels.

Communication in the Studio

One consideration of working in the production studio, especially when recording interview shows, is how to communicate with announcers and guests when mics are open. This isn't nearly as big a problem as it was in the days of live radio, when whole programs such as variety shows and dramas were put live over the air, but knowing some simple cues and signals can prevent the inconvenience of having to stop tape to give an instruction. In addition, signals sometimes prove useful when a speaker is going live over the air.

The hand signals we're going to demonstrate have been around for quite some time, and while you may not have much occasion to use them, they do represent a standard way of communicating in the studio.

You're on This signal (Fig. 7.7(a)) consists of a finger pointed directly at the speaker.

Give me a level A chattering motion with the fingers (Fig. 7.7(b)) indicates that you would like the announcer to give you a voice level.

Figure 7.7   Standard studio hand signals.

(a) "You're on."

(b) "Give me a level."

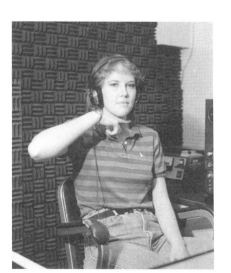

(c) "Kill my mic."

(d) "Wrap up."

(continued)

Figure 7.7   *(continued)*

(e) "Stretch."

Kill my mic Draw a finger across your throat (Fig. 7.7(c)). If you're not using a headset mic, point to the mic, too.

Wrap up This signal is accomplished by a circular ("winding up") motion of the hands (Fig. 7.7(d)).

Stretch Make a motion with your hands as though stretching a rubber band (Fig. 7.7(e)). This tells the person on-mic to keep talking and stretch out the program.

Remember, these signals aren't foolproof, and not everyone knows them. If they are standard in your station, fine; and if you work out signals in advance with talent and guests, they may prove useful.

■   SOUND EFFECTS IN   ■ STUDIO PRODUCTION

Sound effects have been discussed in various contexts in other chapters. Here we examine how they are used in studio production. The most useful sources of sound effects available to the producer are disc libraries sold by various firms. These discs carry quite specific entries, also listing the number of seconds each cut lasts. For example, the entries in the car horns honking category might be listed this way:

‣ Number 17: Horn honking, Model T Ford, :05
‣ Number 18: Horn honking, modern car, :06
‣ Number 19: Horns honking in city traffic, :10

The cuts usually have generous amounts of space between them, so you'll be able to drop the stylus in the widely separated grooves, which indicate silence. Since many of these records contain dozens of cuts per side, counting them is often difficult. Count aloud as you move the tonearm over each cut.

Sometimes, you won't be able to find what you need, and a sound effect will have to be custom-created. Most of us are familiar with the standard tricks of the trade for producing sound effects, such as crinkling cellophane to produce the effect of flames crackling. Most of us also know that the results—unless one is a real expert—are often less than satisfactory. Many experienced production people who are willing to take the time and effort can custom-make sound effects, but in most radio production that amount of effort isn't expended.

Most of the sound effects you will have to create yourself will consist of standard background noise, such as the hubbub of a restaurant. Common sense and some experimentation will guide you on this; just be aware that you and the microphone hear differently. While your brain can filter out noise in a restaurant, the mic is likely to pick up every clink of dishes and scrape of silverware. So, when producing a sound effect, be prepared to try some different mic techniques, and don't hesitate to try various sound levels to create the sound you want.

▪ COMBINING ELEMENTS ▪
IN PRODUCTION

The process of mixing music, voice, and sound effects is, essentially, a matter of feeding signals through the console or manipulating them with an editing process to construct the ultimate product.

A major consideration in combining these elements in a production studio setting is to ensure that the final product contains as few generations as possible (that is, the smallest possible number of rerecordings of the same segment).

While the specifics of various production processes are discussed in appropriate chapters, this is a good place to point out the ways in which you can efficiently construct production pieces; using the minimum number of generations is one such practice. During production, you will find a number of ways to save generations on the tape. The basic principle is to do as many operations in one step as possible; for example, make the whole music bed in one step, if you can, rather than adding elements gradually and dubbing the tape several times.

Another aspect of combining elements in production is to keep an open mind and use as many of the options available to you as possible. Is there an easier way to do things? Think about it, and don't always use the same routine out of force of habit. Utilize splicing and dubbing techniques to their fullest in studio production. Remember, you can use a splice to:

› Remove flubs from an existing tape.
› Attach leader.
› Insert questions or breaks.
› Insert **actuality** sound.
› Repair broken tape.
› Tighten up and remove lapses in any program.

You can use a dub to:

› Playback a sound source in a more convenient format (for example, putting a short selection of music on cart, to make it easier to locate).
› Take the place of a splice, when you don't want to cut the tape and you're not concerned about adding another generation to the tape.
› Free up a piece of equipment.
› Mix two or more sources together.

Remember, working in the studio environment will almost always entail striving for excellent quality and efficiency of operation. While some deviation in quality might be acceptable in live coverage of a news event, something produced in-studio must sound good, with no lapses in mic technique or production values.

At the same time, remember that nowhere is the "time is money" equation more obvious than in the modern broadcast studio. There may be several people clamoring to use the studio, and doing your work in task-oriented sequence will be more efficient.

SUMMARY

Many programs are recorded in advance because they are too complicated to be assembled live, on air; in addition, program elements such as commercials that will be used over and over are recorded in advance so that the air person does not have to keep reinventing the wheel to produce them.

Production studios vary widely in size and complexity, from small setups in the corner of a room to large operations complete with state-of-the-art equipment.

The most efficient production work is done in task-oriented sequence; that is, production is organized according to the demands of the production schedule, meaning that the work is not necessarily produced in final sequential order, from start to finish. It may be more convenient, for example, to produce the end of the spot first, then the middle, and finally the beginning.

Music is an important element in recorded program production. It comes from many sources, including the station's standard airplay library and specially licensed production libraries; sometimes, music is specially recorded for a particular commercial or other spot.

Miking multiple speakers usually involves setting up enough mics and channels so that the natural variance in the power of the individuals' speaking voices can be accommodated by the console operator.

APPLICATIONS

▪ **Situation 1** ▪ *The Problem* The producer was setting up for a show in which he would be running the board for an interview with three guests. He had set up one omnidirectional mic. Everything worked fine, but one of the guests happened to have a very, very soft voice.

One Possible Solution Although it is a good choice under other circumstances, the one omnidirectional mic wasn't right for this situation. Instead, the producer set up two cardioids, making sure that the patterns didn't overlap. The two strong-voiced guests were in one pickup pattern; the weak-voiced guest was in the other. Thereafter, the levels could be matched.

▪ **Situation 2** ▪ *The Problem* The news director of a small station wanted to use a portion of a large office as an adjunct studio during election coverage. Unfortunately, the room was so lively that it sounded as though candidate interviews were being done in the shower.

One Possible Solution The news director went down to the local home-supply store and purchased some heavy-grade cardboard. She made a frame of two-by-fours and used the cardboard as a partition, making the room (for all intents and purposes) smaller. She also taped some old egg cartons to the wall to help deflect ambient sound and deaden the room noise.

EXERCISES

1. Prepare a commercial for a hypothetical upcoming concert. This very difficult production task is representative of the kind of activity you might be asked to undertake.

   This particular promo calls for the use of four cuts of a popular singer; although you generally don't use vocals for production work, you'll have no choice when the assignment is to publicize a performance by a singer.

   To produce this spot, pick out a vocalist's album from your personal collection or from your college's or station's production library. Here's the copy you will use to produce the spot:

   APPEARING LIVE AT THE CIVIC CENTER ON JUNE 12, _____ IN PERSON!
   (first cut up, fade down)
   JOIN _____ ON HIS/HER FIRST TOUR OF THIS AREA. HERE'S THE MUSICAL EVENT YOU'VE BEEN WAITING FOR.
   (second cut up, fade down)
   TICKETS ARE $15 AND $12, AND CAN BE PURCHASED FROM SMITH TICKET AGENCY OR AT THE CIVIC CENTER BOX OFFICE.
   (third cut up, fade down)
   DON'T MISS THIS CHANCE TO SEE _____ IN CONCERT AT THE CIVIC CENTER, JUNE 12 AT 7 P.M.
   (close with vocal)

   Your assignment is to produce the foregoing commercial by dubbing the music onto cart and doing the commercial in one take, starting the carts and cross-fading as the copy is read (by you or by an announcer).

2. This time, first prepare the music bed by dubbing the cuts onto a reel-to-reel tape. You won't be able to cross-fade, so butt the songs together. Now do the commercial by reading copy over the music bed.

3. Produce the same commercial, this time cueing up one disc at a time, and stopping the tape after you've played the cut and read the appropriate piece of copy. Do the same with the other discs.

Note: There's no right or wrong way to produce this commercial, but trying it with all three techniques will give you an idea of the advantages and limitations of each.

·8·

Live, On-Air
Production

O ne of the surest tests of production ability is to pull an airshift. An airshift usually involves announcing and running the console. This is the point at which all other production techniques come into play; thus, during the airshift, you are using all your skills to produce the flow of sound that marks the unique character of your station.

You will, indeed, use all the skills discussed so far. The primary activity in an on-air situation is mixing sound sources through the console. Those sources, of course, go to the transmitter and over the air instead of onto tape. It goes without saying that mistakes are to be avoided at all costs. There are no retakes, and a mistake such as a commercial that doesn't play because of an unrecued cart, which would be a mere nuisance in studio production, is a big problem on the air. For one thing, **dead air** is sloppy. To make matters worse, the commercial will have to be rescheduled (called a *make good*) and, in some cases, an apology given to the angry sponsor.

An overall consideration of on-air production is the rapid transition from source to source. This, really, is the essence of on-air performance. Most fast-moving formats center on what's called the *tight board*, meaning that there is hardly any space (in some cases, there is overlap) between sound sources. Experienced on-air producers develop a rhythm, a sixth sense of timing. Developing that sense is largely a matter of practice, although a thorough understanding of the job at hand will help.

▪ **TYPICAL AIRSHIFT** ▪

On-air production is done by two types of radio station employees: the announcer who runs a board combo, and the engineer who runs a board for an announcer. The setup used at your station will largely be determined by a combination of station practices and union rules. In general, only the largest markets have a separate engineer running the board for the announcer. Combo operations (Fig. 8.1) greatly outnumber engineer/announcer setups, and it is likely that you will be running the board combo in your initial radio jobs.

Duties of the On-Air Producer

The combo operation is, of course, handled by an on-the-air producer: the staff announcer or disk jockey. This type of production is complex and stressful, and it usually involves most or all of the following duties:

‣ Running the console
‣ Cueing records and tapes
‣ **Riding levels** on sound sources going over the air
‣ Selecting music
‣ Announcing music, reading commercial copy, and in some cases reading news
‣ Taping programs coming in from networks for delayed broadcast
‣ Answering the telephone
‣ Monitoring the Emergency Broadcast System
‣ Ripping copy off the **teletype** (known as **stripping the wire**), checking for important news items, and saving appropriate material for others in the station
‣ Doing general maintenance, such as changing paper on teletypes, cleaning heads, and sometimes (in very small stations) doing the vacuuming
‣ Taking meter readings (Fig. 8.2)
‣ Keeping the program **log**
‣ Refiling records and tapes
‣ Playing back news actualities during newscasts
‣ Performing off-air production work (sometimes done on the audition channel) when a long program, such as a baseball game or taped show, is airing
‣ In some cases, assembling and reading the local newscast

Figure 8.1 Working combo.

If you think these duties can be murderous, you're right. Pulling an airshift can be exhausting. While listeners might think that playing records and doing a little talking for 4 hours at a stretch is easy, anyone who's tried it knows that exactly the opposite is true.

In addition to the hard work involved, acting as an on-air producer involves some potentially critical duties. In times of emergency, for example, the on-air personality must communicate very important information to the public. Cases of weather emergency often call for the on-air operator to relay news and information from local and area authorities.

There are many configurations of emergency systems. Your local authorities may have a system tied in with area stations, be it a radio transmission system or a telephone network. In addition, federal authorities require all stations in the nation to have a monitor for the **Emergency Broadcast System** (EBS), a network linking the government and the public.

An on-air producer must log all test signals received on the station's EBS monitor and must perform and log scheduled tests from the station; performing these tests involves reading a brief announcement and activating an attention signal.

It is important for an on-air producer to understand the station's procedure for handling EBS *completely*. In particular, you must know the method for authenticating the message known as the Emergency Action Notification; stations that subscribe to major wire services and networks typically post the instructions and authenticator codes (in a sealed envelope). But experience has shown that many operators do not know where

Figure 8.2 Taking meter readings.

the instructions are. Ask station management for such details before you are left to operate the station alone.

Remember, although the duties of an on-air producer may in fact be fun, those duties can also involve enormous responsibility.

Typical Schedule

How are these duties integrated into the working day? We've pieced together what is, from our experience, a pretty standard schedule for the morning and evening announcers at a medium-sized station (Tables 8.1 and 8.2). We've broken down the duties into on-air and off-air tasks.

Both of these schedules reflect a typical shift, although it's important to remember that there can be infinite variations on the themes presented.

Remember, the announcer is also responsible for introducing the records, and must be informative and entertaining in the bargain.

▪ SOUND OF THE ▪ STATION

The primary responsibility of the on-air producer is to provide programming that reinforces the format and goals of the station. The identifying characteristics of the radio station are encompassed and expressed in what's

Table 8.1 | ▸ **Morning Schedule**

Time (A.M.)	On-Air	Off-Air
5:30–5:59		Arrives at station, warms up **transmitter,** checks with news reporter for update on top local stories, pulls records and makes other preparations for show, turns on power for console and other equipment.
5:59	Runs sign-on tape with station ID.	
6:00–6:05	Puts network news over air.	Cues up first two records, pulls commercials for first half-hour of show, puts local news intro into cart machine.
6:05–6:07	Hits local news intro cart, cues news reporter, opens reporter's mic, rides level.	Plays reporter's audio cuts.
6:07–6:09	Says hello, introduces show, does some patter about weather, intros first record.	
6:09–6:12	Plays first record.	Puts together sports report from **wire service** and local newspaper.
6:12–6:13	Reads commercial.	
6:14–6:15	Reads weather forecast.	
6:15–6:18	Plays record.	Catches up on log entries, answers phone calls, takes some notifications of weather-related school closings.
6:18–6:19	Plays spot on cart.	Cues up next record, gets next cart, times instrumental opening of next musical selection to allow for talking up to the vocal.
6:19–6:22	Reads sports report, plays spot for sponsor of sports report.	
6:22–6:25	Plays record.	Records ski report phoned in from correspondent, puts previously played carts away, cues up reel-to-reel tape of "Today in Business" program.
6:25–6:29	Plays "Today in Business" tape.	Gets carts from news reporter for expanded local news report, records local road report phoned in from AAA.
6:29–6:30	Plays commercial, leads into local news report.	

Table 8.2 | ▸ Evening Schedule

Time (P.M.)	On-Air	Off-Air
6:45–7:00	Runs console for local talk call-in show (screens calls, puts calls over the air, runs second tape-delay system).	
7:00–7:05	Network news.	Pulls music for record show.
7:05–7:07	Reads local news headlines and weather, intros record show.	
7:07–7:10	Plays record.	Starts tape recorder to record network program for delayed broadcast.
7:10–7:12	Gives time and temperature, ad-libs spot from **fact sheet.**	
7:12–7:15	Plays record.	Clears wire (news reporter has gone home), monitors network for beginning of sports pregame show.
7:15–end of shift	Sports pregame show and game.	Monitors game for insertion of local commercials and station ID, files records, produces several spots.

known, loosely, as the station's *sound.* The elements of the sound are not only the types of music played. Also dictating the sound are the pace, content, announcing style, and blending of the program sources.

Pace

The schedules shown earlier reflect a rather slow-paced station. In many of the more frenetic stations, the program elements come fast and furious— a jingle here, a joke there, and then a spot or commercial cluster.

Maintaining a pace means checking yourself to ensure that your on-air segments are not too long (or too short, depending on the station). The delivery, too, will vary according to the pace of the programming at your particular station.

Content

The content of a station is what you say and play. It sounds obvious, but maintaining continuity of content isn't as easy as it might seem. From the standpoint of an on-air producer, continuity of content is maintained by not playing a blaring rock record on an easy-listening station, or by not using a rapid-fire, teenager-type delivery when you are host of the Saturday Night Big Band Program.

Announcing Style

Although the focus of this book is production, on-air operations require a brief discussion of announcing. In combo situations, announcing and production duties are intertwined. The announcer is the producer, and vice versa.

The voice of today's radio announcer is a far cry from the characteristic golden-throated male voice heard on the air during radio's so-called Golden Age. The announcer of that era was expected to speak more dramatically than is the announcer today. A deep male voice was standard for announcers, and perfect diction was expected. The style of delivery was formal, with artificial variations in pitch and volume that would sound very odd if used in normal conversation.

The requirement for a deep baritone voice has disappeared in favor of men and women who can communicate effectively with the audience. Radio speech today closely resembles conversational speech. Announcers are expected to convey the impression of one-to-one communication with the audience. To do that effectively, radio personalities must be well-versed in the tastes, interests, and life-styles of the audience the station wishes to attract.

Achieving the proper style of delivery is a matter of matching the style of the station's format. A country music station and a classical music station require different styles of communication. Where the country jock may talk over the music at the beginning of a recording and talk about the artists who performed the music being played, the classical announcer will use a more formal style of delivery, leaving a gap between spoken introductions and the beginning of the recordings being aired. And the classical announcer will provide more information on composers than on artists.

To develop the skills that will help you become competent as an announcer, try to get as much practice as possible. If one is available, take a voice and diction class. Take every opportunity to read copy in various radio styles, constantly striving for a conversational style (it's not as easy as it sounds). One major-market announcer says he developed ad-lib skills by describing the scenery as he drove his car to work each morning. The point to keep in mind is that, when it comes to broadcast announcing, very few people are naturals. Hard work and constant practice are necessary for nearly everyone.

Blending of Sound Sources

Some fast-moving rock stations have almost no on-air silence; in fact, some of these stations frequently combine as many sound sources as possible. The weather, for example, is read over the instrumental lead-in to a record; commercials always have background music; another sound source is always brought up as a record fades. You would not, however, want to blend sound sources this way on an easy-listening station. A country station may or may not utilize this style of blending sound sources, depending on the station's programming strategy.

Making sure your production values and techniques integrate with the sound of the station is one of the keys to successful on-air production. Following are some other suggestions that may prove helpful.

▪ SUGGESTIONS FOR LIVE, ▪ ON-AIR PRODUCTION

We can't address every specific situation, because content, formats, and equipment vary widely. But here are some general suggestions for on-air work, along with some cautionary recommendations derived from experience (sometimes unpleasant experience).

Console Operation

You're usually better off closing keys and zeroing pots. However, with cart machines you may want to leave the pot set at the appropriate level. With turntables, it's a good idea to zero the pot, to avoid cueing over the air. Be extremely careful of pots and keys that control the network lines and telephones. They have a habit of being left open when nothing is on line. When a signal is fed, it can come as something of a shock to the air person who left the pot open.

Establishing a Routine

However you choose to run the console, do it consistently. Get into the habit, for example, of always checking to make sure the mic is not up on the console before you say anything. Incidentally, make it a habit never to swear while you're in the radio station. If you make this a personal rule, you'll never let an obscenity slip over the air. The problems engendered by swearing over the air can be pretty serious, and it does happen, so make it part of your routine to banish cuss words from your vocabulary the moment you get near a mic. Mics can be relied on to be open at exactly the wrong time.

One other helpful routine is always to make sure that the turntable is set at the correct speed. If you mix $33\frac{1}{3}$- and 45-rpm recordings, checking the control as a matter of routine can save you considerable embarrassment.

One other caution: Check the patchbay for patchcords that might have been inserted, and make sure that everything that is supposed to normal does normal.

Planning in Advance

A good console operator has to be like a good pool player, who thinks several shots in advance to avoid getting into the position of not having a good shot. Think the same way in pulling an airshift. Pull as much music in advance as you can; get as many carts ready as possible. One phone call or other interruption can set you back significantly; and once you're "in the hole," it's hard to climb back out.

Being Aware of False Endings

A **false ending** on a record is music that sounds as though it's going to wrap up—but doesn't. The announcer, by this time, has probably started talking and will step all over the real end of the song. Sometimes commercials suffer from the same problem. You can avoid embarrassment and confusion by clearly labeling program material that has false endings. You might write *FALSE ENDING*, for example, right on the record label, or on the cart label.

Many stations label carts with other endings. For example, if a cart ends with music fading out, the words *FADES OUT* are added to the cart label. Often the last three or four words of the commercial script are written on the label. This can be helpful to the operator in determining when a cart is coming to a close. It makes running a tight board easier, and it also avoids those embarrassing moments of silence known in the trade as *dead air*.

Recueing Carts

We would estimate (this is pure guesswork) that a good 50 percent of on-air foulups are caused by carts that, for one reason or another, have not been recued. If you must remove a cart from a cart machine before it has been recued, make sure to put it in a special place where you'll remember to recue it before putting it back in the rack.

Listening to the Air Monitor

It's a good idea to keep the air monitor playing loudly. A low volume from the air monitor won't always allow you to hear, for example, the network line leaking over the air, or a scratch in the disc that is playing over the air. It is also important to monitor the station's broadcast through the off-air or air monitor source. Usually, audio consoles allow you to choose between program, audition, and off-air sources. Though most experienced producers know this, many inexperienced operators have been surprised to find that the program they thought was being aired without a hitch was not broadcast at all because a patch was thrown or some other technical problem occurred without their realizing it. Why? Because the neophyte operators were listening to the program output of the board instead of to the off-air source. By the same token, keep your headset volume reasonably high.

Clearing Equipment

Don't let tapes and carts stay on the equipment; clear them out as soon as possible. If you don't, a time will come when you need a tape machine in a hurry and there won't be one available. You'll also be more likely to put a previously played cart on the air accidentally. Clearing the equipment as you go along is one of the best habits you can develop for efficient on-air production.

Planning for the Worst

Nowhere is a mistake more evident than in radio, where an embarrassing silence underscores the fact that the on-air producer has lost control. One way to mitigate this problem when it occurs is to keep emergency material on standby (a 1-minute public-service announcement, a long record, or the like).

You will also want to prepare for engineering difficulties. Learn how to find and run a mic cord in case the control-room combo mic fails and you have to run another one (assuming, of course, that there are no union restrictions barring you from doing this).

<h1 style="text-align:center">▪ WORKING WITH ▪
SATELLITE SERVICES</h1>

An increasing amount of radio programming is beamed to the ground by **satellite,** received by special dish antennae at the station, and then rebroadcast over the local station. Such programming ranges from what is still anachronistically referred to as *wire-service* programming, to a complete program schedule.

Wire services, of course, are the news-supplying organizations described elsewhere in this book. Wire services, along with network feeds, most often do not enter a station by hard wire anymore. But while satellite reception of news and network programming has been standard practice for about a decade, delivery of entire formats by satellite transmission is a relatively new practice. Even so, it has already gained widespread acceptance.

Basically, when a station receives programming via satellite, it is the final step in a series of actions known as the *satellite feed.*

The Satellite Feed

First of all, the program material is produced at the syndicator's headquarters and is beamed up (in technical terms, **uplinked**) to the satellite. The satellite acts as a relay: it picks up the signal, amplifies it, and rebroadcasts it to the earth. Because of the extremely high position of the satellite, the signal coming to earth covers a wide geographic range, eliminating the need for multiple transmitters to reach remote stations. Satellites are able to perform this function because they are **geostationary**—parked over the equator in an orbit that is exactly synchronized with the earth's rotation, so that the satellite always maintains the same relative position to the ground. Satellites can retransmit several signals from varying networks. The satellite used by many radio networks is called *Satcom I-R* and is operated by RCA.

The station receiving the signal uses **downlink** equipment—a large dish often located on station property—to bring the signal into the console and eventually to the transmitter.

Programming from Satellite

Today, many types of program material are available. Examples include:

▸ *Services that provide complete music programming in various formats.* Such services typically have a carefully constructed format and top-class announcers. One example of a successful service is the Satellite Music Network, headquartered in Dallas, which beams programming to about 700 affiliates in the United States. SMN has seven different formats: a hard-rock format called Z-Rock; a rhythm-and-blues format called Heart and Soul; Pure Gold; Country Coast to Coast; Rock 'n' Hits (top 40); Stardust (older standards); and StarStation (adult contemporary).

▸ *Networks that provide specialty programming in part-time or full-time talk and information formats.* These services are enjoying growing popularity on the AM band, where music programming is on the decline, primarily because listeners who enjoy music prefer higher-fidelity FM stations. Such services include national call-in programs and such specialized format areas as personal motivation. Two recently developed motivation services include "SuccessNet," and "Winners News Network: The Motivation Station."

▸ *Services that provide short-form programming for integration into member stations' existing formats.* Some of these programs are fairly substantial, such as a 5-hour weekend program called "Open House Party," offered from "Superadio," a Boston-based weekend radio network. Thousands of discrete programs are beamed down to stations, including news-and-information magazine programs, news reports, sports programs, and many business programs.

How to Utilize Service Material

An on-air producer has many options in dealing with material downlinked from satellite, depending on the particular station's format.

Live Broadcast If the material is to be broadcast live and inserted into a locally produced format, the on-air producer treats the transmission as he or she would any other network program. Engineering staff will have wired the input from the satellite downlink into the console. You simply open a console pot at the time—the exact time—the program is due to start. Newscasts, business reports, and special music programs can all be broadcast in this fashion.

Delayed Broadcast Often the material is recorded for later airplay; sometimes this function is automated. For example, large all-news stations typically receive a plethora of satellite news feeds from various services, and opt to automate a bank of recorders to save this material. News producers then sort through the feeds at their convenience and edit particularly useful material for inclusion in newscasts. If there is no automation, the on-air personality is often responsible for recording the feed while performing other on-air duties. This usually involves patching the feed into a control-room tape recorder and starting the tape deck manually.

Local Insertion In other cases the on-air producer receives the complete program by satellite and must insert local programming, which usually accounts for a very small portion of the broadcast day. Such programming includes local commercials, news, weather, and locally oriented public-service programming.

   Generally, satellite services will provide local affiliates with clear guidelines as to the exact time periods allocated for local access. One common method is to use a clocklike representation called a *hot-clock* or *pie,* which shows each hour's programming and shows when:

1. The service will be broadcasting music and commercials.
2. Local affiliates can insert their commercials. Each hour, affiliates might be allowed a maximum of 8 minutes of commercial time, with 2 minutes' worth of commercials originating from the network. Time is also allocated for local station identifications and promotional announcements. Some services allow several minutes of optional time, during which satellite programming is still delivered but local affiliates may opt to insert their own material.

   While inserts can be done manually, automation is an increasingly popular option. Ground-based automation can be programmed to function via cue tones embedded within the satellite feed, beginning an automatically replayed local program element (such as a commercial) and then switching back to the network on receipt of another cue tone. Increasingly, satellite networks are devising methods to allow the network announcer to feed, through private lines, local IDs and weather forecasts; these are played back on cue, giving virtually complete local customization to the program. For additional information on computer-based automation, see Chapter 15.

SUMMARY

On-air production usually refers to running the console live during a broadcast program. When the announcer runs his or her own board, this is known as *running combo*. The duties of an on-air producer are eclectic and usually include such varied tasks as playing or reading commercials, public-service announcements, and news; taking meter readings; operating all control-room equipment, pulling records for airplay, and filling in the station log—an official FCC document.

Operating a console during a live program is a difficult chore. Among the operator's responsibilities are to maintain the integrity of the station's sound and to maintain the proper pace, content, and blending of sound sources.

Running the board can be made considerably less complicated if you establish a "safety first" routine: zero pots, close keys, recue carts, and so on. Plan your board operations in advance; think the way a good pool player does, several shots ahead. Above all, be careful around microphones; they have a habit of being left open at inopportune times.

Modern satellite feeds allow the on-air producer to interact with a broadcast fed from one central transmission point. In some cases, all the on-air producer needs to do is insert local news and weather. Sometimes, the producer will have many local time segments that must be filled.

APPLICATIONS

▪ **Situation 1** ▪ *The Problem* An announcer's music show ends at 7 o'clock, when she has to hit the network. One problem she's been encountering is that the end of the show has been sloppy: She is always having to pot down the last record in midsong in order to hit the net.

One Possible Solution The announcer adopted an upbeat instrumental for her theme song and started the cut, which ran 3 minutes, 20 seconds, at 7:46:40. She didn't put the cut over the air immediately, though: The selection was dead-potted until the previous record ended. The announcer then began her outro patter and faded up the dead-potted cut, talking over it.

Because the instrumental—which had a climactic ending—was back-timed to end perfectly, the announcer was able to hit the net cleanly and give a definite ending to her show.

(Many announcers who have a standard theme keep it on cart.)

■ **Situation 2** ■ *The Problem* The station had only two cart machines in the control room, but a great deal of the programming was on cart. On-air people had to pull carts out of the machines before they were recued, to free up the cart machine. Unfortunately, these carts had a habit of being played over the air in an unrecued state.

One Possible Solution The program director (who couldn't talk the station owner into buying additional cart machines) installed a rack clearly labeled UNRECUED CARTS. Air people were instructed to develop a routine of always placing the unrecued carts in the rack, and to recue those carts as soon as they had a chance.

EXERCISES

1. Do a mock airshift that includes these elements: three record cuts, two weather reports, a commercial or public-service announcement on cart, and at least 15 seconds of patter.

   Your airshift should use three styles:

   ‣ Dance-band music and a middle-of-the-road approach
   ‣ Fast-paced rock
   ‣ Laid-back, album-oriented rock

   Don't worry so much about the quality of announcing, because that's not the real purpose of this exercise. You should focus on production values. For example, would you talk over the instrumental introduction of a rock cut? How about the dance band?

2. Pick three local stations and describe their sound in terms of production values. Listen for things like music and talk overlapping. Does the announcer talk for only a couple of seconds at a time? Or conversely, does the announcer spend extended periods in patter?

   Write down your observations and discuss how the production values reinforce the sound of the stations.

3. This exercise is done strictly to time. You must fit all the elements into a 10-minute segment:

   ‣ Exactly 1 minute of reading news copy.

   ‣ Exactly 1 minute of commercial copy.

   ‣ A record cut from 2 to 4 minutes long.

   ‣ Exactly 1 minute of community calendar listings read from the local paper.

   ‣ Enough weather to get you through the remaining time.

   ‣ Dead-pot an instrumental record while you are reading copy; the record must end exactly when your 10 minutes is up.

PART THREE

THE APPLICATIONS

·9·

Achieving an Effect

I f you'll permit us to stretch a point a bit, think of Chapters 6, 7, and 8 as an art lesson in which you learned the basic brush strokes. It's now time to explore ways to create light, shadow, substance, and mood.

As a radio producer, you will be called on to create a variety of effects, utilizing the basic skills explained previously. But producing an effect calls for more than a learned-by-rote recall of mechanics: It involves imagination, experimentation, and a certain amount of trial and error.

This is not to say that producing an effect is entirely a seat-of-the-pants affair. Specific techniques must be mastered, and technical expertise must be matched with creativity. This chapter serves as a bridge between the first eight chapters, which dealt with techniques and mechanics, and the chapters that follow on radio drama and on dramatic elements in radio production, commercial production, and news and public-affairs production. This chapter also reviews many of the elements discussed earlier and touches on some of the aspects to be dealt with later. The mix of elements is important, because the marriage of technology and art—the ability to create an effect—is the heart of radio production.

■   WHAT IS AN EFFECT?   ■

When we refer to the overall mood, impact, and appeal of a radio production, we use the term *effect*. We don't mean a specific sound effect (such as the screeching of a car's brakes).

Modern communication theory points out that getting a message across depends on more than the validity of the message. Reaching people with a message also involves pulling their emotional strings—creating a mood of excitement, perhaps, or a feeling of identification. These emotional activators often can be turned on and off by means of radio production techniques.

A commercial to spur ticket sales for a football team, for instance, would certainly seek to create a mood of excitement: the sound of a kickoff, followed by the roar of the crowd, supported with upbeat, vibrant music. To create this example, the producer would have to know how to dub in sound effects, either taking them from a sound effects record played back on a turntable or recording the desired sound at a game, using basic microphone techniques. All the production techniques, of course, hinge on proper routing of the signals through a console. Essentially, the producer would use production skills to assemble and form the structure of the commercial; but an understanding of creating an effect would be necessary to produce the subtle message, the nuances, responsible for the impact and drama of the message.

▪   KINDS OF EFFECT   ▪

The focus of the message—and the effect you want to create—won't always be the same, even in quite similar situations. Assume, for example, that the radio station's sales manager, who needs a commercial for a restaurant, wants your help in creating an effective 60-second spot.

Soft music, you say? The sound of tinkling glasses, coupled with a mellow-voiced announcer? Perhaps. If the restaurant is an elegant one (or tries to be), your choice of soft music would be correct. But restaurants are as different as people. Digging a little deeper, you may discover that this particular client's restaurant has an ethnic flair; if so, might a polka, waltz, or other specialty selection be more effective? Perhaps this is a fast-food establishment. You, the producer, would most likely seek to convey a sense of fast action; thus upbeat, quick-tempo music would be the logical choice.

Music, like any other production element, must support the theme. You will be wise to etch this principle deeply within your thinking, because straying from the overall theme is the most common mistake of the novice radio producer. Every production element must support the theme, or it will detract from the message.

■ HOW PRODUCTION ELEMENTS ■ SUPPORT A THEME

The upbeat music in our fast-food restaurant commercial conveys a specific impression: that of speed, excitement, and vibrancy. This production element supports the theme of a message for a fast-food establishment; it would certainly detract from a commercial for an elegant eatery.

Such themes aren't always so readily apparent. There's no obvious guideline on how to produce a commercial for a personal computer, for example. In fact, the approach eventually adopted might evolve after months of sophisticated market research aimed at discovering what approaches trigger the emotions of typical computer buyers. Obviously, such intricate planning won't be left up to you, the producer. On many occasions, however, the sales manager and the client know exactly what mood and effect they want. It will be up to you to achieve that effect, and to choose production elements that support the theme. There are many production elements other than music and sound effects, but let's focus on those two for the time being. Later in this chapter, we'll discuss sound quality, voice quality, and so on, and explore their proper use. There are many ways in which the production elements of music and sound effects support a theme and bolster the message. Here are some brief examples illustrating how these elements fit into the overall scheme of things.

Creating Excitement

Soft-drink commercials depend on the capacity of radio production to create excitement to make their product appeal to a market that seeks thrills, activity, and youthful enjoyment of life. The music chosen—apart from the lyrics, which tout the benefits of the beverage in question—must support this mood of excitement.

Think, too, of the music you've heard at the introduction of sports play-by-play programs. Was the music a leisurely, sentimental ballad? Of course not. It was up-tempo, hard-driving music that implied: *The program that follows is going to be a fast-moving, exciting event.*

Creating Immediate Identification

What does the sound of a stopwatch ticking conjure in your mind? If you're like millions of other Americans, you will think immediately of the CBS News program "Sixty Minutes." And that's exactly what the producers would like you to think of.

Why? Because the familiar stopwatch theme is one element that immediately distinguishes "Sixty Minutes" from its competition and creates a certain amount of loyalty among viewers and listeners. In any medium, that is the name of the game. The sponsor of a commercial wants that commercial to stand out; the producer of a talk show wants listeners to distinguish that show from the competition and wants it to have some sort of tag they can identify with.

An important point: Whatever production element is chosen for the task of creating immediate identification, it must support the overall message. The sound of cannons firing, for example, would certainly attract attention, but it wouldn't do much to demonstrate that the upcoming news program is going to be important and dignified. In fact, such confusion within the message would detract from the identification factor; listeners to a news show that opened with the sound of cannon shots probably wouldn't mentally link the show and the signature.

Evoking an Emotion

What does the sound of automobile horns blaring mean to you? Chances are, it evokes the feelings you experienced the last time you sat, hot and frustrated, in a traffic jam. The producer of a commercial for an airline trip to a Caribbean island could utilize this factor effectively. Sound effects are one of the most effective tools for evoking an emotion.

Summary of Effects

The goal of radio production is to achieve an effect. The goal of achieving an effect is to be able to reach a certain group with a message. In many cases, the group and the message may be spelled out for you by an advertising manager and/or the client who wants you to produce a commercial. A more complete discussion is offered in Chapter 11.

When reporting to the producer of a news or sports program, you will be asked to utilize production elements that support the show's theme and create listener identification. As we discussed in Chapter 1, the producer in modern radio is responsible for reinforcing the station's particular sound— the quality that distinguishes it from its competitors up and down the dial.

Remember, you may be responsible for production in a variety of different jobs at various radio stations. You may be a staff announcer who produces commercials and public-service announcements after your airshift (the airshift is also, of course, a product of radio production). You may be a news reporter responsible for piecing together a half-hour's worth of news items and integrating them into an overall theme. Your job in the sales department at a small station may involve hands-on production. You may be the program director, in charge of ensuring that everything that goes out over the air strengthens the format, the sound.

But regardless of the job title, you will be using the basic production equipment and techniques described in the preceding chapters to achieve the effects discussed so far in this chapter. And as we've seen, you will be utilizing various production elements.

■   HOW A PRODUCER UTILIZES   ■
PRODUCTION ELEMENTS

We have briefly touched on how the production elements of music and sound effects are used to create an effect. Other elements can serve the same purpose. We now examine each element and show how and why it creates an effect.

Music

The observation that music reaches deep into the human psyche won't surprise you. Music has moved men to march to war and has waltzed couples into matrimony. Music of all types is instantly available to the radio producer. The sources from which you will draw music include:

‣ Your station's general-airplay record library. The station has paid a fee to various licensing agencies for use of the music, and you can use these records in your production.

‣ Certain types of records for which you must pay per **needle drop**—that is, whenever a cut from such a record is dubbed onto the tape used in a production. This situation is more common at recording studios that are not affiliated with a radio station and do not pay a licensing fee for general-airplay music.

‣ Music beds supplied by a national advertiser for use by local affiliated merchants or businesses. For example, a lawn-mower manufacturer might supply to its distributors a commercial in which the company's jingle is included at the beginning and end of a 60-second spot, with a 15-second hole of background music—a bed—over which an announcer would read copy for the local merchant's store. (More on this in Chapter 11.) These cooperative, or co-op, advertising materials come in a wide range of structures.

‣ Original music composed specifically for a certain purpose, such as the type of jingle music used in beds but also including jingles produced locally for businesses and music composed for use in themes of shows or productions. You may, from time to time, become involved in the recording of such music; that aspect of radio production is examined in Chapter 14.

Music is such an evocative tool that it is used in a great number of radio production tasks; unfortunately, it is also frequently misused and overused. Here are some brief rules of thumb to help you, the producer, use music properly in the aesthetic context.

DO use music:

‣ When you can find a logical reason to do so; when it creates a mood and reinforces a theme.
‣ When the music has a logical purpose and fits into the format of your station. A hard-rock music background for a public-service announcement will not complement the sound of an easy-listening station. As discussed in Chapter 1, the producer must respect the integrity of the station's format.

DO NOT use music:

‣ Strictly as a reflex. Many times you'll be better off without it. Suppose, for instance, that every other station in town uses a brief musical opening (sometimes called a **stinger**) for newscasts. Do you, as a producer, feel compelled to do the same? No, of course not; a "cold" opening can certainly be effective and, in this case, will set you apart from the competition.
‣ Indiscriminately. This warning applies specifically to the novice radio producer who is tempted to utilize currently popular music within announcements or other productions regardless of whether it serves to reinforce the message.

A final note: Be very cautious of using vocals as background for a produced announcement. While lyrics that proclaim something to the effect of "I'll be your friend forever, just give me a call. . . ." might tempt the producer of a public-service announcement for a community health agency, mixing vocals with a voice-over can make both lyrics and announcer unintelligible. Cross-fading and other technical operations, however, can mitigate the problem in some circumstances.

Sound Effects

The example of blaring car horns used in an advertisement for a Caribbean vacation shows the value of appropriate sound effects. (Note the word *appropriate*.) A sound effect is generally considered to be any sound element other than music or speech. Sound effects (SFX) can come from:

▸ Special sound-effects libraries; records the radio station purchases and buys the rights to use. Sound-effects libraries are almost always on disc (rather than on tape) because of the need to access material throughout the recording.

▸ Sound effects recorded by the producer. This practice sounds simpler than it really is. The old-time radio trick of crackling cellophane to simulate the sound of flames often sounds exactly like crackling cellophane. A door slamming, as another example, won't always sound like a door slamming. With certain microphone placements, and certain doors, it can sound like a gunshot, instead. Thus, recording your own sound effects will take some experimenting, both with producing the sound and with placing the microphone to record it.

Regardless of how a sound effect is produced, its appropriate use can add to the message. Inappropriate use can make the message seem hackneyed, amateurish, and off the mark. There are two good reasons for using sound effects.

DO use sound effects:

▸ To save time and words. Another vacation-oriented commercial might start with a blast of wintery wind to reinforce the message. Use of the sound effect has saved the producer some verbiage; there's no need for an announcer to say: "Don't you hate winter and the latest stretch of miserable weather?" The sound effect, lasting only a second or two, has created the desired image.

▸ To inject drama. Audiences have come to expect a bit of drama in all media. A bit of drama that reinforces your message can grab the attention of your target listeners. Can you picture, for example, the kind of audience and the kind of message that would be matched up in a commercial that features the sound effect of a baby crying? of a sports car engine roaring? of a rocket taking off?

DO NOT use sound effects:

▸ Just because they are there. The producer should not even consider using a sound effect in the absence of a definite need and purpose for that effect.

Keep in mind that overuse of sound effects is one of the more common mistakes made by newcomers to radio production. You will surely mark yourself as an amateur by falling into this trap.

Sound effects are an excellent production tool, but if they're used just for the sake of using them, they are inappropriate and can detract from the message. Use a sound effect when it's logical and serves a purpose; the chapters on radio drama and commercial production expand on the ways sound effects communicate a message effectively.

Coloration of Sound

Coloration of sound is a nebulous quality that cannot always be singled out. This production element is difficult to define. However, you will understand it when you hear it. Eventually, too, you'll utilize sound coloration techniques to produce an effect in your own production work.

Some examples may be helpful. Compare the overall sound quality of a screaming-DJ type of radio program to that of a news and public-affairs interview program on a station with a more leisurely format. You'll know there's a difference, even though you can't quite articulate it.

Well, one reason the screaming DJ maintains such an intense sound is the electronic compression of the signal; this is done quite scientifically, we might add, and involves boosting the volume of softer sounds, so the entire presentation is intense (and so that, the program director hopes, the signal will stand out more than the signals of competing stations when the listener twists the dial). Heavy compression would not be appropriate in a slow-moving talk show, because the machinery would insist on boosting the periods of silence between questions and answers, creating an annoying "pumping" effect.

Compression is just one example of a process by which sound is altered to achieve coloration of sound. A mild **echo** is often electronically applied; this effect is covered more thoroughly in Chapter 14. FM stations, which transmit a high-resolution signal, often favor high-quality microphones that reproduce a wide spectrum of sounds, including breath and mouth noises of the announcer, making the voice seem very close up and intimate.

Microphones can have a powerful effect on the coloration of sound. As you remember from the discussion of sound quality (or timbre) in Chapter 5, the way sound patterns are reproduced affects the way we perceive those patterns. Often, the coloration is in fact a desirable type of **distortion**. Examples of sound coloration are presented in the chapters dealing with drama, commercials, and remote and sports production. Some technical methods of achieving coloration are discussed in Chapter 14.

A radio producer should be prepared to confront the coloration concept. Don't be surprised when the program director asks you to produce a brighter sound or requests a promotional spot with a more personal feel.

Timing and Pace

Whether you are producing a music program, a news show, or a commercial, timing and pace will directly affect the mood and the message. This production element is one of the most critical in the entire spectrum of radio production. Yet timing and pace have some effects you might not, at first thought, be aware of. Try this comparison:

▸ Listen to a commercial for securities or other investments. (Such commercials are quite common on radio talk shows, especially talk shows dealing with business issues.) Note the very slow, deliberate pacing. Why? Because we've developed a negative image of fast talkers. The announcer who sells us major investments must be trusted.

▸ Contrast the foregoing approach with soft-drink commercials. Trust, here, is really not a factor. An image of a life-style is being sold, and that image generally represents a youthful and fast-moving crowd.

We cite these examples in the hope that you will develop a critical ear when it comes to determining the timing and pace of your own work. Keep in mind, always, that the pace creates an effect and must reinforce the message.

Walter Winchell, the legendary broadcaster whose radio career peaked in the Great Depression era, entered radio after experience as a newspaper gossip columnist. Initially he was given little chance of success because radio announcers at the time were expected to have a slow, mellifluous delivery. Winchell, however, broke the rules with a rapid-fire, staccato delivery: "Good evening, Mr. and Mrs. North and South America, and all the ships at sea, let's go to press . . . Flash! . . ." His delivery was breathless, punctuated with the dit-dit-dit of a telegraph key, and it accomplished exactly what he wanted. It implied that Winchell had a fast-moving program, figuratively grabbing the listener by the lapels and shouting "Wait 'til you hear this!" That is, timing and pace reinforced Winchell's message.

Veteran broadcaster Paul Harvey is an acknowledged master of timing, and his technique will help us to make an important distinction. While Harvey keeps up a varied, energetic pace, he also captivates his audience by use of the well-timed punch line, usually preceded by a dramatic pause. "And the man woke up the next morning to find," Harvey might say, "that he'd been spraying the annoying mosquito not with insecticide . . . [pause] . . . but with . . . [agonizing pause] . . . a can . . . of *blue spray paint!*"

Timing and pace are also major elements in production of a music program. In many laid-back album-oriented rock stations, the whole format is built around low-key timing and pace. Compare that with the frenetic, nonstop approach of the screaming-DJ top-40 station. Both are trying to project an image.

Voice Quality

This production element doesn't necessarily imply a qualitative difference between good and bad voices. *Voice quality* is the overall image that an announcer's voice projects.

Often, a producer chooses the announcer to be used for a particular production. Sometimes the producer is assigned a particular task and must use a designated voice (or his or her own voice) to maximum effect, perhaps making some subtle changes in delivery.

In any event, matching a proper voice and delivery to the message at hand is the important element here. Many aspects of selection and delivery are reasonably obvious. A news moderator's voice calls for a measure of dignity. A spot designed to convince young people to shop at a particular store might well benefit from a young voice and an intimate "chummy" delivery. Think of other examples. Do advertisements for medicines generally carry a strong, authoritative voice? Why?

Another aspect of voice quality is the lack of distraction. Voices used on the air, it's generally agreed, should not have defects (not necessarily pathological speech defects) that will detract from the message. One of the most common distractions is improper breathing on the part of the announcer. Overly breathy voices, except when they are a well-known novelty, sound amateurish. Often, inexperienced announcers can be heard gasping for air between phrases. Such gasping sounds might not be apparent in everyday speech, but a mic can be merciless. The cure for this is to maintain generous breath support—a good tankful of air—instead of trying to talk until all breath is expended. Plan where to take breaths; breathe at natural pauses in the copy. Don't just read until you can't read any more.

Sound of Words

A radio producer often is responsible for writing the copy that is read on the air. We'll address specific copy techniques below and in appropriate chapters (notably on news and commercials), but one point must be considered here: writing for the ear.

Words can evoke moods. Note how the words *dine* and *eat* create different moods. Likewise with *invest* and *buy*. The physical sound of the words also has an effect. *Businesses* is not a great word for the ear because the three *s* sounds make the word hissy and unattractive. Doesn't *firms* sound better?

Copywriting

Here are three general principles of copywriting:

1. Remember that you're writing for the ear, not for the eye. Long sentences and intricate constructions have no place in radio. Keep your sentences short and conversational. Avoid references such as "the latter option" (the listener can't refer back and decide which is the former and which is the latter).
2. Remember that your writing must be *read*. While that sounds obvious, it is not. It takes practice to write in a rhythm that can be read easily by someone else. Be particularly careful about your use of commas and dashes; incorrect usage can make the copy virtually unreadable.
3. Pay close attention to technical format. Each station has a more-or-less standard way of writing copy. Some stations, for example, use all-capital letters for anything to be read over the air. Most stations use various abbreviations, such as SFX for sound effects. But the technicalities vary from station to station, so be sure you follow local form. Otherwise, the copy you produce can be very difficult for an announcer to decipher.

In summary, production elements are features that are useful in creating an effect and reinforcing a message. Many are obvious; some require a bit of thought. All have an impact on how a radio production will affect an audience.

Production elements also blend into one total package; that's obvious because most radio productions contain a variety of elements. In judging various elements, you, the producer, must always determine whether they make sense within the context of the message. Does this sound effect get the point across? Will the music make the message stronger, or will it be a distraction? Does the announcer's voice convey the right message? Do the words convey the full message? Are the words written for the ear? The key to successful production is not to leave these decisions to chance.

▪ USING ELEMENTS OF SOUND ▪ TO ACHIEVE AN EFFECT

Up until now, our discussion has been pretty much on the theoretical level. At this point, we'll consider exactly how the production techniques you've learned from preceding chapters come into play. The job of a producer usually involves being half artist and half technician. You will use highly sophisticated electronic equipment to translate what you want to do into the technical form of a finished product, something that can easily be played back over the air.

Problems in production often arise when the producer thinks he or she is too much an artist to have to bother with the technical side of things. By the same token, production values suffer when a producer enamored with complex equipment forgets that he or she is in the business of communicating. A musician must know how to blow a horn and finger the valves properly, but must also have the artistic capability to play notes that convey meaning; while machines can be programmed to play trumpets, they generally don't do a very good job. With that in mind, let's see how some simple operations are performed by someone who is a radio producer, not just a person who knows how to run the equipment.

Putting Voice on Tape

You have learned the chain of events that allows you to record a voice on a tape recorder. Now, start thinking like a producer. You want to record a two-person news interview program (one moderator and a guest). Will you use the same type of mic utilized for recording classical music? Do you need the same type of quality and pickup pattern? What about the effect of the equipment on the participants? While the conveniently located studio mic suspended from a boom can do the job, will this large instrument hanging in midair—between the moderator and the guest—have an intimidating effect? You bet it will.

People unfamiliar with radio generally regard the microphone with the same distrust as they would a dentist's drill. As a producer, you must take this into account. You are likely to find that the best results are achieved with two mics mounted inconspicuously on table stands, or even with two good-quality lavaliers. There's more to selecting a microphone than addressing the technical considerations discussed in Chapter 5. See if you can come up with some other examples.

Recording Music on Tape

You've progressed to the point of being able to cue a record, start the turntable, and route the signal through the console and into a tape recorder. Now, let's imagine an actual production.

You have been assigned the task of cutting a 30-second public-service announcement for a local community health hotline. The music you want to use contains some lyrics and some entirely instrumental portions.

The lyric you want to use is "I'll be your friend forever, just give me a call. . . ." But you can't just run the song under the announcement, for two reasons:

1. There are more lyrics following the ones you want to use at the beginning of the spot, and they will make your reading of the script unintelligible.

2. You want the spot to end with a musical climax: to be precise, the instrumental climax that just happens to be at the end of this 3-minute piece of music.

How would a producer working combo approach this dilemma? One possible strategy is to record the final 25 seconds of the song onto cartridge. Since you know (by reading the time on the record label or by timing the piece yourself) that the cut is exactly 3 minutes long, you simply start the record and the timer simultaneously, and start the cartridge recording when the timer reaches 2:35. You have determined that the opening lyric takes about 9 seconds (and you have also timed the copy you will be reading). At this point, you can recue the cart, and follow this sequence:

‣ Start the turntable and fade up the turntable on the console. Remember, if you open the turntable pot before the turntable has been switched on, you will get electronic noise from the switch. Of course, you've already taken levels and know how high to put the volume.

‣ Start the timer as the record makes its portion of a turn to bring the first sound-bearing groove into contact with the stylus.

‣ Record the first 5 seconds of the lyric.

‣ Start the cart 5 seconds into the record, before you open the mic. Remember, you have 4 more seconds before the lyric will finish. The cart is now set to finish exactly when you want it to: 30 seconds from the beginning of the spot.

‣ Open the mic.

When the important line of lyrics ends, begin to fade down the turntable and to read your copy. While reading the copy execute a cross-fade. That is, fade up the cart as you fade down the turntable. Done gradually, and underneath the cover of your voice, the cross-fade may not be detectable. Remember, at this point the music should not overpower your voice. Be sure to use headphones to monitor your mic.

When you have finished reading your copy, bring up the music to the correct level on the VU meter to finish the spot.

You've created a perfectly timed spot that includes the beginning and end you want. And all the production elements reinforce the message and create an effect. In particular, the music reinforces the message. The result is a package that puts the point across, with all the production elements enhancing the message.

(Incidentally, another way of doing things that might prove easier is to record 40 seconds of the song on cart. That way you won't have to start the cart during the spot; however, you will have to keep accurate time before the spot begins.)

SUMMARY

The ultimate goal of radio production is to achieve an effect—that is, to create an image in the mind of the listener, to communicate a message.

Production elements in a piece of production support a central theme in order to achieve an effect. For example, upbeat music in a restaurant commercial conveys vibrancy and excitement. Production elements are also used as signatures, to create immediate identification in the minds of the listeners.

Music is a common production element used to achieve an effect. Music is best used when it explicitly contributes to the communication of an idea. Using music just for the sake of having it is often distracting and counterproductive.

Likewise, sound effects must be used judiciously. Sound effects can be very effective when their use is logical and supports the central theme; when they are used just because they are available, sound effects become pure gimmickry.

Coloration of sound, another contributing factor in achieving an effect, refers to the technical ways sound is manipulated. Other contributors to achieving an effect are timing and pace, voice quality, and the sound of individual words.

APPLICATIONS

▪ **Situation 1** ▪ *The Problem* The producer was given a tough and very important assignment: Produce a commercial for men's cologne. The talent—a woman—seemed to read the copy correctly, but the client didn't like the spot, even though he couldn't spell out what didn't ring true about it. His only comment was: "It doesn't sound like she's talking to *me.*"

One Possible Solution After giving it some thought, the producer changed microphones. Using a higher-quality mic with a cardioid pickup pattern, he instructed the talent to move in closer. The result: greater presence, and a more intimate feel for the commercial.

■ **Situation 2** ■ *The Problem* The producer at an FM station was in charge of preparing a public-service announcement calling for air-pollution abatement. According to the script, the announcer was to read copy outdoors with birds chirping in the background. But when this was tried, the portable equipment didn't produce very good quality: The birds, which really were chirping in the park where the spot was taped, were barely audible on the final product.

One Possible Solution Realizing that the way things sound to the ear is not necessarily how they sound to the microphone, the producer recorded only the birds on one tape. This gave her the option of varying the volume when she mixed the announcer and the background sound effects through the console.

The announcer's voice track presented another problem. It sounded terrible when recorded on the portable equipment, whose quality just couldn't match the studio mics. This lack of quality would be sorely apparent when the spot was played on air. But recording the announcer's copy in the studio made the whole spot sound phony. It sounded not like an announcer standing outdoors, but like a studio recording mixed with sound effects.

The producer remembered what she had learned about the physics of sound and realized that the problems stemmed from the microphone's being in a very lively part of the studio, near several bare walls. Some experimentation resulted in the relocation of the microphone in a dead area. Without the sound bouncing off the walls, the sound was flatter, and the listener could much more readily imagine that the entire spot had been recorded outdoors.

Now the producer was finding that she could achieve the effect she wanted, within the technical restrictions of radio equipment. One problem remained, however. While the bird noises she'd recorded in the park worked well for the background, they weren't of sufficiently high quality to be brought up full, as she had wanted to do in the beginning of the spot. She felt the production needed to open with a couple of seconds of solid sound effects, which would then fade down under the announcer.

She solved this problem by finding the appropriate sound effect in the station's sound-effects library. The only entry she could find ("Bird Calls") would not have been appropriate for the background of the entire spot, but it was perfect for an attention-getting opening. To create the whole package, she used the bird call from the disk and cross-faded it to the ambient sound she had recorded.

The ultimate result? A high-quality public-service announcement that achieved the desired effect.

EXERCISES

1. Construct a script for a 60-second public-service announcement. For this exercise, be sure to include:
   ‣ One sound effect
   ‣ A music bed
   ‣ Narration

   Be sure that everything in your PSA has a purpose. Nothing must seem to be thrown in for its own sake.

2. Under the supervision of your instructor, produce the PSA.

3. If a music library is available to you, have class members select music they feel is appropriate for:
   ‣ The opening of a news program
   ‣ Background for a beer commercial
   ‣ Background for a fashion show

   Discuss these selections, and also discuss class members' impressions about the three scenarios. (Conceptions of a good beer commercial, for instance, will vary from person to person.) Note the difference in class members' conceptions of both the scenarios and the proper selection of music.

4. Cast celebrities for voice-over parts in the following hypothetical radio productions. (Remember, the celebrities will be heard and not seen.) Write down your choices and your reasons for making them.
   ‣ A commercial for aspirin
   ‣ A commercial for an elegant restaurant
   ‣ A public-service announcement for saving wildlife
   ‣ The part of an insane murderer in a radio drama
   ‣ A commercial for high-priced, somewhat frivolous women's accessories

   Discuss your reasoning with class members and your instructor. During your discussions, try to state as directly as possible exactly what it is about each celebrity's voice that would create the proper effects and get the various messages across.

·10·

Drama and

Dramatic Elements

in Radio Production

T he purpose of this chapter is not to demonstrate what is almost an obsolete art form, but rather to serve as an introduction to the principles of radio drama that are present in other forms of radio production.

This very short chapter contains only one exercise. Instead of the usual complement of exercises, we have provided a full-length radio drama in Appendix C. Production of the drama can serve as a class project; merely reading it will give you an insight into the structure of drama and dramatic elements. If time doesn't permit (production of a radio drama is a big project), the exercise at the end of this chapter will suffice.

Radio drama per se is not very common in America any more, and that's unfortunate. Old-time radio drama, as its devotees can attest, involved the audience in a way that television cannot. A radio drama creates images in the mind that can furnish a much more vivid picture than can be produced by even the most sophisticated television production company.

Radio drama, too, is an excellent way to learn the mechanics of editing, miking, and mixing. You'll find the production of the drama provided in Appendix C to be exceptionally challenging but quite instructional, as well. An understanding of radio drama also provides an insight into techniques of inserting dramatic elements into commercials and—in limited applications—into news and public-affairs programs. That's the essential focus of this chapter.

▪ THE STRUCTURE OF ▪ DRAMA

Drama is a composition that tells a story through action and dialogue. It generally involves a conflict: person versus person, or person versus society. A drama, in its broadest form, has a plot; usually the plot has a beginning, middle, and end. A drama includes dramatic techniques, such as suspense and exposition.

Let's review the preceding description and see how each term relates to radio drama and to dramatic elements in radio production.

Action

Because radio is not a visual medium, action must be portrayed through sound. Action in a prizefight, for example, would be dramatized on radio with the ringing of the bell, the roar of the crowd, and the smacking of gloves. A description of the fight could be provided by the dialogue.

Dialogue

Spoken words are very important in radio drama, for obvious reasons. Words provide most of the information and meaning in a scene, and they describe most of the action. The prizefight scene, for example, could be fleshed out with dialogue from a ring announcer and/or conversation in a fighter's corner.

Plot

The plot is the story line. All action and dialogue must advance the plot; that is, each scene of action and/or dialogue must serve to move the plot along and to reinforce the message.

Beginning, Middle, and End

Drama usually has a sequence of events and a conclusion. Although dramatic elements within radio production don't always have a complete "beginning, middle, and end" sequence, there almost always is some sort of resolution, or solving of the problem. In dramatic terms, this is known as the *denouement,* which is the resolution of a conflict.

Conflict

Conflict in drama doesn't always have to be a struggle between two people, which is what we usually call *melodrama.* Conflict can consist of a person's struggle to overcome headache pain, a type of conflict that is portrayed frequently in radio commercials. (Resolution, of course, would come from the sponsor's pain remedy.)

Suspense

Suspense is what compels us to keep listening. To achieve suspense, plot writers refrain from providing conflict and resolution at the same time. Will Mrs. Smith's headache pain be cured? We usually have to wait through about 20 seconds of product pitch to find the answer.

Exposition

Details must be revealed in a logical and realistic fashion. The process of imparting information is known as *exposition,* and it's an important part of all types of drama.

Think about it: Gracefully giving the audience all the information it needs to understand an unfolding scene is a very difficult task. In plays written centuries ago, a popular form of exposition consisted of having two maids, through supposedly casual conversation, set the scene while dusting the master's house. This type of exposition, a clumsy recitation of facts, came to be known as *feather-duster* exposition, and it is usually avoided by modern writers.

More graceful exposition techniques usually involve a short dramatic scene. Let's say the producer of a radio commercial wants to set a scene that supports a family's need to buy a home computer to help a child with math homework. Would it serve the client's purposes to have mother and father—in the role of "maids"—discuss Junior's poor report card? Perhaps, but the scene could be set more effectively and quickly with, for example, a short classroom scene, where Junior demonstrates his lack of mathematical acumen by botching a problem at the chalkboard.

▪ ROLE OF DRAMATIC ▪ ELEMENTS IN RADIO PRODUCTION

While you may find little occasion to produce the kind of full-scale drama included in Appendix C, you will certainly have the opportunity to incorporate dramatic elements in such areas as commercials and news.

Radio Drama in Commercials

"Oh, my head is killing me!"

How often have you heard that line, or one similar to it, in an advertisement for a headache remedy? It's the start of a common drama—a slice of life, so to speak—that can be played out effectively. Note how much more effective it is to use the dramatic scene than to have the announcer prattle on about the fact that Mrs. Smith has a headache. Drama, in effect, serves two purposes in a radio commercial, to capture attention and to compress time.

Capturing Attention All of us are interested in how life unfolds. Why else do soap operas and other similar dramatic forms draw such rapt interest?

In the radio commercial, a dramatic scene serves to engage the listener and to drive home a point. For example, a comedic scene featuring some incompetent mechanics attracts the listener and sets the stage for the upcoming spiel that tells why Joe's Garage does a better job than the bunglers depicted in the commercial. Note how the commercial reproduced in Figure 10.1 uses a similar dramatic scene to attract attention.

Compressing Time Which approach seems more effective from a radio producer's point of view?

1. John works at a newspaper; he is a reporter and the pressure is very intense. Right now he's working under a tight deadline. The pressure gets to him sometimes and results in heartburn and an upset stomach.

2. **SFX** (sound effects): TELETYPES, OFFICE COMMOTION.

   VOICE I: John, deadline for the fire story is in 5 minutes!

   JOHN: Boy, this pressure really gets to me sometimes . . . heartburn, acid indigestion. . . .

```
(PHIL WHISTLING "DECK THE HALL."  SOUND EFFECTS OF PAPER RUSTLING AND BOX BEING

SMASHED ABOUT ON TABLE . . . SOUND EFFECT CARRIES THROUGHOUT.)


LEW:     HEY . . . WHAT ARE YOU DOING?

PHIL:    I AM BUSILY WRAPPING A WONDERFUL CHRISTMAS GIFT IN A DECORATIVE FASHION.

         HOW DO YOU LIKE THE LITTLE . . . OOPS, I CUT A LITTLE HOLE IN THE TABLE-

         CLOTH THERE.  OH WELL . . . I'LL PUT A VASE THERE AND NO ONE WILL NOTICE.

LEW:     LOOK, YOU'RE WASTING YOUR TIME WITH THAT MESS.  IF YOU WOULD JUST. . . .

PHIL (INTERRUPTS):  WAIT.  PUT YOUR FINGER RIGHT THERE AND HOLD IT.  THEN WHEN I

         SAY "LET GO," TAKE IT AWAY REAL FAST.  OK . . . LET GO.

(SOUND OF VIOLENT RUMPLING OF PAPER AND SMASHING OF BOX.  GIFT ENDS UP ON FLOOR.)

LEW:     LOOK . . . INSTEAD OF GOING THROUGH ALL THAT, WHY DON'T YOU TAKE YOUR GIFTS

         TO COUNTY SAVINGS BANK?

PHIL:    COUNTY SAVINGS WANTS MY GIFTS?

LEW:     THEY'LL WRAP THEM FOR YOU.  FREE.  THEN YOU CAN PICK THEM UP IN TIME FOR

         CHRISTMAS . . . ALL NEATLY WRAPPED.

PHIL:    THEY'LL DO THAT FOR ME?

LEW:     YOU AND ANYONE ELSE WHO BRINGS IN THEIR GIFTS BEFORE DECEMBER 16TH.

PHIL:    YOU DON'T SAY?  HEY, YOU DON'T SUPPOSE THEY KNOW HOW TO MAKE A NICE SCOTCH

         TAPE BOW DO YOU?  I WAS JUST ABOUT TO. . . . (FADE OUT)
```

Figure 10.1   Script for a commercial that uses dramatic elements to attract attention. (Script courtesy of Creative Communications.)

Notice that scene 2 would take about half the time needed for scene 1. Similarly, a sound effect of clapping thunder and pouring rain takes much less time than announcer's copy telling how bad the storm is.

Figure 10.2 shows a commercial that compresses its premise by using dramatic elements. Chapter 11 deals with the concepts of attracting attention and compressing time, as well as with other facets of radio commercial production.

```
                    (Open with sound effect of car being driven down road)

WIFE:      IT'S SO HARD TO SHOP FOR A HOME IN SUCH A SHORT AMOUNT OF TIME.

HUSBAND:   YOU'RE RIGHT.  AND WE REALLY HAVE TO FINISH BY TOMORROW. . . . . OR WE HAVE

           TO COME BACK ANOTHER TIME.

WIFE:      (SIGHS)

ANNOUNCER: YOU DON'T HAVE TO GO THROUGH ALL THAT AT JOHN HOLMES REALTY AT

           143 WEST SECOND STREET.  AT JOHN HOLMES REALTY, WE DON'T

           RUN YOU ALL OVER TO LOOK AT EVERYTHING THERE IS FOR SALE. . . . . WHAT

           WE DO IS SIT YOU DOWN IN OUR COMFORTABLE LOUNGE AND LET YOU LOOK OVER

           OUR ILLUSTRATED GUIDE TO HOMES ON THE MARKET.  YOU PICK THE HOMES THAT

           FIT YOUR NEEDS AND PRICE RANGE, AND THEN WE'LL GIVE YOU A TOUR USING

           OUR MODERN VIDEOTAPE EQUIPMENT.  SO IF YOU FIND THAT YOU DON'T LIKE

           THE WALLPAPER, YOU'LL KNOW IT BEFORE DRIVING THERE.  WHEN YOU SEE THE

           HOME YOU'D LIKE TO GO AND LOOK AT, WE'LL TAKE YOU THERE FOR A CLOSE

           LOOK.

           IT'S A SIMPLE PROCESS TO BUY A HOME AT JOHN HOLMES REALTY.  COME AND

           SEE US AND WE'LL SHOW YOU.
```

Figure 10.2 Script for a commercial that uses dramatic techniques to compress time. (Script courtesy of Creative Communications.)

▪ ROLE OF DRAMATIC ▪ ELEMENTS IN NEWS PRODUCTION

The goal of drama is to tell an interesting story in a compelling way. The goal of news is really not so different.

Although a news producer must be extremely careful not to mislead listeners or to falsify information for the sake of dramatic impact, judicious use of dramatic elements is certainly acceptable. Documentaries usually contain some dramatic elements; a story on beachfront pollution, for example, can be bolstered with the sound effects of the plaintive call of seagulls.

Contrast, an important facet of drama, is also used as a dramatic element in documentary production. Thus a politician's claim that tax revenues are insufficient could be directly juxtaposed with a city official's contention that most of the city budget is squandered on salaries for no-show employees or in other wasteful ways. Playing the two cuts back to back, without comment, increases the dramatic value and makes a point that no amount of narration could. Music is also an important element of documentary production, although it is rarely if ever used in hard news production.

Remember that narration of news, public affairs, and documentaries can utilize dramatic elements, too. Don't be afraid to try new ideas in news production. Dramatic elements, as long as they are tasteful and not deceptive, can significantly freshen up what can otherwise be a stale area of radio production. The sound of police and fire trucks racing to a scene, for example, can be cut into a news report to give it extra impact.

■   TECHNICAL   ■
CONSIDERATIONS OF
RADIO DRAMA

The most immediate consideration in producing radio drama or inserting a dramatic element is to create the illusion of place and movement. By *place*, we mean the location of the actors; by *movement*, we mean their physical movement through space.

Giving the Illusion of Place

Acoustic characteristics are important in determining place. For example, would you believe that a lively, reverberating sound was coming from someone on a beach, even with seashore sound effects in the background? No, it wouldn't be convincing (just as the lively studio made the outdoor scene in the Applications section of Chapter 9 sound unnatural).

Would you believe that someone was shouting from across the lawn if the actor was miked 3 inches from his mouth? Would an intimate conversation sound natural if it was being picked up by a mic several feet across the room?

The proper illusion of place is determined by mic technique. The producer will have to move actors farther from and closer to the mic to achieve the proper effect.

Giving the Illusion of Movement

Since radio drama often entails movement of the actors, it's important that the mic setup give the illusion of movement. A script element that requires an actor to leave the room and slam the door, for example, will have to sound believable. As suggested earlier, actually having an actor slam the studio door may not give the effect desired, because the mic doesn't hear the way ears do. A better approach might be to have the actor take small steps, moving just a few feet away from the mic; the door slam can be dubbed in or done live by a studio assistant.

In any event, there must be an illusion of movement within the scene, and the movement must be played to the mic to achieve a realistic sound.

Making the Background a Fabric of Believability

The sounds we hear (or ignore) as everyday background noise would be far too intrusive for a radio drama. That's because in real life we focus our attention on certain sound and exclude other sound from our attention. In radio drama it is very important to plan the background sound effects to create a fabric of believability. If we need to move through busy streets, the sound effects must take us from one location to another. Often, the inexperienced producer mistakenly sequences sounds one after another, instead of weaving and blending sound together. Have the sounds move in and out of perspective. This weaving of sound is accomplished with pre-planning and careful execution of audio levels. It is a vital element of dramatic believability.

The proper perspective is a function of more than just loudness (or in the case of stereo drama, of spatial position). Perspective also includes the way a character would hear sound. A movie sound effect best exemplifies this. In a boxing film, the sound of the blows is far different when the view of the camera (perspective) represents the person being hit. The blows are often portrayed, visually and aurally, in slow motion, as crashing, cata-strophic explosions. When the camera serves as the observer, the blows are not portrayed in such a dramatic fashion.

Mic Techniques to Achieve Illusions of Place and Movement

Creating illusion of place is largely a function of the physical shape and construction of the studio, but as mentioned earlier the distance of the actors from the mic plays a major role. The ideal setup for radio drama in

Figure 10.3 Actors grouped around a boom-mounted mic.

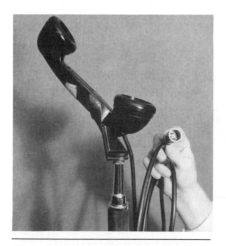

Figure 10.4 This device can come in handy in creating an illusion.

which actors must deal with place and movement is to suspend the mic from a boom (Fig. 10.3) and group the actors around it. This eliminates hazards of tripping over wires and bumping into floor stands.

An omnidirectional mic is best although bidirectional patterns can be used. A high degree of presence is usually felt to be a desirable attribute in radio drama, so a sensitive condenser mic might be a wise choice. The technical device pictured in Figure 10.4 can also prove to be quite handy in creating an illusion.

Always keep in mind that radio in general (and radio drama in particular) is an illusion. It doesn't just happen: It has to be created. A certain amount of technical skill and planning is an absolute necessity for the producer who wants the listener to believe in that illusion. Drama production, from conception to completion, is a long process and must be planned with the final product visualized at every stage.

SUMMARY

While radio drama as a distinct art form is long past its prime, drama and dramatic elements are common tools in a wide range of radio production tasks. Many successful commercials are, in fact, miniature dramas or comedies.

A dramatic element generally has the traditional structures of drama: action; dialogue; plot; a beginning, middle, and end; conflict; suspense; and exposition.

Dramatic elements are commonly used in radio production; they are particularly popular in radio commercials. Dramatic elements can attract attention, and they can compress time by expressing many thoughts in a small dramatic scene. Dramatic elements have some place in news production, although it is essential that they not be used in such a way as to mislead the listener.

Among the major considerations of the radio producer are to create the illusion of place, give the illusion of movement, and make the background a fabric of believability. Achieving illusions of place and movement can be accomplished through mic techniques.

APPLICATIONS

▪ **Situation 1** ▪ *The Problem* A producer was given the assignment of producing a 15-minute documentary on the effects of government loan programs on local farmers. It soon became apparent that the collection of interviews he intended to gather would prove to be extremely dull. One interview in particular, a question-and-answer session with a farmer and the farmer's accountant, promised to be deadly.

One Possible Solution To liven things up, the producer took two steps. First, the narration was done not in the studio but on site at a local farm; background audio lent a dramatic texture. Second, instead of questioning the farmer and accountant, the producer convinced them to talk with each other, to dramatize a frank discussion of how the government's loan policies had affected the farmer's operation. The goal was to listen in on a conversation between the farmer and the accountant, not to question them.

■ **Situation 2** ■ *The Problem* A producer at a New England radio station was given the task of developing commercials for a glove manufacturer and retailer. Previous ads had featured nothing but announcer's copy extolling the toughness and warmth of the gloves; those commercials did not appear to be effective. The sponsor's instructions were: "Give me something with a little more zip."

One Possible Solution In search of that elusive zip, the producer came across the information that the gloves really were tough. The fishermen who operated in the Atlantic coastal waters favored them almost exclusively.

The producer took a portable tape recorder out onto the fishing boats and interviewed some of the fishermen wearing the gloves. The fishermen (who were compensated for their endorsement) spoke of how tough their job was on gloves and how a good pair of gloves made life on a fishing boat a lot easier. One fisherman also described an incident in which his gloves had helped him weather a brutal storm.

With the ambient noise and some dubbed-in sound effects, the producer was able to use the dramatic scenes to produce a compelling commercial that met the client's needs.

EXERCISE

Create a 30- or 60-second spot that tells the story of your first day in college. Consider telling the listener about such first-day encounters as registration, dining-hall eating, finding your classroom, meeting a friend or roommate, getting lost on campus, and discovering third- and fourth-year students. Do this using only sound effects and music. (*Hint:* Voice can be used as a sound effect when we don't hear any particular person speaking.)

·11·

Commercial
Production

C ommercial production, as far as managers and owners are concerned, is at the core of the main purpose of radio: to make a profit. Like it or not, that's how commercial stations survive.

It is extremely important that commercials, which are the tangible result of the sales effort, be done well. As a producer of radio commercials, you will have three responsibilities:

1. To produce commercials that stimulate sales
2. To produce commercials that please the client
3. To produce commercials that fit your station's sound

The producer of a commercial (who can be anyone at the station—a sales manager, a staff announcer, or a production manager) must translate those goals into a radio production that will capture the attention of an audience and be a successful sales tool for the client.

This chapter addresses all the elements that make up a commercial, including general sales appeal, content, and production values. It's important to have a rounded view of the commercial, because most radio professionals will deal with commercial production at a variety of levels at various points in their careers. Keep in mind that your function in putting together a radio commercial will include any or all of the following:

‣ Writing the script, and/or putting the concept together
‣ Narrating the commercial
‣ Doing the hands-on production work
‣ Convincing the client that your approach is the proper one

The last duty is a common bugaboo of the commercial production field; the producer is often caught in the middle between the salesperson and the client, and must act as the final arbiter of what is effective and what constitutes good production.

You may have a great deal of responsibility in determining what elements and production values will make the commercial effective. This will be especially true if you function in both sales and production capacities, which is common in first broadcasting jobs (and sometimes is the only way to make a decent income).

■   WHAT MAKES A   ■
COMMERCIAL
EFFECTIVE?

We are convinced, after a combined half-century of involvement with broadcast advertising, that there are no hard-and-fast rules for determining a commercial's effectiveness. In fact, rules that occasionally get handed down from on high are often proved wrong. Several years ago, top advertising agencies determined that humor was not an effective way to help sell a product; as proof, they pointed to large firms whose very entertaining commercials didn't move the products. But then a funny thing happened: Humorous commercials began to be the crux of very successful ad campaigns. Comedic teams such as Bob and Ray and Dick and Bert began creating extremely successful commercials, and the old "humor is no good" theory went down the drain.

But while there are no firm rules, we feel that the most important general principle of radio advertising is that commercials, like programming, must engage the attention of the audience. Some effective commercials have done this by being mildly irritating, such as the "ring around the collar" television ad.

The important thing about "ring around the collar"—or any other commercial, for that matter—is that it engages attention and appeals to a fundamental human drive. Consider that the dreaded ring always was discovered in a public and often posh environment, such as a cruise ship (never while playing touch football, though). There was always a scene of the poor housewife squirming in humiliation as her husband's ring around the collar was loudly pointed out. But, of course, she discovered the right detergent and all her problems were solved—within the space of 30 seconds.

Why was such an obvious piece of tripe so effective in selling the product (which it must have been, since the commercials ran for years)? Essentially, it appealed to a basic human emotion: the desire not to be humiliated in front of one's family.

While you might protest that such tactics don't work on you, it might be worthwhile to examine your buying habits and determine what role advertising has had in your purchases. On a related note, be aware that while people often adamantly deny that they are persuaded by advertising, research frequently shows otherwise. The story of motivational research in advertising is beyond the scope of this book, but *The Hidden Persuaders* by Vance Packard and *Confessions of an Advertising Man* by David Ogilvy will provide some additional insight.

There are no magic formulas for producing effective commercials; in fact, even the major advertising agencies, backed with millions of dollars for research, bomb every once in a while. Conversely, commercials that fly in the face of research and established practice have done spectacularly well.

Although you generally won't be able to research the effectiveness of the commercials you produce (except for getting feedback from local merchants), you can take advantage of the basic appeals that appear again and again in broadcast advertising, by including the elements of an effective commercial in your productions.

▪   ELEMENTS OF EFFECTIVE   ▪
RADIO ADVERTISING

Essentially, a radio commercial has to be effective in terms of sound. Since there's no picture, the sound must compensate.

That's not necessarily a disadvantage. A picture in the mind can be infinitely more persuasive than a picture on the screen or in a print ad. Writer/producer Stan Freberg demonstrated this attribute quite effectively in a well-known promotional spot produced for the Radio Advertising Bureau. He created an imaginary scene, complete with sound effects, in which he drained Lake Michigan, filled it with hot chocolate, added a mountain of whipped cream, and had the Royal Canadian Air Force drop a 10-ton maraschino cherry on top. Freberg then challenged potential advertisers to "try that on television."

The point is that all the imagination of the listener is brought to bear on the message through the use of music and simple dramatic techniques—many of them the same ones outlined in the previous chapter.

Remember, too, that radio advertising can and should be geared toward a target audience. One of the great advantages of radio is that its audiences are usually clearly defined. Want to advertise acne medicine? Buy some time in the evening hours of the local top-40 station. An advertiser with a Mercedes-Benz dealership would be wise to check out the beautiful music station. The beer company advertising directly certainly will buy some time on the local station that carries the baseball games.

You, the radio producer, can take advantage of both elements of radio advertising (the ability to create mental pictures, and the targeting of advertising) to create effective commercials. But it means that you must think in terms of radio. This sounds obvious, but it's not.

For one thing, the producer of radio commercials is often at odds with the client. This is because many merchants have the idea that the only effective commercial consists of an announcer reading as many store items and prices as can be crammed into a 30-second spot. We're not overstating the case. If you are in charge of at least some of the creative concept of a commercial (as is often the case, especially if you are involved in the sale), this is a situation you will probably experience time and time again.

The producer dealing with such a client faces a ticklish situation. The easy way out is to give the client what he or she wants, which may not be particularly effective, meaning that the account could soon be lost. Alternatively, the producer can lobby for a more enlightened approach, which could conceivably produce much better results and bring about an increase in advertising. However, keep in mind that even the most cleverly constructed commercial can fall flat.

In the long run, you and the client will both be better off by shying away from the approach of listing the entire contents of the client's store. Here are two examples of how Lew O'Donnell and Phil Benoit, who once owned an advertising agency, handled the problem. We're not saying that these are the best approaches or the only approaches; they're simply alternatives that were effective.

A Shoe Store Advertisement

A local merchant had, for years, run back-to-school ads listing ten or eleven brands of children's shoes and their respective prices; results were middling. Although the shoe store owner initially opposed the idea, a radio campaign was developed in which the nostalgic excitement of back-to-school time was recreated in the minds of the parents (Fig. 11.1).

A Car Dealership Advertisement

Another merchant, the owner of a car dealership, was convinced to alter his advertising from a recitation of cars and prices to an approach that

ANNOUNCER: REMEMBER THE EXCITEMENT OF GOING BACK TO SCHOOL WHEN YOU WERE A KID?

THERE WAS THE SLIGHT SADNESS THAT SUMMER WAS OVER, BUT THERE WAS ALSO THE SENSE OF

ANTICIPATION. . . . NEW BEGINNINGS AND A FEELING OF GOOD TIMES AHEAD FOR THE NEW

SCHOOL YEAR.

ALONG WITH THAT SENSE OF EXCITEMENT CAME THE TIME WHEN YOU WENT SHOPPING FOR NEW

CLOTHES. THEY ALWAYS HAD A SPECIAL KIND OF "NEW" SMELL TO THEM. AND WHEN YOU

SMELL IT TODAY, YOU PROBABLY THINK OF GOING BACK TO SCHOOL.

BEST OF ALL, THOUGH, WAS GETTING NEW SHOES. YOUR OLD RELIABLES HAD JUST ABOUT

MADE IT THROUGH THE PAST YEAR. AND NOW IT WAS TIME TO GET THOSE BRAND NEW ONES

THAT WOULD GET YOU OFF TO A GOOD START.

WELL VONA SHOES, 122 WEST SECOND STREET, IS THE PLACE THAT CAN BUILD

SIMILAR MEMORIES FOR YOUR CHILD. AND WHILE THEY'RE AT IT THEY'LL SEE TO IT

THAT YOUR CHILD GETS QUALITY AND A GOOD FIT. THE TOP BRAND NAMES IN CHILDREN'S

FOOTWEAR IN VONA'S EXTENSIVE INVENTORY MEANS THAT YOU'LL FIND THE SIZE YOU NEED

AND YOU'LL GET VALUE.

THAT'S IMPORTANT FOR YOU. BUT FOR YOUR CHILD, THERE WILL BE EXCITEMENT AND THE

FUN OF GOING TO BUY SHOES FOR BACK TO SCHOOL. A TIME FILLED WITH SIGNIFICANCE IN

A YOUNG LIFE.

VONA SHOES . . . WHERE THEY UNDERSTAND YOU.

Figure 11.1 Script of a commercial that uses an appeal to nostalgia to persuade its audience. (Script courtesy of Creative Communications.)

encouraged potential customers to browse on Sunday. The script (Fig. 11.2) also conveyed a low-key attitude.

Notice how the listing approach is avoided by major advertisers. Grocery store chains, for example, may note one or two specials, but the thrust of the commercial is: Our stores are friendly and convenient, offering the largest selection at the best prices, and so on and so forth. Much of this message can be communicated through dramatic technique, or through

ANNOUNCER: SHOPPING FOR A CAR IS AN IMPORTANT PROCESS. ONE THAT TAKES TIME AND
THOUGHT. YOU LOOK AND YOU TALK. . . . YOU DEAL AND YOU DECIDE. BUT THERE ARE
TIMES WHEN YOU WOULD LIKE TO BE ALL ALONE AT A CAR DEALER'S LOT AND JUST TAKE
YOUR TIME TO LOOK OVER THE SELECTION OF CARS WITHOUT TALKING TO A SALESPERSON.

        WELL AT BURRITT CHEVROLET ON BRIDGE STREET IN OSWEGO, WE UNDERSTAND
THAT NEED. SO HERE'S A SUGGESTION. COME ON SUNDAY. ALL OUR CARS ARE ON THE
LOT . . . AND THERE'S NO ONE THERE. YOU CAN BROWSE TO YOUR HEART'S CONTENT.

        OF COURSE, ONCE YOU'VE HAD A CHANCE TO LOOK OVER OUR FINE SELECTION OF
BRAND NEW CHEVROLETS AND OUR GREAT A-1 USED CARS, YOU'LL PROBABLY WANT TO COME BACK
FOR A TEST DRIVE.

        THAT'S WHERE OUR SALESPEOPLE CAN COME IN HANDY. THEY'RE AROUND THE
OTHER SIX DAYS OF THE WEEK, AND THEY'LL BE HAPPY TO SET YOU UP WITH A TEST DRIVE.
AND THEN THEY'LL WORK WITH YOU TO COME UP WITH THE BEST DEAL AROUND ON THAT CHEVY
OR USED CAR.

        SO PLEASE . . . BE OUR GUEST. VISIT BURRITT CHEVROLET ON WEST BRIDGE
STREET, OSWEGO. DO IT ON SUNDAY AT YOUR OWN PACE. THEN COME BACK ON MONDAY, OR
TUESDAY OR ANY OTHER DAY, AND FIND OUT WHY WE'RE THE DEALIN'EST GUYS IN TOWN.

Figure 11.2   Script of a commercial that tries to lessen the pressure of the car-buying
process. (Script courtesy of Creative Communications.)

music. But almost any approach will be better than the crammed-
in list. For one thing, a list of products and prices, while effective in a
newspaper ad, might not even be comprehended by a radio listener. Second, a list of products and prices doesn't exploit the strengths of radio
advertising.

What does exploit radio advertising's strong points? Essentially, any ad
that creates mental images and proves a benefit to the consumer. That
benefit may be tangible (saving money) or perceived (avoiding the humiliation of ring around the collar).

▪ PRACTICAL APPROACHES TO ▪
RADIO COMMERCIALS

This section discusses the specific appeals radio advertising can make, as well as the nuts-and-bolts construction of a radio commercial.

Advertising Appeals

We're going to provide a rather cold-blooded listing of some of the emotional triggers that are frequently used in advertising. These appeals aren't usually discussed in this manner, but if they are to be used, it's only right to recognize them for what they are. Although there's no universal agreement on the effectiveness of all these appeals, since advertising is an area of few cut-and-dried truisms, we believe that the following appeals represent motives used in modern advertising.

We refer to a number of well-known television commercials to illustrate the appeals, because spots aired on network television will be familiar to almost all readers; radio commercials are usually done on a local or regional basis and would therefore be less useful for this discussion.

Each of these commercials is aimed at an individual. Too often we tend to think of our audience as a group of listeners, but actually our audience is made up of individuals. Think about when you listen to radio. You listen, perhaps, in your car on the way to work, or with a personal headset-type radio at the beach. Commercials should always address an individual and get him or her involved in the message. This is far more effective and appealing than the stereotypical "Hey all of you out there in radioland" approach.

Appeal to Personal Fulfillment   The army's promise to help you "be all that you can be" typifies this appeal, which offers a subtle promise that the sponsor's product can help you be the person you always knew you could be. A credit-card firm, for example, devotes a commercial to a woman in a college classroom, fulfilling her personal ambitions because, apparently, she was able to charge her tuition bills. Although we might quarrel with the approach of the credit-card commercial, isn't it more effective than reciting a list of all the places where a credit card can be used?

Appeal to Authority   Don't we all want a person who knows how to take us by the hand, figuratively, and tell us about a product? Notice how actor Robert Young, famous for his portrayal of a doctor, used the authority appeal in touting a caffeine-free coffee or an arthritis remedy.

Appeal to the Bandwagon Effect "More and more people every day are discovering. . . ." A desire to get in on a trend is a powerful human emotion. Be in with the desirable people! Use the same products as the "in" crowd! Do you recognize several major advertising appeals that stem from this approach?

Appeal to Fear of Rejection This is subtly different from the bandwagon effect, because it illustrates the negative aspects of not being on the bandwagon. Commercials dealing with personal hygiene products are, without a doubt, the ultimate exploiters of the fear of rejection appeal. Note how the people turn away from the poor unfortunates with bad breath, dandruff, and so on. You don't want to wind up like them, do you?

Appeal to Sexual Success This appeal can be as blatant as a well-known commercial that implied that a certain brand of toothpaste would improve one's love life. This category overlaps a number of other appeals, including personal fulfillment and fear of rejection. In many cases, the message is so obvious as to be offensive to some: Consider the stocking commercials featuring what is ostensibly a career woman—but people just can't stop looking at her legs.

Appeal to Reinforcement of Listener's Ego "You know that this product is better, because you're an intelligent . . ." is a common approach. In effect, the commercial gives the listener a chance to use the product or service and prove that he or she is, indeed, as smart as the commercial maintains. Remember the series of car commercials aired several years ago that pointed out what a large percentage of college graduates owned autos of a particular make?

Appeal to Prestige "Don't you deserve a [fill in name of car]?" Were it not for an innate need for prestige, such items as luxury cars and designer clothes probably wouldn't sell at all. The appeal to prestige hits that sensitive nerve that prods us to prove, through our cars, clothes, and club memberships, that we're a little better than other people.

Appeal to Value and Quality This appeal cuts across several categories, including prestige and reinforcement of ego, but the sum total of this approach is to convince the listener that the product or service is worth the price. Car commercials often state that the consumer can save money in the long run by buying a high-quality car that will hold up. Other commercials touting brand-name products use the same appeal. Sometimes direct comparisons are utilized.

Appeals to Other Emotional Triggers Nostalgia, family ties, guilt, loyalty, tradition, and even simple acquisitiveness, all play roles in reaching listeners.

Execution of Radio Commercials

The various techniques for reinforcing the appeal of a commercial make the message effective. Most of these techniques have been covered in other parts of the book, but here we deal with some of the specific applications to radio commercial production.

Music in Radio Commercials Music is very effective in establishing a commercial's mood or an overall set of conditions—perhaps even the attitude of a person acting out a dramatic element. For example, music that features other singers joining in is a strong motivator for the bandwagon effect. (Think of soft-drink commercials, which utilize bandwagon tactics heavily.) A commercial that appeals to nostalgia can quickly set the scene by using old songs. In this case, music becomes a sort of shorthand way of communicating a message. For example, it's far more efficient to set the stage with some dance-band music than to load up the precious time with spoken copy designed to indicate the time frame.

Music, then, is very helpful to the commercial producer in creating a mood and reinforcing a message. However, music is not always a favorable attribute in a commercial. As we're already noted, popular songs tend to be overused. And to make matters worse, a currently popular song may detract from the message, because listeners tune into the song and ignore the thrust of the commercial.

Music for commercials can come from sources other than the station's airplay library. To review, music can be obtained from:

▸ *Generic commercial music libraries.* These collections feature music and lyrics for a wide variety of applications, such as "Do your shopping downtown," or "Your business is important to us." This type of production music is often quite useful; but it can become repetitive, and the lyrics tend to be on the corny side. Moreover, once a lyric becomes associated with one retailer, it loses its usefulness for other applications.

▸ *Jingles from a national advertiser's ad agency.* When large manufacturers provide a contribution to local merchants' advertising budgets, the result is known as cooperative or co-op advertising. The same types of jingles are used by large organizations that have local franchises. Most of this prepared music comes in a form known as a **donut,** whose "hole" is filled in by the local merchant's copy. An example of a script for a donut co-op ad is shown in Figure 11.3.

```
                                                           Radio Script
                                                           JOAN MAYER
                                                           30 seconds
                                                           Co-op



         USE WITH TAPE CUT #2


         MUSIC OPEN:  (10 seconds)

         FADE MUSIC UNDER

         ANNOUNCER:  THAT'S RIGHT, THERE IS NO BETTER WAY TO GET INTO SPRING THIS YEAR

                     THAN TO BUY YOURSELF A COMPLETE COORDINATED SUIT AND SHOES OUTFIT

                     BY JOAN MAYER.  YOU'LL FIND A WIDE SELECTION RIGHT NOW AT

                     _____.  A JOAN MAYER OUTFIT
                              (STORE NAME AND ADDRESS)
                     MAKES IT EASY TO SAY "I'M READY," READY FOR SPRING.  THE WIDE

                     SELECTION OF TWO-PIECE SUITS IN LIGHTWEIGHT DACRON WITH COLORS TO

                     MATCH AND COORDINATE WITH OUR QUALITY BRAND OF SPRING FOOTWEAR

                     MEANS THAT YOU'LL HAVE NO TROUBLE FINDING THE OUTFIT OR OUTFITS

                     THAT MAKE YOU LOOK YOUR SMARTEST FOR SPRING.  SO STOP IN SOON AT

                     _____ AND MAKE YOUR

                     SELECTIONS FROM OUR SELECTIONS.

         MUSIC UP:  (5 seconds)
```

Figure 11.3 Script of a commercial that uses a donut. (Script courtesy of
Philip Benoit.)

‣ *Original music produced locally.* Local advertisers or advertising agencies
often engage recording studios to compose original music for radio advertising. This usually isn't as difficult or as expensive as you might think,
and some locally produced music can brighten a spot considerably. Some
radio stations use musically talented staffers and freelancers to produce
musical spots in-house.

In the use of any music, the producer will generally follow the guidelines expressed in Chapter 6; the editing structures (blending music and voice) are used extensively in the production of commercials.

Voice in Radio Commercials The producer's role in dealing with vocal execution in commercials often extends to doing the actual announcing or choosing an announcer. The producer is also responsible for ensuring that the correct phrasing is used. Although guidance in announcing skills is beyond the scope of this book, it is important for the producer to know that anyone who reads copy must stress key words. The meaning must be clear; if the goal of the commercial is to express value, the word *value* must receive its proper stress.

Likewise, the announcer must be believable. In the most basic terms, someone portraying a senior diplomat should not sound like a 21-year-old. Another aspect of believability is consistency of the message: Does the announcer extolling the virtues of the friendly neighborhood bank sound friendly? Remember that booming bass tones don't make an announcer's delivery believable. In today's radio, the announcer is being supplanted by the communicator, who communicates *with* an audience, rather than orating *at* them.

Another aspect of choosing an announcer is the compatibility of the announcer's voice and delivery with the approach of the message. For example:

▸ The *hard-sell* approach requires an announcer with an authoritative, strong voice (not necessarily a deep voice, though).

▸ The *sincere* approach calls for an announcer who is casual and does not have the disc jockey type of artificial delivery. An announcer with the sing-song artificiality commonly found in top-40 radio (especially small-market top-40 radio) would be an extremely poor choice for a commercial requiring sincerity, such as a spot for a bank.

▸ The *whimsical* approach often borders on the comedic. This approach (remember Lake Michigan being filled with hot chocolate?) requires an announcer with a good deal of flexibility and acting ability. An offbeat voice often fills the bill quite well. An affected, booming, announcerish voice does not work well in this type of commercial, unless it's a parody of affected, booming announcers.

▸ Any *dramatized* element in a commercial requires an announcer with acting ability. Proficient announcers are not necessarily good actors, so careful screening must be done when casting a commercial that contains dramatic scenes.

The major point here is that, to take advantage of the different approaches available in radio advertising, the producer must be able to match the proper style of delivery to the message.

■   ## SUGGESTIONS FOR PRODUCING EFFECTIVE COMMERCIALS   ■

The basics of producing good commercials are closely tied to the basics of any good radio production: a clear message and clean production. The elements spelled out in this chapter will help in defining the message and in structuring it properly. Finally, we would like to add some specific suggestions concerning the specialized case of radio commercial production.

Avoid Gimmicks

For some reason, producers—and local merchants—seem to fall in love with echos, sound effects, and so forth. A commercial that depends on gimmicks often has its essential message weakened. In addition, producing all your commercials with gimmicks becomes repetitive.

While electronic effects and sound effects certainly have a place in commercial production, be sure, before you use them, that they reinforce the message and have a direct bearing on the commercial itself.

Summarize the Thrust

You should be able to summarize the thrust of a commercial in a few words: "The clerks in this store are very knowledgeable about their wares," or "This bank is friendly and wants to give you personal attention." The shotgun approach—mentioning every possible benefit of a product or service—usually doesn't work very well in a radio commercial, primarily because of the listener's short attention span and because time itself is limited. If the message seems scattered or fuzzy, rewrite the commercial.

Don't Blast the Listener

Some producers have become enamored of the idea that louder is better and take considerable pains to make sure that every sound element peaks the VU. While there's no question that you should strive for bright technical quality, excessive loudness and abrasiveness can often detract from the message.

Read the Spot to the Client

If you're in the position of writing the spot and getting approval from the client, you can wind up with a better product by reading the script to the client rather than handing over a piece of paper. Why? Because people tend to pick at words, instead of grasping the whole concept. They also tend to drastically overestimate the amount of copy that can be squeezed into a given time frame, and reading your spot aloud leaves no doubt in the client's mind that it is, indeed, 30 seconds' worth of copy.

By reading the spot aloud to the client, you project the thrust of the commercial as it should be presented, and you don't get involved in a 10-minute argument over the choice of a particular word. Some salespeople choose to bring along a roughed-out tape of the produced spot; this approach has pros and cons, and its effectiveness will probably depend on your individual situation.

Don't Force Humor

If there's any doubt about whether a spot is funny, it's probably not. Nothing falls as flat as a failed attempt at humor.

Achieve High Technical Quality

Strive for the best possible technical quality in your commercials. Commercials tend to stay unchanged for quite a while, and they get frequent use, so use as few tape generations as possible, and put the spot on a new cart. (Checking the rack in many radio stations often turns up commercials produced years ago.) If the commercial is on a bad tape to begin with, the quality will only deteriorate.

It's a good idea to save reel-to-reel copies of all commercials in the event of cart failure; otherwise, you'll have to reproduce the whole spot. Incidentally, always save hard-to-reproduce production elements, such as jingles or elaborately created sound effects, in case you want to recut the commercial with a new slant while retaining some of the original production elements.

Don't Overuse a Particular Piece of Music

There's a tendency to seize on a piece of music that works well for production purposes and use it constantly. It is a tendency to be resisted. If you use music from your station's airplay library, keep alert for new selections that would lend themselves to production work.

An index of the musical beds used for various productions is sometimes a good way to ensure that a particular piece does not get overused. Tape an index card to the back of an album cover and list the spots and dates you used certain cuts. (Imagine how embarrassing it would be to find that you and another producer had recently used the same cut for two different banking commercials.)

Keep the Message Simple

Too many ideas in one commercial, as we've discussed, can muddy the whole concept of the spot.

Avoid the "Big Five"

In general, steer clear of what we call the Big Five mistakes of commercial production, some of which have already been touched on. To summarize, avoid the following:

1. *Lack of focus.* The listener must be given a simple message that doesn't wander from idea to idea.
2. *Poor technical quality.* This includes commercials that are too loud, too soft, or on bad tape. Take pains to recut or redub a commercial when the tape starts to wear.
3. *Lack of completeness.* As pointed out in Chapter 10, a message is more effective if it has a beginning, a middle, and an end. A commercial that just sort of peters out, ending without a satisfying conclusion, loses some of its impact.
4. *The assembly-line approach.* All of us develop certain working habits, but when a producer makes several commercials that sound the same, there's a serious problem. The commercials will lose impact, and clients— who, after all, have ears, too—will complain. Make an effort to vary your approach from time to time. Use different announcers and production music.
5. *Fear of experimentation.* Don't shy away from trying a new approach just because it hasn't been done before in your station or your city. You may make mistakes, but never allowing yourself the freedom to experiment limits both your creative potential and the potential benefits to your advertising clients.

Radio advertising offers a viable outlet for your creativity—an outlet that will permit your creativity to be strongly appreciated. And while advertising can sometimes be a pretty cold dollars-and-cents affair, radio advertising producers have shown that creative advertising, done honestly and in good taste, can be effective.

SUMMARY

Producers of commercials must meet a number of goals, including producing commercials that stimulate sales, producing commercials that please the client, and producing commercials that fit your station's sound.

Many elements help make a commercial effective. Often, those elements run deeper than what you might at first imagine. For example, it is not enough simply to run lists of merchandise and prices in a radio ad. Radio requires entry into the theater of the mind.

Many appeals are involved in radio advertising, including but not limited to appeals to personal fulfillment, to authority, to the bandwagon effect, to fear of rejection, to sexual success, to reinforcement of the listener's ego, to prestige, to value and quality, and to other emotional triggers.

Music is an important tool in radio production, but it is helpful only when it reinforces the central theme of the spot. The voice of the announcer obviously plays a critical role. It is not enough, however, that the announcer have a good voice; he or she must also have an appropriate voice for the particular spot.

Commercials should have a narrow thrust; that is, you should be able to summarize the commercial in a sentence. If it is too complex for quick capsulization, it is too complex to be a radio commercial. Simplify!

APPLICATIONS

▪ **Situation 1** ▪ *The Problem* The production director of a radio station was putting together a commercial for an ice-cream parlor. The client insisted on copy that touted the old-fashioned atmosphere of the store; the copy included a physical description of the ice-cream parlor and a dissertation on old-fashioned value. As it stood, the commercial was flat, talky, and unfocused.

One Possible Solution About 15 seconds of the copy was deleted, and a bed of Gay Nineties music was substituted. The banjo and piano music, which was bright and cheerful in addition to conveying a sense of period, augmented the message, which now could be clarified and refined.

■ **Situation 2** ■ *The Problem* A local bank, one of the station's largest customers, had become extremely unhappy with the lack of results from its radio advertising. The commercials, which were elaborately produced, with music and narration by the station's young morning woman, stressed the honesty and dependability of the bank and its people. But the message didn't seem to get across.

One Possible Solution The music and fast-paced delivery were scrapped, and new commercials were cut. The new spots featured the voice of the station manager, a woman in her late fifties, who stressed, in a conversational, low-key tone, that the bank and its people were honest, dependable, and an asset to the community.

Now, the production values supported the message.

EXERCISES

1. Replace the following announcer's copy with a shorter dramatic scene or sound-effects sequence. Your goal is to shorten the message, focus it clearly, and give it greater impact. This assignment can be done either as a hands-on production exercise or as a mental exercise with the solution scripted out.

   "Rolling Hills Apartment Complex is more than a place to live. It's a place to enjoy—there are tennis courts, a swimming pool, and a golf course. You can enjoy all these facilities, and families with children are welcome. Everyone can have a lot of fun at Rolling Hills. . . ."

   (*Hint:* Would sound effects work here?)

   (*Hint:* How about a dramatized scene of happy residents?)

2. A bank has come to you with a desire for commercials to entice more young professional customers. Write a 60-second commercial that meets this need. One hook might be a young doctor saying that she doesn't have time to manage her money thoughtfully, and the people at the bank are a great help. Could sound effects or dramatic elements help clarify this message? If time and lab facilities are available, produce the spot.

3. Write a treatment (a description of the approach and production elements) for each of the following situations. Tell why you think each will be effective.

   a. A shoe store that wants to reach blue-collar workers with a message about its tough workboots.

b. A drugstore that has a new line of cosmetics for men. The store's manager wants to reach young adult males and convince them that it's all right to use cosmetics. (Would a well-known local athlete—whose manhood certainly isn't in doubt—be a good choice to pitch cosmetics?)

c. A hardware store that wants to attract apartment dwellers, rather than just homeowners. (What products at a hardware store would be of interest to apartment dwellers, and why should they go to a hardware store to buy them instead of to a department store?)

·12·

Radio Production
for News and
Public Affairs

N ews production is a critical portion of the work done in a typical radio station. For one thing, news is a very visible part of the station's product, so the production values stand out clearly. And since news is aired frequently on most radio stations, particularly on the AM band, the news producer is called on to do new production and to change production values at a quick pace.

It isn't always possible to change the content of a news story every hour or half-hour, but it is possible to change the production/editing structure. For example, the news producer may decide to eliminate an actuality quote used at 8 A.M. and instead read the quote as part of the news story at 9 A.M. The producer might also elect to use two actualities within a story instead of one, and recut the news story for the next hour.

The hectic pace of news requires that you be able to do the work quickly. In addition, you must do the work well: The radio network news may play immediately before or after the local report, and it is incumbent on the producer to offer production that doesn't suffer by comparison.

Don't assume that, because you want to specialize in another area of radio, there's no reason to become proficient in news. Virtually everyone involved in radio has, at some time, been required to do and understand news production. Air personalities in smaller stations often are expected to be able to come up with an acceptable newscast; even sales people will be called on to discuss the newscast in detail.

Regardless of your particular role in preparing news programming, the important thing for you to remember is that radio is a medium of sound.

More and better sound doesn't necessarily guarantee a good newscast, but it does add to its impact and appeal.

What do we mean by "more and better sound"? Essentially, the goal of radio news programming is to offer something more than an announcer reading the copy. Additional sound elements—such as an interview conducted with the subject of the story; a live, on-the-scene report from a radio station staffer; or the noise of a riot taking place—add to the variety and maximize the impact.

These attributes relate to the strengths of radio and the qualities news radio can stress. Radio is unsurpassed for timeliness—getting the story on the air quickly. Radio is also a personal medium, a one-on-one method of communication, and as such can effectively relate the human interest values in a story. Also, the personal medium of radio can bring a listener into close proximity to a story, directly on the picket line or at the scene of the fire. Sound sources can help a great deal in this regard.

It's important to emphasize again that sound sources do not make the newscast. Good journalistic principles must be followed, and the voice and delivery of the on-air person must be appropriate. The news producer—whether he or she is the actual gatherer and reader of news or the executive in charge of the station's overall news effort—is responsible for a wide variety of duties. The total gamut of these duties (which may be split among several people) involves news gathering, news writing, assembling the elements of a newscast (including stories and sound elements), and news reading and reporting.

Let's take a look at these aspects, and examine how production plays a role in their execution.

▪   NEWS GATHERING   ▪

One of the limitations of radio news is that the newsperson is often tied to the studio. In smaller stations especially, the news director may be the only newsperson. Although a good reporter will make every effort to get out into the field, at least to make rounds at the police station, city hall, and so forth, much news gathering must be done from the studio. In larger stations, street reporters do on-the-spot news gathering.

In either event, news gathering consists of the process of obtaining facts from which stories are written. It consists of collecting actualities, the recorded segments of news events or news makers. An actuality can be an interview segment or a recording of the **wild sound** resulting from an event, such as a funeral march or the wailing of fire sirens. Although the terminology varies across the country, wild sound or interview actuality is often referred to as a **sound bite;** however, that term is more widely used in TV than in radio. *Sound bite* generally refers to an interview segment. News gathering for radio also involves a great deal of recording off the telephone.

In smaller stations, much of the news gathering is done by perusing the local paper. Although it's not generally admitted, many local newscasts involve the announcer reading directly out of the paper. Sometimes the listener can even hear the pages being turned! More often, though, stories are rewritten. In small and even medium-sized markets, the radio news-person won't have many sources at all other than the newspaper, although overreliance on the paper must be avoided. For one thing, papers are wrong on occasion, and when the paper is wrong, you are wrong. In addition, most newspapers are quite sensitive about the reuse of their material by another profit-making organization. Many newspapers are copyrighted, and could take legal action against a station that makes a wholesale appropriation of its material.

Another drawback to relying too heavily on the newspaper is that radio news is expected to be "up to the minute," while newspapers are generally several hours out of date by the time they reach the reader. It's important for a radio news staff to develop its own system of news gathering (sources, routines of calls to police, and so on) because listeners generally aren't tolerant of old news, which has about as much appeal as yesterday's newspaper.

■ NEWS WRITING ■

Words—their order, their meaning, and their rhythm—can be considered to be a production value. The style of writing influences the sounds, and writing does, of course, put the whole package together. Writing also involves the way sound elements are assembled.

While a treatise on news writing is beyond the scope of this book, it is important for a news producer to keep in mind that what is written must sound right when it is read aloud and must be conversational. Stilted, ponderous writing has no place in radio. Be aware that the listeners have only one opportunity to understand what is being said; they cannot look back, as they can with a newspaper article. Clarity is critical.

Another difference between newspaper and radio writing (and another reason for not reading out of the newspaper) is that newspapers use the **inverse pyramid** writing style, in which the important who, what, where, when, and why are listed in the first few sentences. Its advantages in the print media notwithstanding, this format is generally both confusing and boring to the listener. Radio news demands shorter sentences and active verb tenses, and this style of writing is really quite different from newspaper journalism. To repeat a popular and worthwhile phrase, radio writing is written for the ear, not the eye.

For example, a newspaper **lead** might read: "Twenty-four-year-old John Smith, of 91-B Mechanic St. in Centerville, was killed in an accident today near the Jefferson Street on-ramp to I-100, when his car collided with a truck that was traveling the wrong way on the ramp, police said." That sentence (which is not extremely long as newspaper leads go) would be confusing to listeners, who would be better served by: "A local man died today when his car collided with a truck police say was heading the wrong way on an expressway offramp." Now, the details can be presented in ear-pleasing, bite-size fashion.

Sentences in broadcast news writing should be kept short (twenty to twenty-five words, or fewer). Attribution is usually put first. In other words, "State Police Captain David Smith said today that there is no word on the fate of the missing hunter," rather than, "There is no word on the fate of the missing hunter, said Captain David Smith of the state police."

Proficiency in news writing will come from journalism courses and on-the-job training, so we won't expand on it here except to remind you that, if you don't know how to type at this point in your career, it is imperative that you learn. Many radio stations simply won't hire newspeople who can't type; in any event, typing is a skill that will come in quite handy in almost any broadcast career.

▪   NEWS ASSEMBLY   ▪

An important responsibility of a news producer is to fit the pieces of the newscast together and decide what will go on the air. (We're talking here about a newscast, although other facets of radio news production are examined later in this chapter, along with more specific details of newscast structure.) The assembly process can involve choosing stories and story order, and choosing the proper sound elements.

Choosing Stories and Story Order

What goes on the air? What goes on the air first? Often the responsibility for answering these two questions will fall on you, and it requires a sense of news judgment. Running a story first makes it, in effect, the lead story and imbues it with additional importance. Although news judgment is a subject better addressed in journalism classes, the radio news producer must

be aware that it is often necessary to shuffle news stories from hour to hour
to provide variety in the news. A story is often pushed up in the rotation
simply because it is new. The time element is an important consideration
because radio is a medium that thrives on timeliness; in fact, it can provide
news more quickly than any other medium.

Choosing Sound Elements

Next you may select an actuality and integrate it into the copy. In addition
to the actuality and wild sound described earlier, you will often have access
to reports filed by journalists in the field. These reports usually come in
the forms of voice reports, or **voicers,** and **voice-actuality** reports.

Voice Reports These straight news items are reported by a journalist and
signed off in a fashion such as: "This is Jane Roberts reporting for WXXX
News." Voice news reports usually run between 30 and 90 seconds, although
there's no hard-and-fast rule.

Voice-Actuality Reports A voice-actuality is constructed in the manner of
a voice wrap, the editing/production structure explained in Chapter 6. A
voice-actuality is simply a report from a journalist with an actuality segment inserted. It is signed off in the same way as a voice report.

■ NEWS READING AND ■
REPORTING

In small stations the role of producer is combined with the roles of reporter
and news reader. Again, the broad topics of news reading and the technique
of filing reports are beyond the scope of radio production, but it's important to remember that they do play a role. Inflection and tone are as eloquent as the choice of words. Pace of the delivery certainly is a production
value. Another production value is the quality and style of the ad-lib type
of report filed by journalists in the field, which may involve use of the
telephone or two-way radio. As a news producer, you should be aware that
this kind of ad-lib report is done with some frequency in radio news, and
is in fact the kind of thing radio does better than any other medium.

Many radio stations have used timeliness to their advantage by calling
themselves "newsleaders" or "the news authority" in the community. Such
slogans need to be backed up with good coverage and accurate reporting,
but time and again radio has demonstrated its ability to go live at a moment's
notice. Often, this can be done with a simple phone call. Anyone who has

ever listened to "All Things Considered" or "As It Happens" knows of radio's superior ability to cover breaking stories immediately.

Gathering, writing, assembling, reading, and reporting the news are the basic tasks that constitute the structure of news programming. These tasks can be integrated into various types of programs, which for the sake of discussion we will group into public-affairs programming, newscasts, and talk shows. (Talk shows are often a part of public-affairs programming, but they are different enough to merit separate discussion.)

■   NEWS AND PUBLIC-AFFAIRS   ■
PROGRAMMING

Although it really has no precise definition, **public affairs** differs from *news* in that it is less immediate than breaking news. Public-affairs programming is usually directed toward a specific topic, which is examined at greater length than is possible in a news report. The role of a producer in public affairs can involve selecting the topic for discussion or examination, choosing guests, making all the organizational arrangements, and even setting up the mics.

The mainstay of public-affairs programming is the interview or talk show, which is discussed in detail shortly. Public-service announcements also are the responsibility of the public-affairs producer.

Public-service announcements, known as PSAs, are generally short announcements, similar in structure to commercials, that are provided at no charge on behalf of nonprofit organizations. PSAs are usually 30 or 60 seconds long, have the same structure as commercials, and can be approached with the production techniques described in Chapter 11.

■   NEWSCASTS   ■

In radio, the newscast is often a 3- to 5-minute program inserted into the music programming of the station. In most cases, the station offers the newscasts on the hour or on the half-hour, although the local news may follow the network news and may therefore be presented starting 2, 3, 4, or 5 minutes after the hour, depending on where the station breaks away from the network newscast. (Radio networks structure the newscasts so that local affiliates can break away gracefully at various points.)

The newscasts produced locally are usually put together in a newsroom, which contains a variety of equipment to facilitate construction of the newscast (Fig. 12.1).

Figure 12.1 Typical radio newsroom. Note the recording
equipment.

Equipment in a typical newsroom includes means for recording off the telephone, a vital part of radio newsgathering (although some stations choose not to use telephone interviews). There are usually cart machines in the newsroom and a reel-to-reel tape recorder. Wire-service teletypes are also usually located in the newsroom. In some cases, the newscast is done directly from the newsroom, so a mic and console are found in some facilities.

The content and structure of the newscast vary greatly among stations. Following are some of the typical mixtures and arrangements.

Exclusively Local News

Many stations carry network newscasts and have their news staffs devoted entirely to local news. News staffs typically gather, write, assemble, and read the newscast over the air. The local news in such stations usually includes two or more pieces of actuality. Much of the local news coverage is rewritten from the paper; if staff size permits, local meetings are covered (usually in the evening) and a voicer is left for the morning reporter.

Local News with Wire Copy

Many stations integrate international, national, and state copy into locally originated newscasts. By and large, radio stations get their state, national, and international news from wire services, most notably Associated Press

```
˅ 39851a1--
r h AP-9THNEWSMINUTE       09-02 0178
^ AP-9TH NEWSMINUTE
^

  HERE IS THE LATEST NEWS FROM THE ASSOCIATED PRESS:
^

  THE NATION'S UNEMPLOYMENT RATE PUSHED BACK UP LAST MONTH -- RISING
TWO-TENTHS OF A PERCENTAGE POINT TO FIVE-POINT-SIX PERCENT. THE JOBLESS
RATE HIKE CAME AS A FOUR-MONTH HIRING ACCELERATION IN THE RETAIL AND
FACTORY SECTORS CAME TO A SCREECHING HALT.
^

  A TITAN ROCKET BLASTED OFF FROM CAPE CANAVERAL, FLORIDA THIS
MORNING, CARRYING A SECRET MILITARY SATELLITE ALOFT -- IN A LAUNCH THAT
WASN'T ANNOUNCED BY THE AIR FORCE. A CIVILIAN EXPERT SAYS THE SECRET
SATELLITE IS CAPABLE OF EAVESDROPPING ON SOVIET MILITARY AND DIPLOMATIC
COMMUNICATIONS.
^

  MEDICAL INVESTIGATORS SAY THE 13 PEOPLE WHO DIED IN THE CRASH OF
DELTA FLIGHT 1141 AT THE DALLAS-FORT WORTH AIRPORT WEREN'T KILLED BY
THE IMPACT. INSTEAD, ALL DIED OF SMOKE INHALATION -- MANY TRAPPED BY AN
EMERGENCY DOOR THAT WOULDN'T OPEN.
^

  SOLIDARITY LEADER LECH WALESA (LEK VAH-WEN'-SAH) IS MEETING WITH
STRIKING MINERS IN SOUTHWESTERN POLAND, TRYING TO PERSUADE THEM TO GO
BACK TO WORK. FIVE STRIKES CONTINUE ACROSS POLAND, DESPITE THE
COMMUNIST GOVERNMENT'S AGREEMENT TO HOLD MEETINGS WITH WALESA.
^


AP-NP-09-02-88 0908EDT<+
```

Figure 12.2   Sample of wire-service copy. (Associated Press.)

(AP) and United Press International (UPI). There are other news services, and some are syndicated through the mail.

Although today much of the transmission is via satellite, the name *wire services* is still used, a reminder that all news was once fed over telegraph and telephone wires. The wire services offer special feeds to broadcast outlets—feeds that differ from the service given to newspapers. Essentially, the stories are shorter and are written in broadcast style. The stories are often constructed in such a fashion that they can be updated quickly, with new information plugged in. The wire services specify where the new information is to be inserted.

The offerings of wire services include extensive news summaries, which are fed at predetermined times during the day; briefer summaries, which provide a couple of minutes' worth of copy; headline summaries; stock reports; agricultural news; commentaries and feature pieces; sports; and weather. Wire services also feed special features that relate to current news items. A newsperson can utilize these features, which are fed well in advance of an upcoming event, to bolster a station's coverage of a major news story, such as a political convention. Wire-service material is slugged (a **slug** is a brief identifying or clarifying phrase) with the time of transmission, along with other relevant facts (Fig. 12.2).

Wire services provide what's known as a *state split;* that is, the circuits of the services are turned over to state bureaus, and state news is fed to the appropriate stations. Much of this news is gathered by local affiliated stations and phoned in to the wire services. Traffic fatalities, for example, are almost always phoned in by local affiliates. The weather is also delivered in a split. Several forecasts will be fed, and the local newsperson picks out the appropriate forecast. (It might be slugged, for example, SEVEN WESTERN COUNTIES.)

Wire services are very useful and provide material that a local station couldn't easily obtain anywhere else. Unfortunately, the excellent job done by wire services, combined with the fact that many radio stations are badly understaffed, leads to the rip-and-read syndrome, wherein the newscast gets no more attention than reading 5 minutes of whatever's available.

In smaller stations, the rip-and-read approach to news often results in a newscast's being torn from the wire service printer and read by a staff announcer, rather than by a full-time newsperson. Rip-and-read often sounds exactly like what it is: a half-hearted and somewhat sloppy approach to a station's news commitment.

If you utilize wire-service material in your newscasts—and you almost certainly will do so at some stage in your radio career—proofread the wire copy in advance. Keep an eye out for state and regional stories that have a direct impact on your community. (The rip-and-read newscasters often overlook state and regional stories that might relate, for instance, to the health of a local industry or to a current or former local resident.)

Wire services provide such an excellent resource that many people involved in radio news production often overlook some important working principles. Here are some brief suggestions on utilizing wire services effectively in radio news production.

Acquaint Yourself with the Schedules and Workings of the Service Very often, the schedule of transmissions isn't posted; if that's the case, track it down and learn it. The wire services provide working manuals and other descriptive literature that can be very helpful but often don't filter down to the newspeople. Asking for and reading through this material will be of great benefit.

Check Copy for Typos and Pronunciation Problems During a reading on the air is the wrong time to puzzle over a typo. Typos do happen on wire-service feeds, and since the transmission systems are subject to interference, you may encounter garbled material.

Likewise, don't take the chance of stumbling through an unfamiliar name or word. Use a dictionary if you're in doubt, and ask someone at the station for advice on how to pronounce names of local people and communities. Wire services generally provide pronunciation guides for difficult-to-pronounce words. Learn to use these guides, and you may save yourself and your station some embarrassment.

Always Verify the Time of Transmission on a Story You Will Use In a pile of wire copy, one piece of paper looks just like another. That's why it is important to check through copy to make sure that an old and dated story doesn't get included in copy scheduled to go on the air. Monitor wire copy to be sure an update on your story has not been sent.

Keep a Close Eye on the Paper Supply Teletypes have a habit of running out of paper before the material you need is fed. It seems simple, but paper problems are the bane of many newsrooms. Always familiarize yourself with the paper-changing process, and find out where paper boxes are stored; even if it's not your job, you may be called on to change paper in an emergency. Have someone show you how to change printer ribbons, too.

If you miss a story, you can often call the wire service and have the item fed again, but it is an inconvenience for everyone.

News with Wire Copy and Network Audio

In addition to newscasts, some wire service and networks provide voicers, actualities, and voice actualities to affiliated stations. This kind of arrangement allows you to be very creative, provides more flexibility in sound, and also gives the newscast a very professional sound. Correspondents report the news from all over the world, and actualities from breaking news stories are fed as soon as they are gathered.

A wire service can feed a hard-copy description known as a **billboard** (Fig. 12.3). The billboard describes the piece, tells its length, and states whether it is a voicer, a voice-actuality, or an actuality. The individual pieces are counted down ("Rolling in three . . . two . . . one. . . . In Washington today, there was . . .") so that the person in the newsroom can start the cart machine at the proper time.

Remember, the audio service is a different entity from the wire-service copy, which comes over the teletype; the audio service is an extra. This type of product is also available from private organizations seeking to provide news features free in return for the publicity. Colleges and universities often run such services as a part of their public-relations operations. For example, Dickinson College in Carlisle, Pennsylvania, offers a sound-bite service to radio stations in Pennsylvania via an (800) telephone number. Figure 12.4 shows a promotional flier for the Dickinson news service.

```
ˇ 3960aPr--
r r AP-NETWORK8:32AED 9-2-88 (TWOTAKES) 09-02 0166
^ AP-NETWORK 8:32 AED, 9-2-88 (TWO TAKES)
^
   AIR SHOW CRASH
   ^
   105-V-35-FRANKFURT, W. GERMANY-(KEVIN COSTELLOE)-TWO AMERICANS
IDENTIFIED AMONG AIR SHOW CRASH VICTIMS.
^
   THE CONTENDERS (REFEED)
   ^
   106-W-1:36-WASH-(LOUISE SCHIAVONE W- GEORGE BUSH, REP. PRES. CAND.
AND MICHAEL DUKAKIS, DEM. PRES. CAND.)-THE CONTENDERS: ENVIRONMENTAL
AND EDUCATION ISSUES TAKE CENTER STAGE IN PRESIDENTIAL CAMPAIGNING.
^
   FOCUS: MIDWEST (REFEED)
   ^
   107-V-33-MILWAUKEE-(ALAN RICHARDS)-STUDY SAYS NEARLY HALF OF
WISCONSIN'S PREGNANT TEENS GET ABORTIONS.
^
   FOCUS: CALWEST
   ^
   108-W-39-SANTA MARIA, CA.-(REBECCA ROBERTS W- ROGER OXBORRO, AIRPORT
MANAGER, PASO ROBLES)-CENTRAL COASTAL CALIFORNIA AIR SHOW TO TAKE PLACE
THIS SUNDAY DESPITE RECENT WEST GERMAN AIR SHOW DISASTER.
   109-V-35-WASH-(DOREEN MCCALLISTER)-INTERIOR DEPT. REPORTS IN FEDERAL
WATERS OFF CALIFORNIA, OIL PRODUCTION SHOULD DOUBLE BY 1992.
   110-W-39-SACRAMENTO-(ANDY FRIEDMAN W- CONSTRUCTION WORKER STEVE
RODWELL)-HEAVY SMOG CHOKING SACRAMENTO. (CUT OPENS W- SOUND)
^

AP-NP-09-02-88 0820EDT<+
```

Figure 12.3   Wire-service billboard. (Associated Press.)

■   **TALK SHOWS**   ■

Talk programs can run the gamut from news-oriented, issue-focused community-affairs programs to celebrity interviews. Often, though, they come under the jurisdiction of the news and/or public-affairs department.

Most often the talk show is prerecorded and features a host and one or more guests discussing a prearranged topic. The two most common forms are the one-on-one show and the panel discussion. A popular variant is the call-in show.

In the *one-on-one talk show*, an interviewer and a guest discuss a topic; the interviewer often runs her or his own board, with the guest on a separate mic in the same studio. Sometimes an engineer runs the board.

The *panel discussion* features a moderator and several participants. Here, proper miking becomes a major consideration. Aside from following the mic techniques outlined in this book, you can deal with the problem of miking a panel discussion by keeping the number of interviewees as small as possible. Some panel discussions on radio are truly awful because they

NEWS ADVISORY

THE DICKINSON COLLEGE NEWS NETWORK

will present a special four-part series on

"Labor Racketeering and Other Organized Crime"
Interviews with investigative experts who lectured at the
Pennsylvania Crime Commission's annual seminar
held at Dickinson College earlier this month

June 27-30

Monday, June 27
G. Alan Bailey
Deputy Executive Director of the Pennsylvania Crime Commission

Tuesday, June 28
Ronald Goldstock
Director of the New York State Organized Crime Task Force

Wednesday, June 29
Edwin Stier
First court-appointed trustee to oversee a union local

Thursday, June 30
Michael Goldsmith
Professor of law at Brigham Young Law School

To record stories and actualities for on-air use
call toll free in Pennsylvania
1-800-422-7279

For more information contact Nancy Freiberg at 717-245-1289

Figure 12.4 Promotional flier for a college radio news service.

are impossible to follow. A clamor of disembodied voices makes things very tough on the listener.

From the standpoint of the producer and/or moderator, it's important, in a multiperson discussion, to identify each speaker frequently during the program and to avoid whenever possible having two or more people speak simultaneously. (This happens more often than you might think.)

The *call-in show* is a talk program designed to include the listening audience. Often it is presented around a previously announced topic of discussion, but sometimes listeners call in and speak about whatever is on their minds. What's on listeners' minds is not always suitable for airing, however, so a tape-delay system is often used. That is, the program is recorded live and fed back over the air several seconds later. Producers of call-in shows often screen calls in advance, weeding out cranks and clarifying the topic with the callers. A board operator handles the tape-delay system, monitoring the signal that goes out after the delay.

▪   SPECIAL EVENTS   ▪

The news and public-affairs producer often is charged with responsibility for special events production. Many of the technical aspects are covered in Chapter 13. Keep in mind that you may be called on to cover a wide variety of events, such as store openings, county fairs, and press conferences.

▪   PRODUCTION TECHNIQUES   ▪
FOR NEWS AND
PUBLIC AFFAIRS

Certain techniques are most appropriate in particular types of productions. This section discusses some of the techniques that are particularly relevant to news and public-affairs programming and are not covered elsewhere in the book.

Interviewing

Although a complete discussion of interviewing would be more appropriate in a performance course, certain principles relate directly to production. Interviewing is actually a news production technique, because the way a question is phrased will determine the product that results. Here are some suggestions.

Ask Simple and Direct Questions Try and put yourself in the place of the listener, and determine what the listener would like to ask.

For example, in questioning the spokesman for a utility that is raising its rates, be sure to ask how much the rate hike will cost an individual listener. It is also important to phrase the question in a way that is not vague or overwhelming; that way, the answer you get is less likely to be evasive or too long.

Phrase Questions That Invite Bite-sized Answers, but Don't Ask Yes-or-No Questions Obviously a plain "yes" or "no" will not provide you with much actuality. On the other hand, questions that invite ponderous answers are bad because the answers can be too unwieldy to edit. Here's an example:

DO ask: How much more will a homeowner be paying in property taxes after revaluation?

DON'T ask: What impact will revaluation have on homeowners in the area, and how do they and the city council feel about the situation?

Ask Follow-up Questions In a talk show, it's important to pursue a line of questioning if an interesting conversation develops. Formulate questions on the basis of previous answers. Don't fall into the trap of coming into the interview with a list of prepared questions and sticking to it no matter what. This is a common mistake and can result in an interview that will appear to the interested listener to be almost laughably bad. The listener isn't tensely clinging to a list of questions; he or she may be genuinely interested in the responses obtained and probably wants to hear an intelligent follow-up.

Fill Listeners In This is very important in a radio talk show, because statistics tell us that listeners tune in for a shorter time than do television viewers. The producer/moderator should frequently mention the names of the guests and identify the topic.

Story and Actuality Editing

A knowledge of editing is essential for newscasts. Editing allows you to inject some variety, because you can take different pieces of interview segments, rearrange these actualities, and rewrite the stories around them. In addition to offering variety, editing the actualities allows you to shape the story to be told in the quickest and most succinct way possible.

One of the biggest problems for beginning news producers involves creating a story and editing an actuality from a news interview. What part of the tape should be used on air? Which part should serve as information that will be written into a news story?

Although there are no hard-and-fast rules, it may help to remember that fact usually is better written into the story, while reaction and comment are better used in actuality. For example, the listener is less interested in hearing a politician recite how many votes he or she won by than in hearing the politician's reactions and plans.

Using Sound Sources in Radio News Production

The use of sound sources as background in radio news production is often overlooked. Sound bites can really dress up a news story. Traffic noise, for example, can be a helpful adjunct to a story about highway construction.

If you have been assigned to do a live, on-the-scene voice report, it is generally helpful to get local noise in the background. This will make the story more immediate for the listener. If you're covering a fire, for example, wouldn't it be much more effective to have the noise of the fire engines and roaring flames in the background? Oddly, some news reporters (accustomed to studio conditions) seek a quiet place to voice their report.

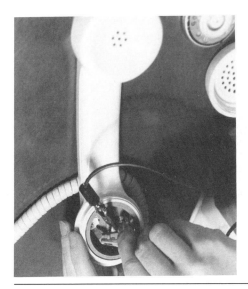

Figure 12.5   Tape recorder output cord with
alligator clips, used to feed a
recording directly into a
telephone receiver. The reporter
simply removes the mouthpiece
and attaches the clips to the
two prongs in the mouthpiece
end of the receiver.

Think in terms of sound elements that can be used in your radio reports
(without, of course, being overly dramatic or misleading). Plan in advance
for the sound bites you want to pick up.

Using the Telephone to Maximum Benefit

You can feed tape over the telephone by using a pair of alligator clips (Fig.
12.5) connected to your tape recorder and to a telephone. This can be done
quickly from a remote location. Your station's engineer will be able to
prepare the clip system for you. Some tape recorders, such as the Marantz
PMD221 portable cassette recorder (Fig. 12.6), can easily be connected to
a phone by means of a modular jack on the machine.

The telephone, of course, is also a newsgathering tool—in fact, one of
the most important newsgathering tools. While you can't always get celebrities to come to the studio or grant an in-person interview, it's surprising
how available they can be to a phone call. Or a routine story, even a state

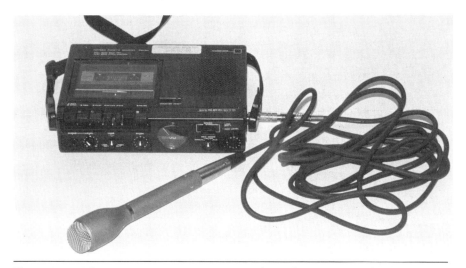

Figure 12.6   The Marantz PMD221, a commonly used cassette recorder that allows radio news reporters to record and play back tape via phone lines. A modular jack built into the machine provides a direct connection to a telephone.

story taken from the wire service, can be given added importance by carefully done telephone interviews.

Recording off the phone is a common practice in radio news and definitely should be exploited by a news producer. You must inform all parties that a recording is being made. Check with your news director for guidance on legal and procedural policies concerning telephone recording at your particular station.

Adding Production Elements to Public-Service Announcements

While you wouldn't want to tamper with a newscast by adding music or staged dialogue, the public-service announcement can definitely benefit by attention to production details. One purpose of the PSA is to draw attention to a message.

Utilizing Modern News-gathering Technology

While the industry is in a state of flux concerning the role of computerized technology in the newsroom, modern gear is making inroads into radio operations. Here are some points to consider.

Use of digital editing (described fully in Chapter 15) is not standard practice in the modern newsroom, although the versatility of the equipment does hold promise. The newsroom of the future may depend on digitally stored sound and computer-generated readouts of audio information, rather than on carts, cassettes, and grease pencils. However, it remains to be seen whether the new generation of digital audio equipment can be made cost-effective for newsroom operations.

Word processing is gaining wider acceptance in radio news, although many large stations still utilize standard typewriters. The primary advantage of word processing is, of course, the speed with which corrections and additions can be made; also, many news-oriented setups allow more than one staffer to have access to a story. But radio managers typically do not purchase equipment for show: It must prove its worth; and as of this writing, microprocessors in the newsroom have not proved themselves to be universally cost-effective.

Modern transmission gear has had a major effect on radio news-gathering practices, and the influence of technology continues to grow. Today's radio reporter is often equipped with a portable transmitter for feeding live reports back to the station; major stations have a series of boosters located throughout the city to ensure quality transmission. Cellular telephones have also made it possible for smaller stations to report live from the scene of a breaking story.

Satellite feeds have had a noticeable effect on news and public-affairs programming. Modern news and information formats allow local break-aways, which create the appearance of an integrated news program.

Making the Newscast a Cohesive, Unified Whole

The elements should follow logically, and the pace and style of delivery should be varied to reflect story content. This sounds obvious, but many newscasters don't alter their deliveries in relation to the story. Thus the piece on the polar bear cubs born at the zoo is delivered in the same style as the report of the two-fatality auto wreck. Avoid a joking style in general, and be particularly wary of light-hearted readings of serious stories.

In essence, the newscast is an entire story, and while the individual elements vary in content, the items should follow gracefully.

Within the newscast you will want to strive for completeness; don't leave the listener hanging, waiting for an answer that never comes. On a related note, don't leave actualities hanging; in other words, don't play an interview segment and then move directly into another story. Have some copy after the actuality, even if it simply identifies the speaker. Incidentally, it is always a good idea to identify the speaker of an actuality before and after it's played. Avoiding confusion in the mind of the listener is one of the primary responsibilities of the radio news producer.

Responsibility, in fact, is a word often repeated in radio newsrooms. Providing the news is a heavy responsibility, and it's important not to forget that. Newspeople don't have to be stuffed shirts, but they do have to realize that they're in a serious business. But while it's serious, it can also be fun. News—and in particular radio news—is one of the fastest-moving and most exciting of all professions.

SUMMARY

Radio newspeople have a great advantage over their competitors in other media because radio is relatively simple and immediate; stories can be gathered and relayed with great speed.

Radio news writing has its own style. Sentences are shorter than newspaper-type stories, and attribution comes first in a sentence.

Wire services provide valuable news and information that can be integrated into a station's news effort. However, it is very important for a news producer to avoid the temptation to rip and read.

Interviewing skills are essential to the radio newsperson. Among the most important points: Ask follow up questions; ask simple and direct questions; and ask questions that invite concise responses. Yes—no questions, though, are best avoided.

Don't be afraid to use sound sources in radio news production. As long as they are not used to distort the facts, sounds of crowds chanting, fire engines racing, and other "wild sound" elements are appropriate—and enormously evocative.

Don't forget that the telephone is one of your most useful tools. You can record off the telephone and, as explained in this chapter, feed recorded stories back to the station with the phone.

APPLICATIONS

▪ **Situation 1** ▪ *The Problem* A news reporter was assigned to cover a potentially violent job action at a local plant. Arriving on the scene, she found that picketers had been instructed not to talk to the press and police would not let her pass police lines to do an interview. The obvious approach was to read her notes into the microphone, but that seemed a particularly dull way to cover the story.

One Possible Solution The reporter placed herself as close to the police lines as possible and voiced her report with chanting and other wild sounds in the background. Later, a scuffle broke out, and she recorded wild noise from that altercation and edited it into another report, which she produced back at the station.

■ **Situation 2** ■ *The Problem* The producer/news reporter on duty Sunday afternoon found that there was nothing going on—and he had a half-hour newscast to fill in 2 hours. The only items available were feature stories in the local paper, and another organization's feature stories are not easily rewritten and adapted to a local radio newscast.

One Possible Solution One state story fed by the wire service dealt with the governor's plans for improving the quality of public education in the state. It was a substantial and interesting story, but had no local angle. The news producer checked through his files of telephone numbers and called:

‣ The principal of a local high school
‣ The head of the local teachers' union
‣ A student at a local state college

He asked for their reactions to the governor's proposals, and recorded the actuality off the phone. Now, he had a good lead story for the upcoming newscast.

EXERCISES

1. Have another student read over a newspaper article. Then interview him or her about the article, as if your partner were a spokesman for one of the parties involved in the article. (Your partner should keep the clipping handy for reference.)

    Try to present a logical discussion of the subject. Because your partner is not really an expert on the topic, he or she will be unresponsive on occasion, but that is exactly the situation you'll run into from time to time in radio news. Your goal is to convert the discussion into a graceful interview, 3 to 5 minutes long.

2. Take the interview you've created, edit out a section, and write up a voice wrap. Make the voice wrap deal with a particular newsworthy segment of the interview, and make it about 60 seconds long.

3. Next, come up with two new leads (new heads and orientations), and redo the story. Rewrite it and recut it as if you were freshening up the story for two upcoming newscasts.

Incidentally, mechanical practice on equipment you're likely to use will be valuable, so if you have the opportunity to practice, use it. Record an audio feed, for example, and practice taking audio off the telephone. Becoming familiar with the operation of portable cassette machines will be beneficial, too.

·13·

Remote and

Sports

Production

R emote and sports production form only a portion of the radio
station's program day, but these areas put radio production people
in the proverbial hot seat. Remote work, whether it involves covering a
news conference or a football game, is a difficult undertaking that requires
a great deal of preparation. Knowledge of equipment and production techniques also comes into play; the operational aspects are important in getting the signal back to the station.

Remote broadcasts often include sporting events, which is why a discussion of sports coverage is included in this chapter. Other common remotes
include having a staff announcer play records from a car dealership, a new
store, a restaurant, or some other business. The goal in such cases is to give
the client (who has paid a fee to have the remote originate from his or her
business) exposure and increased business. Less frequently, remotes involve
news coverage, such as live broadcasts of press conferences. Music presentations are sometimes done on remote; usually, however, concerts are recorded
on site and are not fed live over the air.

Considerations of hardware and technical facilities will largely be determined by the equipment your station has on hand and by the technical
qualifications of your engineering staff. Rely on your station's engineers
for technical advice; they are the experts and will make many of the choices
and installations.

Your role as a producer involves the planning, execution, and character
of these events. While the engineering staff can give you help on the technical arrangements, you, the producer, must have an understanding of all
the program elements and the kinds of effect that make remote broadcasts

successful. Together with a basic knowledge of radio production equipment, your knowledge and planning will be the key ingredients in a good remote broadcast.

In essence, your responsibility is to put the remote together in a way that produces the best quality and provides the sound you need to keep up the standards of your station.

▪   **REMOTE RADIO**   ▪
EQUIPMENT

Most remote equipment is pretty much the same as that found in studio applications, although the smaller models are obviously favored. An exception is the remote console pictured in Figure 13.1, which is designed for easy setup and takedown. Remote consoles usually have turntables built in, and often, especially in smaller stations, double as studio production facilities while housed at the station. Submixers are also used in remote productions, especially when a number of different microphones must be used and the inputs on the console are limited, as they usually are.

Submixers are usually referred to as *portable mixers*. Portable mixers, such as those manufactured by Shure and Sony, are especially useful in news remotes. They are essentially small (some are the size of a brick)

Figure 13.1   Remote console featuring built-in
turntables and folding legs for easy setup
and transport. (Photo courtesy Micro-Trak
Corporation, Holyoke, Mass.)

audio consoles that can accommodate several mic and/or line inputs. Volume controls allow the operator to set a correct mix level.

Incidentally, portable mixers can be ganged; that is, several inputs can be combined in one mixer, and the output of that mixer can be fed into another mixer, along with other audio sources. This is a particularly useful tactic when you are confronted with the prospect of trying to run ten mics into one console.

Cart machines are generally not brought to the remote site, because the playing back of spots is done at the studio. Newscasts are generally done at the studio, too. Back at the studio, the signal from the remote usually comes in on a remote pot, and the board operator handles coordination of other program elements originated from the studio. Sometimes program material from a remote location can be microwaved either to the station or directly to the transmitter. Microwave units are becoming increasingly common in radio broadcasting: In fact, larger stations may have dozens of such minitransmitters in strategic locations throughout the city.

Telephone Lines

In small and medium-sized markets, the link is still by land line, a telephone line known as a *broadcast loop*. The loop is a high-quality transmission line, rented from the telephone company, which connects the remote broadcast site to the station. Lines of different quality are available, depending on the frequency range they can carry. Most stations have a standard policy concerning the type of loop typically ordered; when in doubt, ask the station's chief engineer about the ordering procedure.

When the line is installed, one end of it will, of course, terminate at the station. The other end, called the **telco drop,** will terminate at the site you select for your broadcast. There, your engineering staff will hook up the equipment to the telephone line termination. Usually the operation is not complicated, but it is best left to technically qualified people.

However, you as producer will have to find the terminal block left by the telephone company. This isn't always easy—especially in large environments such as state fairs—so it's essential to check well in advance on the location of the terminal. A crew of production people frantically scrambling to find the terminal a half-hour before airtime is not an uncommon sight in the typical remote broadcast.

Other Equipment

A standard telephone is handy, too, so that the remote on-air person will have a backup method of communicating with the studio. In broadcasting from a store, you may elect simply to use an available telephone—if the store owner will let you—and keep the line open to the board operator at the station. In less accessible locations, the telephone company can install a separate telephone when the transmission line is installed.

The separate telephone is a good idea. Although the remote announcer can communicate back to the station by talking over the air line when the remote signal is in cue (back on the station console), that type of operation can be risky because the communication could wind up on the air. Sometimes, though, the remote announcer and the station board operator won't be able to take time out to chat, and some system of signals or protocol should be worked out in advance to avoid confusion. This will be examined shortly.

Microphones are, of course, part of the equipment needed for a remote broadcast. You will do well to use rugged moving-coil mics, because remote work can be rough on equipment. Determining whether or not to use a cardioid mic depends on the physical environment and on how much background noise you want included. Overuse of microphone directionality can detract from the broadcast; after all, if you are on remote from a store, you want it to sound like a store, not a studio.

Mic technique is also a consideration outdoors. **Wind filters** (also known as *pop filters*), such as the one shown in Figure 13.2(a), are useful in eliminating wind noise, which on a mic doesn't sound like wind at all but more like the rumble of a foundry. Be aware that cardioid mics are much more susceptible to wind noise than the omnidirectional types.

In some instances, you may wish to add a mic to pick up wild sounds. In a basketball game, for example, mics are often placed near the backboards to capture the genuine sound of the game. Separate mics on the crowd also provide color and give additional flexibility to the balance of announcer and crowd noise, since the volume of the mics can be controlled separately on a console or submixer.

Picking up a speaker is often a problem in remote news coverage, whether it is for a remote broadcast live or for recording on the scene. You will be at an advantage if the speaker at, for example, a press conference is standing or seated at a lectern. By placing your mic on the lectern, you can usually obtain reasonably good quality.

Placing your mic on a lectern often involves taping it to a group of other reporters' mics, so a roll of masking or duct tape is an essential element in your package of remote equipment. If there is no other mic on the lectern, and you don't have a table or floor stand, you can improvise with the tape and attach the microphone in a jury-rigged manner (Fig. 13.2(b)). Be careful whenever you tape a mic to a lectern, though, because unless you want to dismantle it during the speaker's remarks, you will be pretty much committed to staying for the entire presentation.

Figure 13.2   Microphone techniques
                 for out-of-studio
                 productions.

(a) Carl Hausman illustrates the
    use of a mic with a wind screen,
    for outdoor assignments.

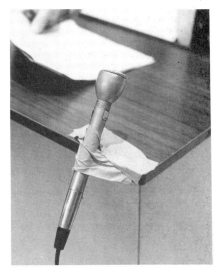

(b) Mic taped to a lectern.

Be sure to pack enough cable to reach your recorder, mixer, or other equipment. More details on planning and packing for a remote are offered later in this chapter.

Another way to pick up audio from a speaker is to tap into the public address system. (PA mics are generally not the best quality, however, and you may wind up with a poor-quality signal.) Many PA systems were set up with this function in mind. If you can't have advance access to the PA block, make sure to bring a variety of connectors; although most PA terminals have standard XLR outputs, some do not.

A variation on the PA terminal is the **multiple,** which is often set up by savvy public-relations people to allow reporters to tap into audio. Public-relations people often provide this as a way to keep the lectern free of a forest of microphones. Professionally supplied multiples often have both mic-level and line-level outputs for the convenience of broadcasters.

In sports applications, headset microphones are often used. In addition to providing excellent noise cancellation (because of the physical qualities of the mic and because the element is close to the speaker's mouth), these are ideal when the announcer will be in a noisy situation, such as a ringside seat in a boxing arena. Headset mics also leave the announcer's hands free and don't crowd the table, a definite asset when you have many statistics and other items to keep track of.

Some headsets are wireless and transmit an FM signal. The director's private line can usually be fed into one earphone, simplifying contact between production and talent—an option primarily used in television. Some have a built-in cough switch to turn the mic off if the announcer needs to cough, clear his throat, or communicate with someone off-air.

■   **PLANNING THE**   ■
      REMOTE

A remote must be well planned. Indeed, one of the major sources of trouble in remote broadcasts has been and continues to be lack of advance planning. Remember that a great deal of detail work is necessary for proper execution of remote broadcasts, and that quite a bit of pressure is associated with these events. Much advertiser money is at stake, along with the prestige of the station. In many cases, rights for a sports broadcast have been purchased in advance, so the producer must be prepared to protect the station's interests by providing a well-considered and airworthy product.

The first step in planning is to secure the contractual arrangement, which might involve a merchant signing a contract with the sales department, or the administration of a college contracting with your station for rights to a sporting event. This is the time to make sure you understand the conditions that will exist at the site from which the program will originate. It is essential at this point to have a clear understanding of what will and what will not be provided for the broadcast: Will you have access to electricity? telephones? a physically secure enclosure for your equipment?

Preparing the Site

The next step is to survey the site. This should, ideally, be done twice: before and after installation of the phone line. On the first visit you can familiarize yourself with the area and make a rough plan showing the locations for various pieces of equipment. During this visit you will also want to determine the availability of power and to assess external noise and wind conditions. Another purpose of the initial visit is to determine exactly where you want the phone line terminated and to prepare explicit instructions for the phone company.

On the second inspection, made closer to the air date, you verify that the phone line (or other transmission facility) is in place, and you ascertain that conditions have not changed since your first visit. Check to make sure, for example, that new sources of noise have not been introduced, or that the recently erected broadcast booth isn't facing directly into the wind.

It's not always possible to make two checks, especially if you are planning a remote to another city, but the truism of better safe than sorry certainly applies to remote radio broadcasting.

Preparing the Equipment

For the lack of a connector, the broadcast could be lost. The same caveat applies to microphones, cables, and power cords. Take an inventory of equipment before you leave for the site and immediately after you arrive. Although particular needs will vary, your inventory list will probably resemble this one:

▸ Console and/or mixers
▸ Microphones
▸ Wind filters
▸ Cable (at least twice as much as you think will be needed)
▸ A variety of connectors and adaptors (male to male, female to female, and male to female)
▸ Power cords and adaptors for two-prong and three-prong outlets
▸ Tape (electrical, masking, and duct)
▸ Portable and accurate electric clock
▸ Portable radio for local pickup of the signal
▸ Recorders, if used
▸ Earphones
▸ Mic stands and clamps
▸ Screwdrivers, scissors, and other tools

Incidentally, an adequate supply of tape is very important for safety considerations. To avoid imposing a hazard on yourself or others, tape mic cables securely to the floor as shown in Figure 13.3. Better yet, string them from the ceiling if possible.

Preparing a Communication System

One of the most embarrassing and unprofessional situations in broadcasting can develop when the remote announcer and the board operator back

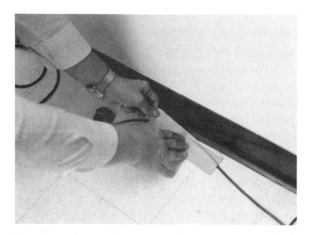

Figure 13.3   Using tape to secure cable to the floor is a
                 good safety measure.

at the station can't figure out who is supposed to do what. Much of this confusion can be avoided by planning out a protocol in advance.

Your role as producer may include acting as either remote announcer or board announcer; if this is the case, work out in advance what will be aired at the studio and when. Is the weather to be read from the studio? If not, how will the weather forecast find its way to the remote announcer? The board operator and remote announcer should have a clear understanding about such matters. The remote announcer can also keep the production flowing smoothly by giving cues to the station board operator, such as "In a moment, we'll go back to the station for the local news, but first let's talk to Joe Robinson, who is manager of the. . . ."

Preparing the communication system also can involve establishing the separate phone line mentioned earlier. Although the individual details will vary, advance thought about the site, equipment, and method of communication is always a necessary part of remote radio production. Next, let's examine some of the particular requirements germaine to sports broadcasting.

■   THE SPORTS   ■
REMOTE

Planning for the sports remote is important, too. The producer of a sports event, who in smaller markets may double as the announcer, will be responsible for assembling, for the announcer's use, rosters of players, color information, and statistics, and will also be responsible for the physical setup. Practice is very helpful. If you can possibly arrange it, try sample coverage (record it on site for your reference) of a similar sporting event, preferably one held in the same location.

In preparation for the sports broadcast, check all connections and mics. Be especially careful of the location of the crowd mic, and be prepared to move it or have another one already strung up; one raucous and/or obscene fan can badly foul up all your plans.

Talk to the announcers about who will handle the starts and stops of the broadcast: who will announce the commercials, who will start talking when the remote starts, and who will be responsible for communicating with the studio in the event of equipment problems or other difficulties. Plan who will toss the program back to the studio for play of taped segments, such as commercials and station identifications.

Finally, be aware that outdoor sporting events are subject to rainout and rain delay. Work out in advance when and if the program will go back to the station in the event of rain delay. Will the board operator play records? Will the announcers fill with talk and feature pieces?

All sporting events offer unique challenges to the producer. Following are some suggestions for the individual problems posed by various sports.

Baseball

The possibility of game delay is one of the biggest factors in planning for a baseball game, so use the preceding guidelines to make contingency plans. As producer, remember that baseball games have many portions of little or no action, so selecting an eloquent and conversational announcer is essential.

From a technical standpoint, the sounds of a baseball game don't always travel back to the point of the announcer's mic. (This is a problem common to many sports.) A shotgun mic or a parabolic mic (a mic positioned in a reflective bowl) can be used to pick up the crack of the bat or the slapping of the ball into the catcher's mitt.

Hockey

The producer of radio coverage for a hockey game has to select very good air people. The action is so fast that it's difficult for an inexperienced announcer to keep on top of it. An action mic adds interest, because the sounds of the hockey game aren't very loud. But be careful, because hockey fans can be raucous and can shout things that are inappropriate for broadcast.

Football

Producers of radio football coverage should be aware that their listeners are among the most technically oriented fans in sports. In-depth analysis is usually called for, and you'll need someone who can handle this task. Also, football sportscasts benefit from a fairly large staff; if you can find someone to keep track of statistics, downs, and penalties, you'll help the announcers do a better job.

Basketball

Basketball is subject to many audio problems. A gymnasium packed with cheering people is a difficult environment from which to broadcast; a half-empty gym can be even worse because of reverberation problems.

In high-school coverage you probably won't have access to a press box, and even in many college games coverage is done from a table set up on the gym floor. The mic must be selected with an ear toward eliminating noise from people next to the announcer, and toward decent **acoustics** at the floor level.

One option is to use a directional mic or headset mic for the announcer and have a separate crowd mic. The two can then be mixed to provide a better-sounding balance. You may suspend the mic from the press box, or even elect to string mics from the structure holding the backboard; this will add some interesting sounds to the coverage.

Basketball involves a great deal of statistical information, so the announcer(s) must have the ability to keep numbers straight. For example, listeners will want to know how many fouls or rebounds a certain player has as the game progresses, and it takes a well-organized announcer—or an announcer with some competent help—to have those stats at her or his fingertips.

Field Sports

Sports played on an unenclosed flat field, such as field hockey, soccer, and rugby, usually are difficult to cover for a number of reasons. First, bleachers or seats to lift the announcer above the action and offer a proper perspective may not exist. Second, wind noise is often a factor when there is no stadium to block air currents. Crowd noise is also a problem, since there may be no place to hang a crowd mic. Spectators may be hundreds of feet away or, conversely, 5 feet from your mic. There also tend to be problems with power and line availability.

In field sports, one of the best options available is to have a parabolic or shotgun mic on hand to pick up **ambient noise** from the crowd and from the athletes. (Wind filters are usually a great help.)

You might wish to build a small platform to elevate the announcer, if no vantage point is available. The top of a building usually works in a pinch. If you can't build a platform and the playing area is far from any structure, the bed of a pickup truck is better than nothing.

Boxing

An auxiliary mic is handy to pick up action sounds, as well as instructions in the corner between rounds. Of course some of the things said in a boxer's corner are not appropriate for airing. The same caution goes for the remarks of ringside spectators. A directional mic is in order because the announcer is within a few feet of spectators, not in a press box.

▪ A FINAL NOTE ▪

The day of a remote is typically a tense one for the people responsible for its execution, and the degree of tension is usually in inverse proportion to the amount of advance planning.

The most important factor in doing a remote broadcast, especially a sporting event, is getting there on time. Arriving on time is a frequent problem in coverage of major sports. Why? Because what normally is a 10-minute drive to the stadium can take 2 hours on game day, when the thoroughfares are choked with traffic. If the event is in your hometown, you'll have a good idea of travel time to the site on game day. If it is an away game, try and book accommodations within walking distance, or plan to leave very far ahead of schedule to ensure that you're on site in time for the broadcast.

One broadcaster of our acquaintance recalls with horror the day he was scheduled to announce play-by-play for a major college game. Traffic was terrible, and he had the distinctly unpleasant experience of hearing the national anthem over his car radio as he waited in traffic, vainly trying to get to the stadium on time.

In conclusion, we'd like to bring up the planning issue again. Problems can and do occur, but advance preparation can make the difference between an inconvenience and a horror story. Having backup equipment can make the difference between executing a quick repair and not going on the air at all.

SUMMARY

Sports and remote production are usually small parts of the job of a typical radio producer, but they tend to be expensive and important affairs that require careful planning.

A variety of remote equipment is available, including portable turntables. Planning in advance is extremely important. Remember, a great deal of advertising money is at stake. The most common source of problems seems to be the coordination of the telco drop or other transmission facility. Be sure to check this out carefully.

For producing a remote, the rule of thumb is to calculate every piece of equipment you might conceivably need, double that amount, and pack it. Be aware that you will need a communications system back to the studio. Work out all of the details in advance.

Sports present a wide range of production problems. The most immediate problem in any sports event involves selecting a competent announcer. After that, the producer must be concerned with arranging mic placements that eliminate extraneous noise.

Finally, plan to be in place well in advance of the scheduled start of the event. More than one remote has been ruined because key personnel were stuck in traffic.

APPLICATIONS

■ **Situation 1** ■ *The Problem* The producer/announcer for a remote inside a grocery store had a great deal of difficulty with noise from the air-conditioning system directly above her location. The setup couldn't be moved, so a directional mic was substituted. Now, however, there was no ambient noise whatsoever; the goal of the remote was to present a program from the new grocery store, but the broadcast might as well have come from a closet.

One Possible Solution A mic was suspended from the ceiling over the cash registers, and the ambient noise was fed into a mixer. A proper balance was struck between the announcer's mic and the ambient mic. Now, there was a sense of location to the remote.

■ **Situation 2** ■ *The Problem* Live reports from the local golf tournament sounded flat and entirely lifeless.

One Possible Solution The radio producer borrowed a technique from television and used a parabolic mic to pick up the swish of the clubs swinging and the plink of the ball dropping into the cup. Now, when the announcer said "We're standing near the eighteenth green, where Lee Leonard is about to putt for an eagle . . ." listeners could hear the ball being struck and dropping.

EXERCISES

1. Test out the sound qualities of various locations by taking a portable tape recorder and mic into various areas and business establishments. Try recording a test tape (with permission from the manager) in an auto dealer's showroom, a supermarket, a locker room, a restaurant, a shopping mall, an open field, and other locations you want to try.

   Briefly jot down the characteristics you feel each location has, and note the problems each might present for a remote broadcast.

2. Write down some of the special problems you think might be encountered in the following situations. Then propose possible solutions. For example, consider the situation of a booth at the fair grounds. You may encounter such problems as a rowdy crowd or a heavy wind from the west. To solve these problems you should (1) ask the fairgrounds manager to station one of the police officers on duty near the booth, and (2) put the remote console against the west-facing wall to keep wind from hitting the mic and, possibly, from dislodging the tonearms (this does happen).

   Now, think of problems and solutions for:
   ‣ Coverage of a high-school swim meet
   ‣ Remote from the construction site of a new building
   ‣ Remote from the opening of the Lilac Festival, held in a city park

3. Plan and execute a remote from the hallway or adjacent room outside your production studio. You and your partners can invent any situation you wish, but there is one ground rule: You cannot iron out problems by opening the door and conversing. Any communication must be done by wires that you and your instructor or lab assistant run yourselves, or by intercom or telephone. Set up mics and turntables, if possible, and run their output back from the hallway or separate room into the board on the production studio. Assign some duties, such as playing commercials or reading the news, to the board operator in the studio.

CHAPTER ·14·

Advanced Radio
Production

T his chapter on advanced production will serve as a jumping-off
point for exploration into other specialized areas. Multichannel
recording of music, for example, is a specialty within itself, and we can
offer only a basic introduction to it in this chapter. As part of that discussion, we'll deal with stereo recording and briefly explore the relationship
of a stereo signal to radio broadcasting. Engineering and other technical
operations are specialties, too. Without writing a primer on electronics, we
nevertheless introduce a few basic terms and concepts that might be useful
to radio production people interested in expanding their knowledge in
these areas.

The applications of audio in other media form a wide-ranging field, and
while those applications typically involve the basic principles dealt with in
this book, many are outside its scope. For a comprehensive guide to these
applications, as well as to more advanced applications of the principles put
forth in this book, we suggest *Audio in Media,* by Stanley R. Alten; you
will find this book an excellent continuation of the information presented
here.

■ MULTICHANNEL ■
RECORDING

Many radio stations today are incorporating multichannel production
facilities within their studio setups. Multichannel recording equipment allows
for high-quality recording and mixing of music and other complex audio
projects, such as sound tracks to multimedia presentations.

Multichannel means pretty much what the name indicates: The console and recorder are capable of isolating a number of channels, depending on the channel configuration of the console and the track configuration of the record/playback system. It's important to make a distinction between tracks (which are associated only with tape machines) and channels (which may be associated with either tape machines or consoles).

A separate audio source can be placed on each of these channels and mixed into the final product. In music recording, for example, drums can be isolated on one channel, the lead vocalist on another, and guitar on yet another. This allows the producer to balance the sound sources properly during recording and to remix the sources afterward. Multichannel audio consoles typically offer a variety of sound-shaping effects that can alter the coloration of the sound.

Common formats for multichannel recording include arrangements of four, eight, sixteen, twenty-six, and thirty-two tracks. In high-quality recording facilities sixteen-track is one of the more popular formats; four-track and eight-track studios are more common in broadcast stations. In sixteen-track recording, sixteen tracks are placed onto the tape. Each track can carry one or more audio sources. A console used for complex multitrack recording is pictured in Figure 14.1(a); a tape machine utilizing 2-inch-wide audiotape, used in multitrack recording, is shown in Figure 14.1(b).

Why is multichannel used? Because it gives greater flexibility and control. In music recording, for example, recording on multichannel offers a distinct advantage. If the recording of a music ensemble were done simply on one track (or in two tracks in stereo, as discussed later in the chapter), the result of the initial recording would be the final result. If the mic position caused the horns to sound too loud, little could be done. With multichannel recording, however, the horns are miked separately, and their volume can be increased or decreased during the following session, called the *mixdown,* when the musical elements are remixed.

But the advantages of multichannel recording don't stop there. Suppose that the horn part was hopelessly bungled during the recording. Since each instrument is separately miked and recorded with multichannel, another musician could be brought in to rerecord nothing but the horn part, which would then be mixed into the final product. Such flexibility also allows a singer to cut several versions of a song, until the desired sound is achieved. A singer can also **overdub** her or his own voice, adding a harmony part, for instance, to a previously recorded song.

Multitrack has another advantage in that multichannel consoles allow for sound shaping; that is, a variety of electronic devices can be used to alter the quality of the audio signal both during the recording and after the mixdown.

Figure 14.1   Equipment for multitrack recording.

(a) Multitrack recording console.

(b) Tape machine using 2-inch audiotape.

Before discussing those features, let's look at a typical console setup. The console pictured in Figure 14.2(a) is a four-channel model. Even though it offers less channel capacity than a sixteen-track model, it functions according to the same basic principles. Always remember that, regardless of the intricacy of the hardware, the principle is the same, namely: In a multichannel mixing console you have a double-duty board. One side of the board controls inputs. The other side controls outputs. This structure relates to the function of a recording engineer and a recording producer; basically, the engineer makes sure that the inputs are correct and the meters are reading properly, while the producer, sitting to the right, governs the mix and remix of the output of the console.

Input Modules

The input side (Fig. 14.2(b)) of the board takes in the signals from the mics (or other sources) and sends them through a series of circuits. A signal is routed through a series of circuits known as modules, the controls for which are located in vertical columns. There are modules for each channel on each side of the console. The circuits in the input modules (not listed in the order of signal flow) include the following.

The Vertical/slide Fader Multitrack consoles utilize vertical/slide faders rather than circular pots, ostensibly because the position of a bank of slide faders is easier to perceive at a glance than the positions of several dials. Most producers also find it easier to control many faders than to control many dials.

Input Selection Controls These include mic-level and line-level selectors. In addition to selection of sources, multitrack consoles offer a **trim control**—a fine-level adjustment of the volume of the input that allows you to keep sliders in the optimal control area.

Sound Shapers Equalizers and filters are types of **sound shapers;** both are located on the input modules. An **equalizer** alters the frequency pattern of an audio source; it can, for example, boost a certain range of frequencies. A **filter,** on the other hand, eliminates frequencies of a certain range. A reverberation effect is typically found on an input module, as well.

Pan Pot The **pan pot** varies the amount of signal sent to each side of the stereo signals. Panning the pot to the left will send more of the signal to the left channel, and vice versa. A pan pot is used in the final mixdown.

Figure 14.2 Typical console setup.

(a) Eight-track console.

(b) Input side of a multitrack console.

Solo The solo mutes other inputs so that the channel being soloed can be heard alone.

Bus Delegation This controls sending the signal from the input modules to the board's output modules, which are known as *buses*. A **bus** is a junction of circuits. Any number of input channels can be routed into a particular bus in the output section of the console. Remember program and audition on a radio board? They, too, are buses.

Figure 14.3 • Output buses.

Output Buses

Output buses (Fig. 14.3) send the signal to the tape machine and to the monitors (although there are additional controls for the monitors, usually above the output buses). The bus feature allows the signals assigned to each bus to be altered in volume, and some effects can also be added at the output level. The important thing to remember is that the output buses correspond to track numbers on the tape.

Monitor Controls

On the multitrack board controls, the signal flow to the loudspeakers is governed by the monitor controls.

Further Note About Multichannel Consoles

The variety of hardware involved in multichannel recording is mind-boggling, and a discussion of multichannel usually winds up surveying the latest technical wonders on the market. However, the important thing about multichannel recording is not the technical features offered. What you should remember is that multichannel consoles have an input section and an output section. The input circuits shape the audio signal and assign it (and any other inputs you designate) to a particular output bus. The output bus is a circuit junction that feeds a particular track on the tape machine. A multichannel board can send signals to a recorder through the same pots that are used for mixdown. Some channels can be premixed; drums, for example, often are put on only one of the sixteen tracks, even though four separate channels may have been used for recording the drums. Because of its ability to shape sound and assign particular signals to certain tracks, the multichannel recording system gives great flexibility to the recordist and allows remixing of the program material.

Although hardware may vary, the principle won't. If you understand the principle, you'll be able to adapt with a minimum of instruction to the particular configuration of any multichannel console.

Role of Multitrack Recording

Radio stations more and more frequently utilize multitrack recording for operations such as recording commercial jingles and recording and mixing music presentations. Multitrack work also has wide application in a number of related audio areas, but it is primarily the domain of the music recordist, and music recording is sometimes encountered by radio station personnel.

While multitrack mixing does offer great flexibility in music recording, it is not the only way to record music. Some musical presentations are recorded simply by mounting a pair of microphones (or a stereo mic) above a musical ensemble. Since most music recording is in stereo, we'll deal with stereo recording and miking next. Then we'll wrap up the discussion of music by demonstrating mic techniques used in multitrack recording.

■   STEREO   ■

Any console routes signals into one or more master channels. In the case of stereo, there are two master channels, usually designated as the left and right channels. Stereo gives a sense of depth and locale to the program material, in much the same way as two ears or two eyes give a sense of depth.

Stereo broadcasting, long a staple of the FM band, has recently moved into AM broadcasting as well, with many stations adopting AM stereo. While some ambiguity remains as to the type of receiving system that will eventually become standardized, it appears that AM stereo will become a major aspect of broadcasting.

Figure 14.4 Typical radio-station stereo console.

Stereo is popular because the balance between left and right gives a feeling of location in space. In a symphony orchestra, for example, violins are seated to the left. In a stereo reproduction, the sound of the violins emanates primarily from the left-hand speaker, giving the listener the same sense of spatial orientation. In terms of physics, this sense of spatial orientation occurs because your ears are attuned to decoding the very slight difference when sound reaches the ears. That's why you're able to tell the approximate position of someone speaking to you, even if you're blindfolded.

A feature of multichannel recording not yet mentioned is that it allows you to artificially assign a spatial relationship to a particular sound. Do you want the guitar to come from the left and the sax to come from the right? It's a simple matter of manipulating the pan pot controls.

Stereo consoles used in broadcasting, such as the one pictured in Figure 14.4, are able to process the stereo signal; they have a separate VU meter for each master channel. Operating a stereo broadcast console is essentially the same as operating a monaural console, but you can control the left and right channels with one pot instead of two.

There is a significant difference involved in stereo versus monaural recording process, however. We've presented the information in this chapter in a specific order, leading up to a discussion of music-recording mic techniques, because the explanation of stereo mic techniques should clarify the roles of sound, stereo, and mixing. Understanding the basics of music recording helps illuminate all areas of audio.

■   RECORDING MUSIC   ■

There are two ways to record music in stereo: **total-sound recording** and **isolated-component recording.** Total-sound recording involves, for example, setting up two mics (one for each stereo track) and recording a symphony concert. As mentioned earlier, this method is a one-shot deal: Your product is essentially the final version. In isolated-component recording, you set up a number of mics on various sections of the orchestra and mix the inputs with a multichannel console.

Which do you choose? Total-sound recording is often used for symphony concerts because the mics pick up the ambience of the concert hall. It is also simpler to set up mics, and—some people contend—this approach does not impart an artificial sound to the music. Total-sound recording also eliminates a lot of problems associated with multiple mics, such as phasing. Isolated-component recording is more common in the recording studio (as opposed to the concert hall) and is most often used for popular music.

Both methods can produce excellent results. For many radio production applications, isolated-component is more useful, because the music (or other program material) can be remixed—a highly practical feature for recording commercial jingles and/or voice-overs.

Total-Sound Recording Microphone Techniques

When confronted with an orchestra or chorus, producers usually place the mics on the ceiling above the audience section, facing, of course, the orchestra or chorus. Cardioid mics are quite commonly used, and in one case a bidirectional mic is mixed in. The most popular methods of orienting the mics are called *coincident, spaced-pair,* and *middle-side.*

Coincident Mics Setting up **coincident mics** (Fig. 14.5(a)) involves crossing two cardioid mics, usually at about a 90-degree angle. This imitates the way the ears hear and results in the kind of sound you would hear sitting in the middle of the house. Why? Because the mic for the left channel picks up most of the sounds from the left side of the stage, the mic for the right channel picks up most of the sounds from the right side of the stage, and the sounds emanating from the middle are balanced between the two. If the mic angle is too narrow, the spatial illusion is lost; and if the angle is too wide, there will be a hole in the middle of the orchestra.

Figure 14.5   Microphone orientations.

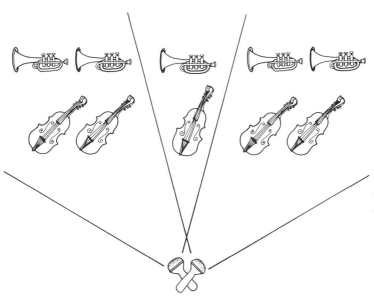

(a) Coincident miking.

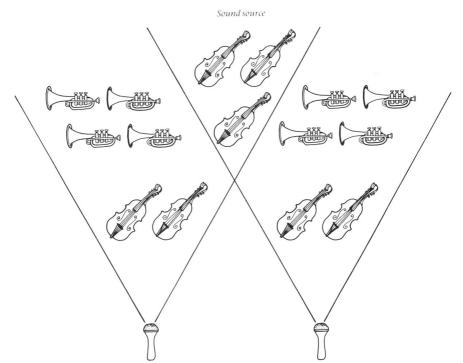

(b) Spaced-pair miking.   (*continued*)

Figure 14.5 *(continued)*

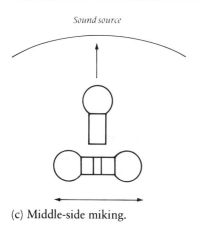

Sound source

(c) Middle-side miking.

Spaced-pair Mics When the mics are parallel, usually 1 or 2 feet apart (Fig. 14.5(b)), you get a very broad sound. Having **spaced-pair mics** heightens the stereo effect, although the mics are subject to some phase-cancellation problems, since their pickup patterns have quite a bit of overlap.

Middle-side Miking The technique known as **middle-side miking** involves using a bidirectional mic to pick up sound from either side, with a cardioid mic facing the middle (Fig. 14.5(c)). Middle-side miking results in an extremely spacious sound, but it requires a special device known as a *phase inverter* to add the signals together properly.

These techniques can be used successfully in a variety of applications for total-sound recording. In addition, they can be used to mic one instrument in isolated-component recording, although most instruments are generally picked up with one mic because the pan pot on the console will be used to orient the instrument spatially.

Isolated-Component Recording

The most common question posed about isolated-component recording is: How can the mic pick up only one instrument? Isolating instruments from one another in the sound studio often involves using baffles or isolation booths, or physically moving one instrument to another room. However, the use of a mic on one instrument results in considerable isolation from the sounds of other instruments, a factor that is often surprising to the first-time recordist.

The following mic techniques are useful in isolated-component recording.

For Singers Most popular vocalists are comfortable with a relatively close mic distance, while classical singers prefer a larger distance. In any event, the distance is almost always less than 1 foot, with the mic placed roughly at mouth level. It is generally not considered good practice to let the vocalist handle the mic.

For Drums Miking drums can be a very complex affair, involving as many as a half-dozen mics. Many recordists favor a separate mic for each unit (high hat, cymbal, snare, tom-tom, and so on), while others prefer to mike the whole drum set from above, often with a crossed pair. It's basically a matter of experimentation and individual judgment.

For Pianos In the method shown in Figure 14.6, one mic is pointed toward the lower strings and another toward the higher strings. This results in a broad mix of the sound. Other methods include pointing a mic toward the open top of a grand piano. Some recordists stick a mic into one of the sound holes. Sensitive condenser mics, such as the AKG 451 shown in the figure, are often favored for piano recording.

Figure 14.6   Miking a piano.

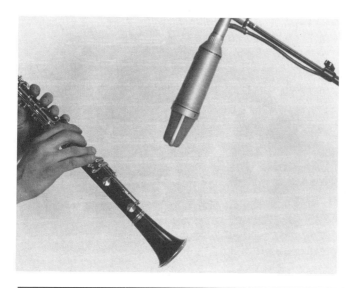

Figure 14.7   Woodwinds are best picked up by placing a mic
near the finger holes.

For Strings An electric guitar (and for that matter, an electric synthesizer)
can be miked by pointing a microphone at the loudspeaker that is fed by
the guitar. Special transformers can be used to route the signal from the
guitar directly into the console.

Acoustic guitars are generally miked by pointing a mic toward the sound-
ing hole. The AKG 451 is a good choice; it is quite sensitive to the subtle
sounds of vibrating strings.

For Brass Brass is usually miked near the bell, since all the sound exits
from the bell. An EV RE20 is a good choice because this durable moving-
coil mic won't be overpowered by the full sound of a trumpet. In addition,
its characteristic warm sound tones down some of the trumpet's blare.

For Woodwinds Because most of a woodwind's sound exits from the finger
holes (not from the bell), that is where the mic belongs. The Neumann U87
is very sensitive to the warm breathiness of a clarinet and gives an excellent
response (Fig. 14.7).

For Ensemble Work With small rock groups, you can easily place a mic
on each instrument. With larger ensembles, you'll want to designate a mic
for sections: one for the violins, another for the brass, and so on. It's largely
a matter of experience and experimentation.

▪ ELECTRONIC EQUIPMENT ▪
AND ITS USE IN RADIO
PRODUCTION

Radio is an ever-changing field, and the equipment utilized can be highly complex. We're going to introduce some of the more advanced radio gadgetry and some of the more interesting applications of technology to producing radio and creating an effect. A radio production professional must keep current with advances in equipment. Read journals, attend conferences, and talk to colleagues; in many areas, radio is very much a state-of-the-art profession, and it pays to keep abreast of developments.

Equipment

First, let's look at hardware.

Equalizers These devices are a fixture in a recording studio and have many applications in all aspects of broadcasting. Essentially, an equalizer alters the frequency response of an audio signal. It can be used to boost or to cut down certain frequency ranges. On one common type, called a **graphic equalizer,** the controls allow you to set a graphic representation of the response curve you would like to effect. By looking at the positions of the faders, you can tell which frequencies within the audible range have been enhanced or diminished. Each equalizer control is usually an octave higher than the preceding one.

Also commonly used in audio is the **parametric equalizer.** The difference between a graphic equalizer and a parametric one lies essentially in the amount of selected frequency that can be manipulated. A parametric equalizer allows you to select one frequency and boost or cut just that frequency or that and surrounding frequencies. You accomplish this by choosing the range above and below the selected frequency you wish to EQ (*EQ* is part of radio lexicon, a verb meaning "to equalize"), using a bandwidth control. For example, you could remove an unwanted 60-Hz hum from a remote broadcast better with a parametric equalizer, because you would adjust it not to cut adjoining frequencies (which might be desirable because they add depth to your remote broadcast sound). Trying to accomplish this with a graphic equalizer might make the remote sound tinny and weak.

The purpose of an equalizer is to change the character of an audio signal. A recordist wishing to make an instrumental piece sound more bassy and powerful, for example, could use an equalizer to boost the bass frequencies.

Filters Sometimes, a producer wants to delete a whole range of frequencies. A hiss, for example, can often be eliminated by a **low-pass filter,** which allows lower frequencies to pass but chops off selected higher frequencies. A **high-pass filter** might be used to eliminate a rumble.

A filter that is set for a single narrow frequency range is called a *notch filter*. Some electronic components called *noise gates* act as filters when there is no audio signal in the circuit. For example, a noise gate is frequently used in studios where a background noise such as air conditioning, although lower in intensity than an announcer's voice, would otherwise be heard whenever a mic was open and no one was speaking. A noise gate acts as an on–off circuit—a gate, in other words—and is triggered by the volume change between the announcer's voice and the air-conditioning noise. Whenever the announcer stops speaking, the gate closes, preventing the noise from passing through the circuit. When the announcer begins speaking again, the gate opens and passes the audio (at which time the announcer's voice masks the background noise).

Compressors and Limiters   These devices are often found in the equipment rack in radio control rooms (Fig. 14.8). A compressor shrinks the **dynamic range** of the audio signal. Low-volume parts are boosted; high volume parts are lowered.

Compression has a number of factors that can be set and varied, including the **attack time** (the length of time it takes for the compressor to kick in after a particular sound affects it) and the **release time** (the length of time the compressor takes to let the signal return to its previous level). A **limiter** is a compressor that severely restricts high-volume noises and has a high ratio of compression. Limiting is useful for keeping sudden loud sounds from overmodulating the signal. (In fact, the Federal Communications Commission demands that radio stations keep their signals within certain tolerances to avoid overmodulation.) Compression is often used in radio stations to maintain a relatively constant signal that won't sink low enough to "fall off the dial."

Equipment for Noise Reduction   A device known as **Dolby**, a trademark name, reduces noise. In a professional unit, Dolby divides the frequency spectrum into three bands, then pre-emphasizes (raises in volume) each band by a certain degree during recording; thus, it raises those frequencies above the noise level. Then it lowers those frequencies by the same amount during playback. In practice, the frequencies are raised high above the so-called *noise floor* and then lowered again, such that the noise floor is lowered, too, and noise is reduced. Dolby units in professional applications are usually rack-mounted and installed in the audio chain between the output of the board and the tape recorder. Dolby is frequently used in the motion picture industry.

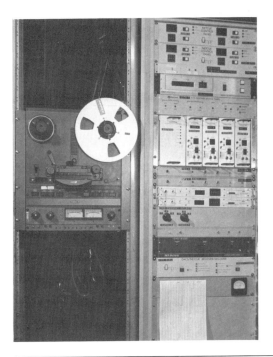

Figure 14.8   Equipment rack in a radio station.

Another noise-reducing device goes by the trade name *dbx*. The dbx has a more pronounced effect than Dolby and uses a more intricate logarithmic formula for expansion and contraction of the sound. It can provide up to 30 dB of noise reduction on tape recordings.

Both Dolby and dbx are processors that must be used in both the record and playback process. Therefore, if a tape is not recorded with either of these two devices, playing a tape back with either dbx or Dolby switched in the circuit will make the tape sound distorted. In addition, Dolby-encoded tapes cannot be played properly with dbx processing, and vice versa.

Harmonizers   Electronic devices called **harmonizers** allow you to vary the pitch, tempo, and **harmonics.** Applications include removing a harmonic to lessen sibilance in a person's voice and altering the harmonics to create an inhuman-sounding voice, such as a "computer" or "Darth Vader" voice. These devices are expensive—often in the $5,000 range—so they aren't usually found in small markets. A medium market station with a harmonizer often tries to solicit business from area ad agencies that might want a recording facility equipped with special effects.

Flangers With **flangers,** you can create a mirror image of a sound and then shift it slightly; this throws the two sounds out of time and phasing and creates a bizarre effect that's been described as something like water rushing through a voice. Essentially the same effect can be achieved mechanically, as described in connection with the technique of doubletracking.

Pressure-Zone Microphones **Pressure-zone mics,** which eliminate proximity effect and phasing problems, are useful for concerts.

Spatial Enhancers By mixing and subtracting components of the stereo signal, **spatial enhancers** produce a signal that gives the impression of having greater presence or a larger spatial environment. The intent is to reproduce more closely the effect of the concert environment.

Techniques

Here are some advanced techniques for special effects (some of which use complex equipment, and some of which don't) that can be useful to a producer.

Echo An echo is the feedback of the original signal from the playback head, passing back through the audio chain into the tape machine's record head. In essence, it produces the same effect as yelling "Hello" into a stony cavern. By controlling the volume of the playback head through the board, you can produce differing amounts of echo.

Reverb Reverberation, or **reverb,** differs from echo in that reverb is accomplished with a discrete unit, an electronic device that produces an electronic delay and adds it back to the signal. Unlike echo, reverb has a constant delay time. Since it is an electronic unit, and not a product of feeding back to a different head, it can be adjusted to fine tolerance. Some reverb units have a control called *depth,* which allows the producer to vary the amount of original signal mixed back in. Reverb is both a technique and a reference to a particular piece of hardware, a reverb unit.

Forward Echo With **forward echo,** the echoes appear before the original sound, and lend excitement. In a rock format ID, for example, forward echo can lend excitement because the echo builds up before the call letters are given.

Accomplishing a forward echo is as simple as playing a tape backward on tape 1 and rerecording it on tape 2 with the tape-2 pot open. Subsequently playing tape 2 backward will give you an echo building up to the announcement—not away from the announcement, as in a normal echo.

Pan Potting Also known as **channel bouncing,** this technique takes full advantage of stereo's unique ability to capture the attention of a listener who is not expecting an announcer's voice to move from one location to another within a spot. Pan potting can also be used to create a dramatic effect of motion (such as a train whizzing by).

Changing Speeds Many tape recorders are equipped with pitch controls, which are actually speed controls. They can vary the pitch between 6 and 12 percent. Many of the new direct-drive turntables allow you to accomplish the same function.

One application of changing speeds is to slow down a recorded voice. In a commercial for a medicine, for example, the copy might begin: "Are you feeling out of sorts? . . ." The effect would reinforce the message.

Doubletracking An interesting special effect that is relatively simple to produce, **doubletracking** involves recording a voice and then altering a copy of that narration—perhaps by equalizing, or by slightly changing the speed. Both voices (giving the identical narration) are played back together. The effect gives the voice an eerie, attention-grabbing aspect. The effect is similar to **flanging,** described earlier in the section on equipment.

We've presented only a limited amount of information on the technical end of radio, and there's a purpose behind that approach. Very often radio instruction becomes a discussion of hardware, and while that's interesting on some levels, it can be counterproductive. Supersophisticated equipment and the equally sophisticated talk that surrounds it seem to cloud the issue of radio production.

Radio production is, in our opinion, an art form. Like any art form, it requires a thorough understanding of the techniques and tools of the trade. But it is more than stringing equipment together and using gadgetry to produce an audio novelty.

To those of us who have spent much of our lives involved with radio, the medium is a very personal form of communication. It's a communication medium that enters the house, travels with us in the car, and even keeps us company while jogging. Radio production is the art of achieving the effects that make radio such an intimate, magic medium.

SUMMARY

Multichannel recording is used when many sound sources must be recorded, mixed, and remixed separately. A typical multichannel board has input modules on one side and output buses on the other. The input side takes in the signals from the mics; the output buses send the signal to the tape machine and the monitors. Each side has a variety of sound-shaping controls.

There are several techniques for recording stereo. The most popular are coincident miking, spaced-pair miking, and middle-side miking. Total-sound recording is accomplished by placing one or more mics in a central place to record the sound as the listener would hear it. Isolated-component recording involves placing separate mics on each sound source and mixing the inputs together; this allows much greater flexibility and also offers a chance to repair bad takes when the music is being performed.

A wide variety of electronic components are used to shape the signal, including equalizers, filters, compressors, limiters, noise reduction equipment, harmonizers, flangers, and spatial enhancers. Techniques used in advanced radio production include effects such as echo, reverb, forward echo, pan potting, and doubletracking.

APPLICATIONS

■ **Situation 1** ■ *The Problem* The producer of a program was recording a church choir for later playback. She miked each vocal section separately and planned to mix the program. The director of the choir listened to a test recording and was not pleased with what he heard. "The choir," he said, "sounds like a group of jingle singers."

One Possible Solution Why did the sound vary so much from what the choir director was used to hearing? Because close-up miking of the sopranos, the altos, the tenors, and so on, did not allow the reverberation of the music through the architectural spaces of the church; consequently the effects of the acoustics—and the sound of the church choir—were altered.

The producer opted for a crossed pair of cardioid mics above the tenth row of pews and was able to achieve a richer, more realistic sound.

■ **Situation 2** ■ *The Problem* A group of jingle singers and musicians were performing a commercial for an ice-cream parlor. Gay Nineties music was called for, with a banjo and piano. Unfortunately, the sound coming through the mics featured the booming, rich tones of the studio's grand piano, which had mics pointing toward its raised top.

One Possible Solution The producer repositioned the mics to a spot directly above the hammers. Now, a lot of hammer was heard, and the piano sounded much more honky-tonk than grand.

EXERCISES

1. Mic a piano in several ways, noting the effects of different mic placements. Position the mic(s) at any or all of the following locations, noting how the mix of mics at various locations changes the character of the sound, too:
   ‣ Behind the soundboard on an upright piano
   ‣ In one of the sound holes inside a grand piano
   ‣ Pointing at the raised cover
   ‣ Above the keyboard
   ‣ Above the strings

2. If multichannel recording equipment is available, record a musical group under the supervision of your instructor or lab assistant. Remix the recording twice, using whatever equipment is available. The goal is to make two recordings of the same program material that sound radically different because of the mix.

3. As a variation of Exercise 2, split the class into two groups and let each, separately, record the same performers doing the same musical number. See if the two versions are identical.

CHAPTER ·15·

Computer Applications in Radio Production

The computer is a valuable tool in radio production, but it is only that—a tool. Technological wizardry is not an end in itself; rather, it is a faster and more capable method of manipulating information, creating effects, and controlling various work functions.

This chapter will address computer technology as it relates to both production and operations. In particular, we'll focus on applications of the computer to computer-generated effects, computer-assisted editing, on-air production, automation, and programming. Our exploration of computers will necessarily repeat some material introduced in previous chapters, both for the sake of continuity and so that this chapter can stand alone as an assignment to be read out of numerical order. However, redundancy and redefinition are kept to a minimum.

Before zeroing in on the specifics of radio applications, let's briefly introduce the computer itself.

COMPUTER BASICS

Few elements of modern life are so shrouded in mystery as the computer. Indeed, it would appear that those privy to the workings of the device make a deliberate effort to mystify the uninitiated with incomprehensible jargon. But the basics of computer operations can be readily understood; and while particular **hardware** (the computer itself) and **software** (the program used to make the computer perform a particular task) vary widely, most computers do roughly the same types of tasks in roughly the same manner.

As with many modern technological devices, computers operate digitally; that is, they work by means of a series of on and off switches, with the on-and-off code expressed in digits. (Chapter 3 provides an introduction to the idea of digital technology.) The concept of digitizing information in terms of on or off dates back to the 1700s. One of the first digital applications was in a weaving loom: Paper punched with holes (later replaced by a card) determined the position of a part of the loom. If there was a hole, the loom would perform a certain operation; if there was no hole, the loom would operate differently.

The on-or-off principle was used in this instance to program the pattern for an entire woven cloth. Later, punch cards were utilized in a wide variety of applications in manufacturing and calculation.

Speedy calculation—the computer's forte—did not become feasible on a large scale affordable by consumers until the development of printed circuits, a direct descendant of the vacuum tube. A vacuum tube is a device for amplifying or otherwise manipulating a signal. Vacuum tubes were hot, fragile, and large. Eventually, scientists replaced the vacuum tube with transistors, solid-state devices that performed the same tasks as vacuum tubes but were much smaller and were mechanically simpler. Because of these characteristics, many transistors could be placed onto a circuit board, the genesis of the integrated circuit.

It soon became apparent that modern scientific techniques could replace the now-cumbersome arrangement of transistors on a circuit board. Using a process involving photography and engraving, scientists could produce an integrated circuit on a chip of material called *silicon;* thus, the silicon microchip was born.

Chips are the brains of the computer, performing the on-and-off tasks—manipulation of digits—that eventually add up to the calculation process. The on-and-off function in each instance is determined by the presence or absence of an electrical signal. A system offering these two choices, on and off, is known as a **binary** process; and through this binary coding the computer represents information. A sequence of on and off pulses is used to denote numbers and letters.

Because these pulses can be generated, tabulated, and manipulated with lightning speed, operations can be performed with inhuman rapidity. Because of this, the computer becomes an invaluable tool for manipulating information. It performs thousands of calculations in an instant, does not become bored or distracted, and possesses perfect precision within the scope of its operations.

The brain of the computer (the place where the master microchip resides) is called a **central processing unit,** or CPU. It is generally accessed through a keyboard, similar to the board on a standard typewriter, and the commands and a readout of the information are viewed on a video monitor.

The computer stores and retrieves information from a program in what is called **random access memory,** or **RAM.** The other type of memory in the computer is the **read only memory,** or **ROM,** which was built into the computer at the factory and cannot be changed.

The information in RAM, which usually is the place where the software program is loaded, along with whatever information you have loaded in or entered from the keyboard, stays there only as long as the computer is turned on, which makes long-term storage in RAM impractical. For this reason, computers are equipped with storage mechanisms, usually in the configuration of a device for writing information on a disc. Discs come in a variety of sizes, including the standard floppy disc (so-called because it bends), smaller computer discs such as cues used in Apple Macintoshes, the larger hard disc, and even the compact disc (the same device used to store digital music), which is increasingly finding applications in the computer industry.

The ability of the computer to manipulate information, as mentioned, is its strength. Simple storage is not a particularly compelling reason to use a computer. For example, 1,000 recipes might more easily be kept on 3 × 5 index cards than keyed into a computer. However, should you desire to sort out all the recipes calling for eggs and parsley, your task would be monumental if done by hand, but it can be accomplished in a few seconds by the computer, which will patiently but quickly check the ingredients of each recipe for a match with the ingredients you identify.

Such inhuman patience and speed also have applications in the field of radio. As an example, consider how the microchip now enables a producer to store and manipulate a variety of sounds.

▪ COMPUTER-GENERATED   ▪
EFFECTS

Radio-station program directors are taking increasing advantage of the versatility of a device known as a *musical instrument digital interface,* called *MIDI* and pronounced "middy." The **MIDI** (Fig. 15.1) is a digital tool that allows a producer to synchronize any number of electronic musical instruments and other sound-production devices, including standard tape-recording units, with a computer. You can think of a MIDI, therefore, as a communications link between electronic musical instruments and electronic controlling or processing devices such as synchronizers and computers. With MIDI devices, it is possible to produce music or special effects, such as "laser beam" sounds used in a science-fiction show.

Figure 15.1   The MIDI, a digital device that enables producers to synchronize various sound sources with a computer. (Photo courtesy of Akai Professional, Fort Worth, Tex.)

A producer with musical skills can also use MIDI in conjunction with a **synthesizer** (Fig. 15.2), an organlike device that can produce a wide variety of sounds. Some synthesizers, for example, produce realistic sounds by combining many different tone and frequency generators together. Each generator is called a *voice*, and many synthesizers can use them to produce the sounds of grand pianos, horns, drums, cars, and so forth; some can produce many sounds simultaneously. When a synthesizer can both simultaneously play several voices that sound like several unique instruments (say, a bass guitar and a piano) and allow you to control those voices separately, it is called *multitimbral*. Utilizing a multitimbral synthesizer, a MIDI sequencer, a drum machine, and a tape recorder, you could reproduce the sound of a small band.

A sequencer is a device that enables you to record different channels of MIDI information into some kind of memory, such as a floppy disc. Computers are frequently used as sequencers and allow you the possibility of recording up to sixteen channels of information. (Note that MIDI has many functions that cannot be covered in this broad treatment.)

By utilizing a sequencer, it is possible to control a multitimbral synthesizer or several synthesizers simultaneously. The sequencer does just what the name implies: It sends a sequence of data to the devices, instructing them to play a certain note at a certain time, make it a certain length, and make it sound like a particular instrument. In a sense, the sequencer acts like a tape recorder, because often you record your music by playing a synthesizer and connecting the MIDI output directly into the sequencer,

Figure 15.2 Synthesizer. This device is often used in conjunction with a MIDI to produce a wide variety of sounds for production purposes.

which memorizes the notes played and the individual timbre and characteristics of the notes.

Let's return to the example of an electronically created small band. Suppose that you wanted to record an original music bed for a local sponsor. Here's what you might do:

1. Start by programming a drum machine to provide a tempo and a beat that meet the requirements for the spot. That information would be recorded by the sequencer. (Remember that the computer records data in the form of digital bits, not in the way we typically think of a tape machine recording a conventional drum set.)

2. Next, program the synthesizer to reproduce the sound of an electric piano; the piano's part is played on the keyboard and recorded by the sequencer.

3. Next, the synthesizer might be programmed to play a bass guitar, and you would play a bass line for our musical bed. Most sequences allow you to set pointers to get the tracks to line up correctly.

4. Now, play back all the channels recorded by the sequencer, which controls the drum machine and all the voices of our synthesizer. If you are satisfied with what you hear, you can dump the output to audiotape;

the music bed for the local spot will then be ready for use in producing the commercial.

If you wanted to create a more sophisticated group—even a symphony orchestra—you could use a time-code generator, a synchronizer, and a MIDI sequencer to control several multitimbral synthesizers and dump their outputs to a multitrack tape recorder. Briefly, here's how it would work:

1. You would use a device called a *time-code generator* to lay down a time code (a constant reference laid down on the tape) on one track of the tape recorder. Track 8 might be our choice.
2. Using that time code to drive a synchronizer (a device that converts time code into information that a MIDI sequencer can understand), you would record your synthesizers on separate tracks—say, tracks 1, 2, 3, and 4—of your multitrack recorder.
3. You would reprogram your synthesizers to new voices and sounds. Again using your time-code track to drive the synchronizers, you would have the synchronizers drive the sequencer to reproduce the new voices on tracks 5 to 7 of the multitrack.
4. Again using your time-code track as a reference to drive the synchronizer and sequencer, you might program a drum machine, and record it while you simultaneously mixed down the seven tracks previously recorded.
5. If you needed some especially sophisticated production, you might also use your MIDI sequencer to control outboard signal-processing devices, such as digital relays and reverb units, during the recording or playback process.

We have obviously simplified the nature of the process for purposes of this discussion.

Be aware that these devices are only slowly gaining acceptance in the radio world, especially in small and medium markets; you probably won't see many of these setups in the next year or two. But the music and recording industries are making wide use of the MIDI, and it is likely that the technology will filter down into mainstream radio production in the near future.

You don't have to be a musician to take advantage of the MIDI. All sorts of audio effects can be achieved, ranging from simple sound effects to aural props in complex comedy skits. Do you need the sound of an alarm clock? Programs accompanying the hardware plugged into certain MIDIs provide just such a sound effect, and it can be loaded into a computer from a disc. The MIDI would also allow you to manipulate that sound, making it seem like a small alarm clock or like Big Ben.

Many firms specialize in providing sound-effects software to users of MIDIs; one company currently offers about 300 sounds on a ten-disc program that sells for only about $60. The variety of sounds, coupled with the computer's ability to manipulate each sound and to create music and musical effects, makes the MIDI an attractive alternative to sound-effects and theme-music libraries on standard LP discs, which can cost upward of $1,000 per year to license.

■ COMPUTER-ASSISTED ■ EDITING

Digital technology may be making progress toward the eventual obsolescence of razor blades and splicing tape, although it appears unlikely that we'll see widespread use of computer-assisted editing in all markets in the near future. But even though the technology is in its infancy, the potential is staggering.

For example, the typical editing suite of the near future (indeed, the technology and its application are in use today) might feature digital storage of all information—music, dialogue, and sound effects—in computer memory, with a video monitor used to chart and manipulate the sounds.

Another version of computerized editing can involve computer controls linked to analog tape machines. (The word *analog* means a "corresponding image," and it is used to refer to the similar image of sound reproduced by standard reel-to-reel tape recorders, cassettes, and cart machines.) The operator of the computer system would use a **mouse**—a device for electronically pinpointing a location on a screen—to indicate the edit points, and the computer would control the stop-and-start motion of the reel-to-reel machine(s). The edit could be rehearsed, and if the edit point proved to be incorrect, the sound could be redisplayed and the edit point chosen again before any "cutting" of the original tape occurred.

An obvious question arises: How can sound be represented visually? As mentioned in Chapter 5, sound is a vibration in the air or in some other medium, and vibration is represented visually by a wave. Most sounds are a composite of many different waves, known as a **complex waveform,** which can be represented on an oscilloscope or on the computer screen.

This representation, sometimes called a **sound envelope** (Fig. 15.3), is much easier to work with and manipulate than you might at first imagine. For example, suppose that, in producing a station promo, you begin by playing back a recording of an announcer speaking; let's assume that the announcer has recorded the words, "WRVO Public Radio." As you play back the words, you will see the varying patterns displayed as the words

Figure 15.3   Sound envelope on a computer screen. This
visual representation of sound can be easily
and precisely edited.

are spoken. Because you can stop, start, or reverse the words, you have the
ability to monitor how the waveform changes with the spoken words. (The
same can be accomplished in dealing with music.)

Suppose that you want to remove the word *public*, and make the ID
simply "WRVO Radio." Here's one way to approach the task:

1. You would move a computerized pointer to the part of the wave that
   indicates the end of "WRVO" and electronically mark that spot by
   entering the appropriate computer command.

2. You would then repeat the process by marking the waveform before the
   beginning of "radio."

3. Through a series of commands (which would depend on the particular
   menu provided with your software) you would then instruct the computer to eliminate the word *public* and splice "WRVO" and "radio"
   together. If there were too much or too little space between the words,
   you could call up the previous menu and rework the edit.

4. Your options don't end here. If you wished to (and if you possess the
   proper equipment), you could add an echo to the words, mix music
   beneath them, or speed up or slow down the pace of the words.

New-generation equipment can accomplish all these effects and more.
The Macintosh computer, a favorite of producers who use MIDIs to interface with computers and synthesizers, can also be used to interface with a

digital editing system. The Dyaxis digital audio system (Fig. 15.4), for example, manufactured by the San Carlos, California, firm Integrated Media Systems, interfaces with certain Macintosh computers and allows the user to visualize splicing and assembling functions on the Mac's screen; and the system's windows and menus mimic a standard audio console, allowing you to mix, pan, cross-fade, edit, and so forth. (Note that in current usage, the term *digital editing system* means a system of hardware that can control all functions of standard editing, while a *MIDI* generally refers to a device used to hook synthesizers and other relatively simple sound-generating sources into a computer. There is obviously some overlap in the functions.)

The Dyaxis system and many other editing controllers allow you to work with what's known as the *SMPTE time code*. (*SMPTE* stands for *Society of Motion Picture and Television Engineers*.) The time code is electronically laid down on tape and identifies a precise address on the tape thirty times per second. Although originally developed for editing videotape, SMPTE time coding is increasingly used in audiotape editing, and in fact some high-tech audio editing is done on videotape.

▪ COMPUTER APPLICATIONS ▪
IN ON-AIR PRODUCTION

At present, a computerized visualization of an audio console would be difficult to utilize while running an airshift, but the technology has almost reached that point. At radio station WEEI in Boston, the Touchstone 2000 Series automation assist system (Fig. 15.5) allows announcers at the all-news station to select one of over thirty sound sources merely by touching a computer screen.

Touchscreen systems allow on-air talent to execute a variety of functions with great ease; some of these are listed on the screen shown in Figure 15.5. For example, a news announcer can call up fast-breaking copy and read it directly off the screen; alternatively, the announcer can put the network on the air simply by touching the appropriate part of the screen. More examples of computer-assisted air work will be furnished in a subsequent section of this chapter, dealing with automation.

The traditional radio console, incidentally, is becoming smarter thanks to microchip technology. Some modern digital consoles use computer software to recall particular settings. For instance, you might have a particular setup for leading into the news: playing a music cart back-timed for the last minute before the news, lowering the volume on the music and opening the mic to promo the songs coming up after the news, music up, music cross-fading to stinger, stinger ending, and network pot opening. All this

Figure 15.4 The Dyaxis Digital Audio Processor. This device makes it possible for a producer to assemble sound elements digitally, using a computer. (Photo courtesy of Integrated Media Systems, San Carlos, Calif.)

Figure 15.5 Modern radio production.

can be programmed into the board's memory, with the correct levels coming up each time. If a level is too high or too low, the adjustment can be made and stored in memory.

Smart consoles, of course, have many applications in off-air production, too. An edit can be rehearsed many times, and settings corrected until the result is perfect.

And while this is only speculation, some industry observers feel that the days of the standard broadcast cartridge may be numbered. Already many stations with fast-moving formats calling for many sound sources utilize digital storage methods and MIDIs to store and recall sounds. Perhaps in the not-too-distant future all sound sources for on-air production will be stored on hard disc, digital tape, or even compact disc, and retrieved virtually instantaneously by computer command. When you stop to consider that, in fast moving formats, an airshift can involve playing more than 300 carts, the idea of calling up all of those sound sources from one centralized location becomes very attractive.

■   COMPUTERS IN   ■
AUTOMATION

Probably the most immediate and visible application of computer technology to radio is in the area of automation and live-assist automation. **Automation** basically means an apparatus for running programs with a minimum or absence of on-site human labor. **Live-assist** refers to automatically sequenced commands designed to help the person running the console to execute a series of commands.

A brief history of radio-station automation will help you understand the current role of computerized automation technology. Automation first came of age in the late 1950s and early 1960s via what now appear to be cumbersome methods of automatically cueing sound sources. The development of the cart machine and its eventual widespread use in the 1960s greatly enhanced the promise of automation: The cart could recue itself and could be loaded into various mechanical devices capable of transporting and playing the cart.

In the early to mid-1970s, cartridge **carousels** became extremely popular. The carousel was a circular device that rotated and brought the carts into contact with the playback device; usually, the carousels were synchronized with reel-to-reel tapes (supplied by a syndicator), which had to be changed by hand every few hours.

Automation appeared to be the answer to the problems faced by many stations, large and small. It drastically cut back on personnel costs and generally provided high-quality program material. The prerecorded voices of the announcers were of the highest quality, and the music was carefully selected according to ostensibly heavily researched criteria.

But station owners found a funny thing happening on the way to the bank: Automation, the apparent answer to any station's financial woes, could actually drive listeners away. Audiences soon tired of the transparently canned format of many of the syndicated programs offered for automation systems. Many stations brought back live announcers for the entire schedule or for certain high-listener periods, and used automation for slow times such as overnight shifts.

Just when automation appeared to be on its way out, though, computer technology brought it back to the forefront of radio operations.

Modern automation uses computer technology to accomplish tasks difficult or impossible to do with older-generation systems involving complex hardware and mechanical relays. The on-air function can utilize traditional automation or it can use sophisticated computer programs to interface with satellite-delivered programs. Such programs use microcomputer hardware in conjunction with software packages that control station programming.

For example, in stations where programming is received by satellite, the computer system senses cue tones that are fed along with program material. The tone is separated from the program signal and fed to the satellite-interface equipment. Such tones then activate local program elements, which are integrated into the satellite-fed programming.

Here are some examples of what cutting-edge automation technology can do:

▸ A satellite feed beams down modern music in a tightly controlled format; music is back-announced by a highly professional announcer located at the system headquarters in a major city. As one song is about to end, the satellite beams down a 35-Hz tone which activates a cart machine at the local station airing the satellite-fed program. The cart says, "You're listening to [local station's call letters]." Then the satellite feed takes over, with the announcer saying, "That was [name of song and artist]."

▸ What's happened is that the automation system has customized the satellite broadcast service, ensuring that the automation doesn't have that canned quality. Certain automation systems even have a method for the announcer to feed a local weather forecast to the particular market; that forecast would be recorded and called up by the automation system at the appropriate time. (Additional details about satellite service are given in Chapter 8.)

▸ A radio newsroom features a central computer with several terminals; reporters and editors can tie into a single system and exchange information with each other, as well as accessing network and wire-service news feeds. There's no one running back and forth trying to find copy; it's all instantly accessible. In addition, reporters carrying portable computers can feed pages of copy back to the newsroom via telephone.

› An automation system based on storage of digital tape allows up to 7 days of continuous programming, with the whole system operating untouched by human hands.

While some would argue that automation is not in the best interests of the industry as a whole—in point of fact, jobs are lost as a result of the expanding technology—automation does offer certain advantages to radio employees and to listeners.

For employees, live-assist automation makes things easier on the person who runs the console. Now he or she may only have to push one button to trigger a sequence of five or six events. Computer-driven systems make it possible for many time-consuming tasks to be accomplished with the touch of a button or, as in the touchscreen system, with the touch of an appropriate part of the video monitor.

An increasing number of radio professionals will have to become computer-literate and comfortable using the new technologies. There is a perceptible trend toward requiring announcers to run combo, even in large markets; for example, a number of CBS-owned and -operated stations, as a money-saving measure, are requiring talent to work combo.

What benefits does automation offer to the listener? Points can be made on many sides of the issue, but it is reasonable to say that many listeners do enjoy the concept of top-quality satellite programming supplemented, thanks to computer-control, with local inserts. Even small markets can have top-quality music formatting and announcing coupled with locally originated material.

While it is too early to make a definitive decision either way, it does seem that in some cases small-market personnel originally assigned to spinning discs (the same records available anywhere in the country) have had their job focus changed to local news or community service when the station changed to satellite services. In some markets, jobs of announcing staff have simply been eliminated.

News and public-service programming, however, can benefit from computer technology. KCBS in San Francisco is one example: The station is equipped with more than a dozen terminals and special news software known as Newstar. While not strictly a form of automation, the system does provide a method of speeding operations by computer.

Ed Kavagnaro, the KCBS director of news and programming, summed up the situation in a 1987 interview reported in the trade journal *Broadcast Management/Engineering*. "Newstar allows us to get news on the air much faster than was previously possible," he said. "Breaking news is radio's niche, and we're in business to provide people with information—not *Wheel of Fortune*."

▪   COMPUTERS IN THE   ▪
PROGRAMMING FUNCTION

While the word *programming* has many meanings in the context of radio production and operations, the activities comprehended by one specific definition—the process of planning and documenting the material aired over the station—are greatly speeded and enhanced by computer technology.

Scheduling music, commercials, and other program elements is extremely time-consuming and complex. But the situation is eased considerably by specialized software. Radio station WHDH in Boston, for example, uses Columbine programming software and an IBM computer to accomplish the following tasks:

▸ Keep track of all program elements, and provide a printout (log).
▸ Make a record of all commercial availabilities.
▸ Ensure that commercials for directly competing products (two airlines, for example) are not scheduled within a certain proximity of each other.
▸ Provide salespeople with a way to program a flight of spots immediately and to let the sponsor know the airdates.
▸ Automatically generate bills for spots aired.
▸ Allow sales management to compare records of individual salespeople and to issue projections (quotas) for each salesperson.

The possibilities for computer use in all areas of radio—producing special effects, editing, on-air production, automation, and programming—are virtually limitless. But even the most devoted apostles of high-tech are quick to warn that gadgetry is not an end in itself. The computer can perform work faster and can make it easier, but it cannot make good radio.

Good radio is made by the skill of the producer and is played out in the brain of the listener. Radio, after all, is center stage in the theater of the mind—and imagination will never be supplanted by gimmickry.

SUMMARY

The modern computer uses hardware (the system itself) and software (the program) to accomplish its goal. The computer can calculate at incredible speed.

One particularly useful function of the computer in radio is to create effects, including music, using a musical instrument digital interface, known as a *MIDI*. You don't have to be a skilled musician to use a synthesizer and a MIDI; the programs for creating music are highly user-friendly.

Computer-assisted editing is finding greater acceptance in radio, although it is far from the norm. In computer-assisted editing, the information is stored digitally and manipulated through visual representations on a computer screen.

Perhaps the most visible impact of computer technology in radio is in automation and live-assist. Automated gear can be incredibly flexible, and live-assist can allow an operator to handle many complex tasks with the touch of one button—or in some cases just by touching the computer screen.

Computers have an important role in the programming function. Today, even small stations use computers to generate logs and schedule program elements.

APPLICATIONS

■ **Situation 1** ■ *The Problem* The producer wanted to put together a station promo package featuring a chorus chanting the station's call letters. Unfortunately, only two announcers were on duty and volunteers for a chorus were nowhere to be found.

One Possible Solution Utilizing a MIDI and sound-processing equipment, the producer laid down two voices in digital storage, changed the characteristics of the voices slightly, laid them down again, and repeated the process until he had what appeared to be a chorus of more than 100 voices.

■ **Situation 2** ■ *The Problem* The production manager of a station that was interfaced with a satellite service did all her production on a digital editing unit. Her most recent effort, though, needed some work. Unfortunately, a voice-only commercial cut to fill a 60-second hole ran only 57 seconds. There was no time to call the announcer back in to recut the spot.

One Possible Solution   One aspect of digital storage is the ability, in some hardware, to speed up or slow down the playback. Slowing down a playback excessively would distort the voice, but stretching it by 3 seconds was hardly noticeable—much less noticeable, certainly, than 3 seconds of dead air on an all-hit station.

EXERCISES

1. Should the appropriate equipment be available, record the following effects. The content is not the central issue; what is important is to note how manipulation of the sound changes the effect produced. Produce and record:

   ‣ A series of notes or tones of steady pitch, with a fast attack followed by a diminution of volume

   ‣ A series of notes of steady pitch, where the tone builds up to a crescendo at the end

   ‣ A series of notes of steady pitch, with no change in volume—just an abrupt on-and-off attack

   ‣ A series of notes in which the pitch changes rapidly, or warbles

   ‣ A hissing noise similar to the white noise of a running shower or the static of snowy television

2. Again, if the equipment is available, draw representations of the waveform (envelope) pictured on the screen for each production in Exercise 1. (Do them to the best of your artistic ability, but remember that drawing skill is not the point here.) Show the drawings to, and then play the sounds for, someone who is not familiar with this exercise, and see if he or she can match the pictures with the sounds.

3. The following is a pen-and-pencil exercise for those who do not have access to computerized equipment. Write a paper (your instructor will specify length and format) focusing on whether, in your opinion, the technological revolution in radio has a good influence or a bad influence on the medium. For example, do you feel that technology is replacing the human touch in radio? Do you believe that it has fostered an over-reliance on gimmickry in production? Or do you feel that the types of technology available are improving radio, freeing people to be more creative?

Regardless of your viewpoint, argue your case by using information from this chapter, information you have gathered in other classes and through research, and:

a. Facts gathered from trade journals. *Broadcasting* and *Broadcast Management/Engineering* will probably be most helpful, and these are widely available in libraries.

b. An interview with a local veteran of radio, preferably an on-air personality.

APPENDIX

·

A

Troubleshooting Chart

There are, of course, an infinite number of problems that can occur during radio production. But what follows are some common and easily remedied problems, together with their possible solutions.

Problem	Possible Cause	Action
1. Unwanted reverberation, constantly increasing in volume.	Cart machine is in record and is potted up on board, causing signal to be amplified and reamplified.	Close cart pot. Stop and erase cart (it's recorded the reverb, so whatever is on it is now ruined), and start over.
2. High-pitched squeal.	(a) Mic is feeding back into headphones or speakers. (b) Tape machine is in record and is potted up on board.	(a) Find and fix source of feedback from sound source to mic. (b) Close tape machine pot.
3. Hissing or white noise on tape; low signal-to-noise ratio; muddy-sounding tape.	Head configuration on playback machine does not match original configuration of record deck. (In other words, you may be playing a half-track tape on a full-track machine.)	Play back tape on compatible machine.

(continued)

Problem	Possible Cause	Action
4. Cart makes "whup . . . whup . . . whup" sound during playback.	Dirty cart—not properly bulk erased.	If you can re-record the cart, erase the cart completely and redo it.
5. Can't get audio from a particular piece of equipment.	Patch has circumvented the normal audio path.	Check patchbay; remove patches, if appropriate.
6. Can't get audio from any piece of equipment.	(a) Board power is off. (b) Master pot is down.	(a) Turn on board power. (b) Return master pot to normal level. Remember, don't use the master pot as a volume control; it should be calibrated at one level and left in place.
7. Cart won't automatically stop at beginning.	(a) Someone has pulled the green wire and not plugged it back in. (b) In extreme heat, some cart machines won't stop at the cue tone.	(a) Replace the green wire. (b) Cool the cart machine.
8. Humming sound on audio.	Interference from an electrical device.	Check nearby lamps and other outboard electrical devices. If no cause is found, call for engineering help.
9. Crackling when pot is turned up or down.	Inside of pot is dirty.	Ask engineer to clean pots.
10. Buzzy audio.	Overmodulation.	Check levels. Pay particular attention to the recording levels on the tape-recording machines; they can be set to overmodulate even when the console VU meter reads normally.
11. Popping noise where splices have been made.	Magnetic field was placed on tape by partially magnetized razor blade.	Bulk-erase the razor blade, just as you would bulk a tape.

Problem	Possible Cause	Action
12. Muddy sound on tape playback.	If the head configurations on record and playback are compatible, the cause may be dirty heads.	Clean heads according to instructions supplied by your station engineer.
13. Blank spot on reel-to-reel tape.	Tape may have been twisted when wound or rewound onto reel, making oxide side of tape face away from heads.	Fast-forward or rewind through entire reel of tape, checking for twists in tape.
14. Popping plosives (p's and b's).	Announcer is working too close to mic or is simply pronouncing p's and b's too vigorously. This is especially troublesome on ribbon mics.	Move announcer farther from microphone. A wind filter or pop filter (see page 228) can produce excellent results when dealing with this problem: It not only provides a physical barrier to air motion, but also (if the filter is big enough) induces the announcer to move back from mic.
15. Odd lack of apparent volume or sound quality from certain mics during multiple-mic setups.	Mics are out of phase. (See page 85.)	Move mics farther apart, or use fewer mics.
16. Pumping or whooshing noise during silent moments in program.	Too much compression.	Adjust time settings on compression unit, or simply turn compressor off. Ask engineering staff for permission first, though.
17. Wowing at beginning of audio selection.	Playback unit (usually turntable or cart machine) does not get up to speed quickly enough.	Turn plate on turntable farther back when cueing up record. Be sure cart is locked into place for several seconds before you press play button.

APPENDIX

B

Typical Formats

Format	Description	Typical Demographic	Advantages	Disadvantages
Country	Refers to a wide variety of music, but generally has a twangy flavor; songs often have roots in rural context.	Format appeals to wide range of age groups. Many listeners (but by no means all) are blue-collar. Audience is split among devotees of certain strains of country; pure country fans often dislike crossover country, which has more of a pop flavor.	Audiences are increasingly upscale and often very loyal to the music. Typically a solid ratings performer, although generally not number one in individual markets.	Some advertisers may feel that this format reaches only blue-collar and rural listeners. Can be difficult to program because of listeners' strong likes and dislikes of various strains of music.
Adult Contemporary (AC)	Usually features modern popular music with a mix of oldies; the modern music is usually neither too hard nor too soft.	Broad range, usually fairly young adults. Listeners usually have good buying power.	AC fans usually tolerate a fairly broad range of musical styles, so tune-out is not such a problem as with other formats, where fans often are devoted to a particular strain or genre of the music. Good performer, often a ratings leader.	Very tight competition in typical markets. Because news and information exchange is important in AC, the format needs good on-air talent.

(continued)

Format	Description	Typical Demographic	Advantages	Disadvantages
Middle of the Road/ Nostalgia	Not all MOR is nostalgia, and vice versa, but usually stations in this broad format category play many ballads, band arrangements, and modern music that resembles the genre.	Usually older adults, a segment that sometimes feels disenfranchised from current radio offerings.	Strong loyalty, easily definable niche in market.	Some advertisers perceive older audiences as poor buying audiences, but this is not always true. The "gray market" is emerging as a powerful buying force in the American economy.
Top 40/Contemporary Hit Radio (CHR)	Top 40/CHR has a limited playlist, consisting of a limited number of the latest hit rock'n'roll songs.	Usually older teens and young adults, although many listeners are in their late 20s, 30s, and 40s. Young teens are emerging as an increasingly important component of the Top 40/CHR audience.	A good ratings performer and not as complex to program as many of the other supersegmented formats.	Extremely tight competition within this format, and occasional oversaturation within markets. The audiences for this format do not tend to be loyal to particular stations.
Religious	Usually gospel music, with increasing use of mainstream soft rock or country. Gospel music itself is becoming more mainstream.	Wide range of ages and incomes. Sometimes a good performer in rural areas.	Audiences are usually quite loyal.	Not a traditional money-maker.

Format	Programming	Audience		
Easy Listening	Usually instrumental versions of popular songs, along with soft vocals. Some easy-listening stations use contemporary soft rock.	Usually middle-aged adults; easy listening often appeals to high-income professionals.	Appeals to affluent demographic. Many radio advertisers like this type of music themselves.	Finicky audience. Pretty much limited to FM, because lower-quality AM stations do not adequately reproduce orchestral music.
News-Talk	Usually a mix of news, public-affairs programming, and call-in talk shows.	Wide range of ages and incomes. Appeals to many listeners who tune in and out quickly for news and information, enabling stations to build high numbers in certain categories of ratings.	A good format for producing high-looking ratings because frequent tune-in takes advantage of peculiarities in ratings methodologies. An easily distinguishable format; easy to carve out a niche in the market.	Good talent is essential to pull off this format. News programming is expensive to produce.
Album-Oriented Rock (AOR)	Longer cuts of rock, sometimes mixed with blues; often fairly hard rock.	Young adults.	Because the music appeals to a distinct life-style, advertisers like the idea of reaching a defined and highly researched audience.	Music appeal is often very narrow; aficionados of one style of AOR may strongly dislike music from other AOR genres. Advertisers often view the audience as being less affluent than listeners to other formats.

(continued)

Format	Description	Typical Demographic	Advantages	Disadvantages
Specialty	A catch-all term for the many small formats that exist in modern radio. Such formats include all-news, ethnic, classical, urban, oldies, and jazz.	Variable, of course, depending on the format, but almost always a well-defined group.	A fairly easy audience to identify and research. If the market is affluent—as with listeners of classical music—premium rates can be charged for advertising.	Very narrow specialty formats typically do not produce high ratings numbers. They usually can exist only in very large markets, seizing a small piece of a very big pie.

APPENDIX

·

C

Another Time

a Play by Richard Wilson

Production of this play can serve as a good exercise in understanding the construction and flow of an outstanding drama. It probably will—as intended—pose a great technical challenge. In fact, we considered less difficult and less sophisticated plays for inclusion in this appendix, but decided that the challenge presented here would provide an excellent learning experience. It also graphically demonstrates what we mentioned in Chapter 10 about the need to maintain a fabric of believability.

The late Richard Wilson was a prize-winning author of fiction and nonfiction. He won the Nebula award of the Science Fiction Writers of America for his novelette, *Mother to the World*. Wilson wrote more than 100 published science fiction stories and three novels. He also wrote a history book and was a reporter and editor in Chicago, Washington, New York, and London.

And now, *Another Time*. . . .

SOUND: *KEYS IN DOOR, DOOR OPENS, TWO MEN WALK INTO ROOM.*

NEIGHBOR (DON): Come up to my place and have a nightcap, Harry. It's still early.

HARRY: No thanks. I've had too much already.

NEIGHBOR: You only have a birthday once a year.

HARRY: Is that all? Lately they seem to come along more often.

NEIGHBOR: None of that, now. Fifty-three is young. Besides, you don't look a day over 52. This is a nice apartment. You've lived here a long time, haven't you?

HARRY: About 30 years. Me and my memories.

NEIGHBOR: Of Helen? Sorry, but people in the building do talk.

HARRY: It's all right. Helen died here. We were going to be married. Meanwhile, we were living here. The Ninth Avenue El was still up then. The trains rattled right outside these windows. What a racket they made! But we didn't mind. We kept the shades down and felt all the more secluded.

NEIGHBOR: I didn't mean to stir up painful memories.

HARRY: It's never painful to think of Helen. I miss the El, though. They started tearing it down the day of her funeral.

SOUND: NEIGHBOR SHUFFLES NERVOUSLY.

NEIGHBOR: Look, I better go.

HARRY: It's all right. I live in the past a lot, except when somebody snaps me out of it, like you. Thanks for the pub crawl, Don. It's been years since somebody dragged me out.

NEIGHBOR: Don't mention it. I've got to go.

HARRY: Want some coffee or anything? Want to sit with me and watch TV?

NEIGHBOR: No thanks. Good night, Harry. Happy birthday.

HARRY: Good night.

SOUND: DOOR OPENS, NEIGHBOR EXITS.
SOUND: HARRY PULLS UP CHAIR, SNAPS ON TELEVISION, TWISTS TV CHANNEL DIAL. THROUGH SOUND OF TELE-VISION SPEAKER, COMMERCIALS COME ON. THEY ARE CHANTED AND BUILD TO AN OFFENSIVE CRESCENDO.

VOICES: Better! More! Bigger! Newer!
Best! Most! Biggest! Newest!

Pain! Pain! Pain!
Relief! Get relief! Get instant relief!
Cramps? Irregularity? Aching back? Hurt? Hurt?
Eat! Smoke! Drink! Diet! Lose weight! Exercise!
Go! Come! RUN! ASK YOUR DOCTOR! ASK YOUR GROCER!!
ASK YOUR. . . .

*SOUND: TV CLICKED OFF. FOOTSTEPS AS HARRY WALKS
ACROSS ROOM. CLICK OF RADIO BEING TURNED ON. . . .
CHARACTERISTIC SOUND OF STATIONS SLIDING PAST AS
DIAL IS TWISTED.*

VOICE *(calm and friendly as Harry moves the dial):* We have
brought you the Atwater Kent concert. . . .

NEW VOICE *(as dial is turned):* This is station WEAF signing off. . . .

NEW VOICE *(as dial is turned):* And so it's good night again from
those sweethearts of the air, May Singhi Breen and Peter de
Rose. . . .

NEW VOICE *(as dial is turned):* This has been Raymond Knight, the
Voice of the Diaphragm, enunciating.

NEW VOICE *(as dial is turned):* Tune in again tomorrow to WJZ for
Billy Jones and Ernie Hare, the Happiness Boys.

SOUND: HARRY CLICKS OFF RADIO.

HARRY *(not believing it):* WEAF. WJZ. I'm back in the past . . .
when I was happy . . . young. When life was uncomplicated.
(Laughs.) I am *happy.* I am *young. (He begins to believe it.)*
    It's true. Why not? As long as I want it to be it's true, here in this
room, right now. As long as I don't look in the mirror—as long as I
don't switch on the TV.
    And I'm 25! Helen's alive! But where is she? She's gone down to
the corner, I guess. She'll be back in a minute with our midnight
milk and oatmeal cookies. . . . Maybe a couple of charlotte russes.

*SOUND: IN DISTANCE, THE RUMBLE OF THE EL. IT GROWS
LOUDER, LOUDER, AND CLOSER.*

HARRY: The El . . . but if I look, it won't be there.

RADIO VOICE: *Yes it will.*

HARRY: Who said that? The radio? You . . . but . . . I want it to be, but it isn't.

RADIO VOICE: *Yes it is.*

HARRY: I have to meet it halfway. Have faith. I have to go out. Then it will be there. *I know. I know.*

SOUND: THE VAGUE RUMBLING OF AN EL PLATFORM.

HARRY: This is the El platform. . . . And the gum machine . . . and the mirror—I'm *young.* (*His voice is reflecting change in age.*)

APRIL: Of course you are. Handsome, too.

HARRY: Who are you? Are you Helen?

APRIL: Helen? No. Have you got a buffalo nickel? To get me through the turnstile?

HARRY: Buffalo nickel?

APRIL: Jefferson won't do. He hasn't been minted yet. *You* know that.

HARRY: I'm not sure I know what you mean.

APRIL: Yes you do. Have you got two buffalo nickels for a Roosevelt dime?

SOUND: CLINK OF COINS AS THEY EXCHANGE.

HARRY: How could you know about Roosevelt dimes? He wasn't — isn't even president yet. FDR, I mean. Wouldn't he still be governor of New York?

APRIL: I'm not good at current events, but I think it's later than that. Just a minute, let me get through the turnstile.

SOUND: COIN DROPS AT TURNSTILE AND TURNSTILE TURNS. APRIL'S FOOTSTEPS.

HARRY: You're not from here either—are you? Your clothes look right, though. How did you get here? (*Laughs.*) I don't even know what year it is. It was too dark to see the license plates and I couldn't find a newsstand—to buy a paper.

APRIL: You don't need a paper.

HARRY: I seem to be about your age. How old are you?

APRIL: Twenty-four.

HARRY: And I'm twenty-five. Let's see—I was born *(he figures to himself)*—and if I'm 25 this is 1936. Is that right?

APRIL: It doesn't matter. Everything is relative in the duoverse.

HARRY: In the what?

APRIL: Never mind. You don't have to understand.

HARRY: I really don't want to—to push it too far. It's too fragile.

APRIL: It's not really. But I can understand your feeling.

HARRY: Can you? I was listening to the radio—it's an old Atwater Kent—because I was mad at the television. . . . You know what television is?

APRIL: Yes, of course.

HARRY: That's right. You know about Roosevelt dimes and Jefferson nickels. Maybe you know about Helen. She died, but if this is. . . .

APRIL: I'm sorry. You won't find Helen. You can reverse time but you can't cancel death.

HARRY: I didn't *really* think you could.

APRIL: You said you were listening to the radio—steeping yourself in the past.

HARRY: I didn't say that.

APRIL: That's the way it happens.

HARRY: It happened to you, too.

APRIL: Not exactly *happened*. I planned it.

HARRY: Well, I certainly didn't—what's your name?

APRIL: April.

HARRY *(formally)*: Hello, April. I'm Harry. Where are you going, April?

APRIL: I'll be going with you . . . while you do your sightseeing in 1936. Then I'll go home with you.

HARRY *(surprised and embarrassed)*: Oh? Home with me?

APRIL: It'll be all right.

HARRY (*not so sure*): Of course. But—home where the TV set is? You'd be—wouldn't you be—old—?

APRIL: Don't worry about anything, Harry. Enjoy yourself. That's what you came back to do, isn't it? Aren't you happier?

HARRY (*after a pause*): Yes, I am.

APRIL: Where do you want to go?

HARRY: First? First to the Staten Island Ferry. Because—because it was there—

APRIL: You don't have to explain. Not in the duoverse.

SOUND: TRAIN RATTLES INTO STATION. . . . SOUND DIS-SOLVES TO WIND, LAPPING WAVES, HARBOR SOUNDS SUCH AS FOGHORNS IN DISTANCE.

APRIL: I'm glad you had two buffalo nickels for the ferry.

HARRY: I'm really here? Literally?

APRIL: What do you think?

HARRY: I don't know. Here—now. It's too—could I meet myself? If I looked, could I find another Harry? The one who's living through 1936 the first time?

APRIL: No. You're the only Harry in this 1936.

HARRY: This 1936? I—is that what you mean by—what do you call it—the duoverse? There are more than one?

APRIL: Yes, but you mustn't think I understand everything I have a name for. I do know you couldn't be here—and neither could I—unless there was something controlling the paradoxes. That's the duoverse, they tell me—a twin universe to keep time travelers from running into themselves.

HARRY (*troubled*): Who tells you that? No . . . don't tell me. I don't need to know. I'm just so glad I found you.

APRIL: I'm glad I found you. I'd been looking for so long.

SOUND: FOGHORN.

HARRY (*almost as a prayer*): Let's not lose what we've found. Let's keep it forever.

APRIL: And thou beside me—under the branches of the time-tree . . . ? Something like that? Oh, Harry!

SOUND: THEY EMBRACE AND KISS.

APRIL *(with infinite regret)*: It's impossible, Harry . . . I'm going the other way.

SOUND: HARRY AND APRIL WALKING TO DOOR OF HARRY'S APARTMENT. SOUND OF EL IN BACKGROUND. DOOR OPENS. SOUND OF HARRY AND APRIL WALKING IN.

APRIL: We haven't done much sightseeing in your beloved past. We haven't seen the Hippodrome—the streetcars on Broadway—

HARRY: No, don't turn on the lights yet. You're all the past I want. *(Concerned.)* Is it all right for you to be here?

APRIL: It's the way it has to be. There's no other.

HARRY: But here I'm old—and you—?

APRIL: Not till we turn on the TV, Harry. Not till then. I'll turn on the lights now.

SOUND: LIGHT SWITCH.

HARRY: I'm still young. I'm—sit down, please. What can I get you?

APRIL: Coffee?

HARRY: I just have to heat it up. It's already been percolated once.

SOUND: WALKS ACROSS ROOM.

APRIL *(calls to him)*: I might have known you'd have real coffee. No millions of tiny flavor buds for you, eh, Old Timer?

HARRY *(calls to her)*: I don't have the room.

SOUND: HARRY WALKS BACK INTO ROOM, SOUND OF CUPS CLINKING AND HARRY AND APRIL DRINKING. HARRY STARTS TO SAY SOMETHING, BUT EL TRAIN DROWNS HIM OUT. FINALLY:

APRIL *(puts down cup; sound of her chair scraping back as she stands)*: Thank you for the coffee—and everything.

HARRY *(sound of him jumping up)*: Don't go! Please!

APRIL: I must. It's a long way. Turn on the TV, please.

HARRY: No—I won't! I won't make you old!

APRIL: You don't understand.

HARRY: Please! It's too early. There's nothing on. Wait. . . .

APRIL: I *have* waited, Harry. You don't know how long.

SOUND OF EL.
SOUND OF APRIL MOVING PAST AND TURNING ON TV.
SOUND OF TV VOICE. AS TV VOICE COMES ON, SOUND OF
EL DIES OUT.

TV VOICE: . . . And now, kiddies, it's time for your Uncle Jack to tell you about a wonderful surprise waiting for you and your mommies in the supermarket. . . .

SOUND: TV CLICKS OFF.

HARRY *(the age once again in his voice)*: You're the same! I'm old— but you're twenty-four! Even though we're back in the present!

APRIL *(sadly)*: I told you we were going different ways. Your way was back. Mine was—is—forward. Oh, my dear, I'm sorry. I had to use you. I had no choice.

HARRY: You came from the past—but in 1936—you weren't even born!

APRIL: I wish—I'm so afraid this will hurt you—but I'm not from your past, or even your present . . . I'm from the future.

HARRY: The future—then I'm just—a stop on your journey . . . where you're going . . . I'm dead!

APRIL: No, Harry. It's all—relative. It's what you are *now* that matters. Not what will be, or what was.

HARRY: I know I hoped for too much. I wanted my youth and I wanted you—and I can't have both. I can't have either.

APRIL *(distressed at his unhappiness)*: It was to have been so simple, so scientific. I was to go back—they have machines—and make notes. Saturate myself in the atmosphere of the past. Oh, it doesn't matter! You're what counts. I've hurt you and all I wanted was to give you what happiness I could, in passing—

HARRY: It doesn't matter. I'm just a phantom in your life—in your real present. Where you belong, I'm only a corpse in the graveyard.

SOUND: APRIL STARTS TO CRY.

HARRY: Let me finish. Be realistic. I'm just a complicating factor who got in your way. You mustn't compare yourself with—with someone who doesn't exist in your own time, but think of me occasionally . . . up there in twenty-hundred and—whatever it is.

APRIL: Harry, stop it! Don't kill yourself in your own lifetime . . . I'll stay with you, my dear. I will! I can't do this to you.

HARRY: No, I won't let you. Look, I'm a sentimental man who's been privileged to know his youth again. Knowing that youth, I know yours. I won't let you sacrifice yourself—for a phantom who died before you were born.

SOUND: APRIL SOBS.

HARRY: Come on, child. Wash your face. Off with that lipstick. Cupid's bows are passé. *(Indulgently, fatherly)* Scoot! You've got to fix yourself up and find somebody who can make change for a coin that hasn't been minted yet. . . . Forgive my vanity, but I hope this time it's a woman.

SOUND: APRIL WALKS TO BATHROOM, DISTANT SOUND OF WATER RUNNING. SOUND OF WALKING BACK INTO ROOM.

HARRY: When you go, don't say goodbye.

APRIL: All right.

HARRY: I hate long goodbyes. Leave as if—as if you were going down to the corner—to get some—some milk and oatmeal cookies.

APRIL *(tries to pretend)*: All right. I guess I'm ready. Is there—anything else you want while I'm out?

HARRY: Maybe a charlotte russe?

APRIL *(the pretense fails)*: Oh, Harry, I don't even know what that is!

HARRY: Never mind.

SOUND: DOOR OPENING, APRIL WALKS OUT. THERE IS SILENCE. SUDDENLY, THE DOOR BURSTS OPEN. APRIL'S FOOTSTEPS AS SHE RUNS IN.

HARRY: You didn't go!

APRIL *(panting, barely able to speak)*: Y-yes.

HARRY: You couldn't have, and been back so soon.

APRIL *(panting)*: I could have come back to yesterday, if I'd wanted, traveling in time. At least there *is* a yesterday.

HARRY: Of course there's a yesterday. That's where we—you mean where you went back to—ahead to—whatever you say—it's not—it's been—?

APRIL: There's no tomorrow.

HARRY: What do you mean?

APRIL: Where I was going I'd have been a corpse—without even a graveyard. I mean when I got close to where I wanted to go I realized it wasn't even there any more. Something wiped it out—or it finally blew itself up—I don't know what. I just know it's gone.

HARRY: . . . and so you came back to me.

APRIL: That's not very flattering, is it? I'm sorry.

HARRY: You're here. The details don't matter.

APRIL: You're the one I turned to.

HARRY: That matters. Very much. You're welcome. But the one you've turned to is an old man.

APRIL: Hush. You're not old. You've lived in a suspended life. I'm the one who's aged, dashing back and forth between the centuries.

HARRY: You lie—adorably. But stay with me. At least until you find your bearings in this crazy time.

APRIL: I *want* to stay with you. You're the same person I met on the El platform. Do you think you've changed—inside?

HARRY *(lightly)*: Inside, I always think of myself as 19—much too young for a mature woman like you.

APRIL: Oh, Harry, I *can* love you. I will. Just give me a little time.

HARRY: You have all the time I have left.

APRIL: . . . I want to stay with you forever, Harry. And if we only listen to the radio all our remaining years, that'll be all right, as long as we're together. And one night, Harry, who knows—we'll turn on the old Atwater Kent—and hear the Street Singer or the Happiness Boys—and then the program will be drowned out by the Ninth Avenue El—I can almost hear it—rattling its way through that magic time when you're twenty-five and I'm twenty-four.

SOUND: THE EL IS HEARD. ITS SOUND SWELLS AND THEN FADES TO SILENCE.

Glossary

acetate A substance similar in composition to Scotch tape, used for manufacturing audiotape; it is rather brittle and can snap easily.

acoustics The study of sound. Also, the properties of a studio, room, or concert hall that contribute to the quality of the sound heard in it.

actuality The sound of an event, recorded or broadcast at the time the event took place. Also called a *sound bite*.

ad-lib To speak over the air without a prepared script.

air monitor A source on the console that monitors the output of the station as it is received over the air (in other words, the actual output of the transmitter, rather than an output from the console or any other piece of equipment along the audio chain).

airshift Period of time during which any particular radio operator puts programming on the air at a radio station.

ambient noise Noise randomly occurring in an environment.

amplification The raising of the volume or strength of a signal.

amplifier A device used to raise the volume or strength of a signal.

amplitude The property of a sound wave or electrical signal that determines its magnitude.

analog In radio, a type of recorded sound source that produces a sound wave similar to the original wave. Traditional methods of reproducing sounds, such as phonograph records and standard audiotape, use analog methods, as opposed to *digital* recording.

ASCAP American Society of Composers and Publishers, a music-licensing agency.

attack time The length of time an audio processing unit takes to activate the compressor after a particular sound affects it.

audio Electronically transmitted or received sound.

audiotape Thin tape used to record sound that has been transduced into a magnetic signal.

audition A mode of console operation in which sound can be channeled into a speaker without being fed to the on-air transmitter. Also, a session for assessing material or talent in advance of production.

automation Machinery for putting program elements on the air, taking the place of human workers.

backtracking Counterclockwise rotation of a disc on a broadcast turntable; part of the sequence of functions used to cue a record.

bed A piece of music used as background for a commercial.

bidirectional A microphone pickup pattern in which sound sources are accepted from two opposite directions—in front of and in back of the mic, but not from the sides.

billboard A rundown of information to be fed by an audio service; usually printed, but sometimes spoken.

binary The digital computer's method of using two pulses—on or off—to encode computer language.

blast filter See **pop filter**.

BMI Broadcast Music International, a music-licensing agency.

board An audio control console.

bus A junction of circuits where the outputs of a number of sound sources are mixed together.

capacitor A device for storage of electrical signals, used (among other functions) as an element in a condenser microphone. *Condenser* is an old-fashioned term for capacitor.

capstan A revolving metal post on a tape deck that determines the speed of the tape's movement; it turns the pinch roller.

cardioid A microphone pickup pattern that is unidirectional, and heart-shaped.

carousel A circular, rotating device for automatically playing cartridges.

cartridge The element of a turntable assembly that converts vibrations of the stylus into electrical energy. See also **cartridge tape.**

cartridge machine A unit that plays and/or records cartridge tapes.

cartridge tape A continuous loop of recording tape housed in a plastic case. Usually called a *cart*.

cassette Two small reels of tape enclosed in a plastic case.

central processing unit The brain of a computer; the circuitry that performs calculations.

channel The route followed by a signal as it travels through the components of a system. Also, an input or output designation on an audio control console.

channel bouncing A production technique that moves sound from one speaker to another. Sometimes called *pan potting*.

coincident mics Two cardioid mics set up to cross at approximately a 90-degree angle; used as a standard method of recording.

coloration The nuances of sound that give it a particular character.

combo Combination of operating the

audio console and announcing over the air. Doing this is usually called *working combo*.

compact disc A small disc that is recorded digitally and is played back by laser-beam readout.

complex waveform A visual representation, usually on a computer or oscilloscope, of the various sound waves that make up a particular sound.

compression Process used to minimize distortion by reducing the differences in level between low- and high-volume segments of a recorded or broadcast sound.

condenser mic A microphone that contains a capacitor as an element and typically requires an external power supply; changes in the position of the vibrating diaphragm of the mic alter the strength of the charge held by the electrical element.

console A device for amplifying, routing, and mixing audio signals.

cross-fade Gradual replacement of one sound source with another. One sound is faded out, and the other is simultaneously faded up; at one point, their sound levels are the same.

crossover A song that bridges two categories of music, such as country and pop.

cue To ready a record or tape playback device so that it will play at the first point of sound or at some other desired starting point. Also, to indicate by hand signal or other means the desired time to begin a performing activity. Also, a channel on a console that allows you to hear a sound source without putting it on the air.

cue tone A sound meant to convey a signal to an operator or to an automated device.

cut A segment of recorded sound on a disc or tape. Also, to record a segment of audio production such as a commercial or public-service announcement.

cycle One complete movement of a sound or electrical wave through its naturally occurring pattern to its starting point.

dead air Silence over the air.

dead-potting Starting an audio source with the pot closed; usually done at a carefully calculated moment, with the goal of finishing the audio source (such as a song) at an exact time.

decibel As applied to sound, a relative measure of volume.

deck A device for playback. The term is usually used in conjunction with the word indicating what the device plays, as in *tape deck* or *cassette deck*.

delegation switch A device that allows the operator of a console to choose which of two or more sources is to be controlled by a particular pot.

demographics Statistical representations of a population; usually used in radio to refer to the characteristics of the listening audience.

diaphragm The portion of a microphone that vibrates in response to sound.

digital Based on the translation of an original sound source into binary computer language.

digital audiotape Audiotape combined with an audiotape recording system that allows sound to be recorded in binary computer language.

directional mic A microphone that picks up sound from only one direction. Also called a *unidirectional mic*.

disc A phonograph record or compact disc.

disc jockey A staff announcer who acts as host of a music program.

distortion A change or alteration in the quality of sound that impairs the listener's ability to identify it with its source.

Dolby A trade name of a noise-reduction system.

donut In radio production, a recorded audio segment that provides an introduction, an ending, and a music bed; an announcer uses the segment as a production aid by reading copy over the music bed, thereby filling the hole in the donut.

double audio A sound problem that occurs when one sound source is recorded over another; usually it is a mistake brought about by not erasing a cart before recording over it.

doubletracking Recording a voice, and then recording another version of the voice that has been slightly altered electronically; when both voices are mixed and played back, an eerie effect results.

downlink The method by which a receiver on earth can pick up a transmission from a satellite.

drive wheel In a broadcast turntable, the wheel that moves the turntable plate.

dubbing Recording sound from one recorded source to another.

dynamic mic A mic in which a coil moves through a magnetic field in response to sound vibration sensed by the diaphragm of the mic.

dynamic range The difference in volume between the loudest and quietest sounds of a source.

echo Repetition of a sound, usually caused by the reflection of the source bouncing off a hard surface. Also, an electronic special effect created by using a delay unit or by feeding back the output of a tape machine's playback head while recording.

editing In audio production, the alteration of a recorded sound—most commonly through the physical cutting and splicing of the tape or through the electronic transfer of the tape from one source to another.

editing block A plastic or metal block used to align audiotape properly for cutting and splicing.

editing/production structures Patterns of editing commonly used in radio production: establish music; voice under, voice up; cross-fade; voice out, music up; music wrap; voice wrap; and various combinations of these patterns.

editing tab A specially manufactured piece of tape used to splice tape together.

edit point A location on a tape or other playback source where the producer wants the edit to begin or end.

electromagnetic field A magnetic field—an area where there are patterned magnetic waves—produced by electricity.

electronic splicing (editing) The removal of portions of a recording and the subsequent reassembly of the remaining material by means of electronic equipment, rather than by physically cutting or splicing the tape.

element The part of the microphone that transduces sound into electrical energy.

Emergency Broadcast System A federal network for broadcasting information to the public, activated in times of war, natural disaster, or other dire circumstance.

equalization Alteration of a sound source as a result of varying its frequency balance.

erase head The part of the head system of a tape unit that removes the recorded signals from tape.

establish To play a recognizable and noticeable portion of a sound source. For example, a producer may establish a music theme before potting it down.

fact sheet A listing of facts given to an announcer as a guide for delivering an ad-lib commercial.

fade To bring a sound source up or down on an audio console at a given rate of speed (usually slowly).

false ending In some recorded material,

an apparent end of the recorded segment that is in fact not the end.

feedback Reamplification of a sound, resulting in a loud squeal from a loudspeaker; often caused by mic pickup of the output of a speaker that is carrying the sound being picked up by the mic; also occurs when the record head of a tape machine receives the output signal of the same recorder.

filter An electronic system that reduces or eliminates sound of designated frequencies.

flanger Device for throwing a sound and its mirror image out of phase to produce unusual sound effects.

flanging Slightly delaying reproduction of a source, and then mixing the reproduced sound with the original source of the sound to produce a special effect.

flat response A faithful response by a microphone.

flux A random magnetic field produced by the erase head in a tape recorder. Flux scrambles the electronic signals already on the tape.

format A radio station's programming strategy to attract a particular audience; the mix of all elements of a station's sound, including type of music played and style of announcing.

forward echo An echo in reverse, used as a special effect; the echo comes first, and then the sound follows.

frequency The number of times a sound wave repeats itself in 1 second—expressed in cycles per second (cps) or hertz (Hz).

frequency response The range of frequencies that can be produced by an audio system.

full-track A method of recording in which the signal is placed over the entire width of a tape.

generation The proximity (for purposes of gauging the diminution in sound quality) of a sound recording to an original sound source. Thus, a tape copied once is first-generation; a copy of that copy is second-generation; and so on.

geostationary (Of a satellite) staying in an orbit over the same part of the earth, as a result of moving in tandem with the earth's rotation.

graphic equalizer A device for tailoring sound; the controls produce a visual representation of the frequency response, hence the term *graphic*.

grooves The continuous narrow channel in a phonograph record that the stylus tracks.

half-track A method of recording in which signals are simultaneously placed on two tracks (one-half of the tape width each) of a tape, thus making stereo recording possible. Also called *two-track*.

hardware The physical equipment of a computer.

hard-wired (Of equipment) physically wired together.

harmonics Frequencies related to a fundamental frequency that are multiples of the original; the mixture of harmonics with the fundamental gives a sound its particular timbre or tonal color.

harmonizer An electronic device used to vary pitch, tempo, and the harmonics of a sound source in order to create special effects.

heads The devices on a tape machine that impart a signal to the tape; they generally consist of an erase head, a record head, and a playback head. The erase head scrambles the iron oxide particles on the tape, the record head arranges the particles in order, and the playback head reads the pattern formed by the record head.

headset mic A mic that fits directly on the head, utilizing earpieces; useful for sports announcers.

headstack A post on which multiple

recording heads are placed one on top of the other.

hertz (Hz) A unit of frequency (identical to cycles per second) named after Heinrich Hertz, whose discoveries made radio transmission possible.

high fidelity Giving high-quality, faithful reproduction.

high-pass filter A filter that only allows high frequencies to pass, chopping off lower frequencies; used, for example, to eliminate a low-pitch rumble.

hot-potting Starting a sound source with the pot open.

hypercardioid A microphone pickup pattern that is very narrow, heart-shaped, and one-directional.

inverse pyramid A method of news-writing whereby the most important details of a story are given at the beginning, or top. The story can then be cut from the bottom.

iron oxide Rust; the substance on a magnetic tape that holds the signal.

isolated-component recording Recording various components of an orchestra or other multiple-component sound source, using a separate mic to record each component. The output of each mic is recorded on a separate channel, and these are mixed after the recording session.

key On an audio console, the device for turning a pot (and through it, a sound source) on and off.

lavalier mic A small mic that hangs from a string around the announcer's neck or clips to the announcer's clothing; not widely used in radio production.

lead The beginning sentence or sentences of a news story—ostensibly the most important part of the story.

leader and timing tape Colored tape that neither records nor plays back; used to separate cuts on the tape and also at the beginning or end of the tape to protect the recorded portion from damage. Some varieties of leader tape show marks that allow the operator to time the segments between cuts accurately.

levels The volumes of signals, usually as read by a VU meter.

limiter A device used to suppress dynamic levels of a reproduced sound above a preset limit, in order to provide a more constant output level.

live-assist A method whereby automation is used to help the operator perform tasks more simply and efficiently.

log The station's official record of what will be and what was aired during a broadcast day.

loudspeaker A device for reproducing sound by transducing it from audio into sound.

low-pass filter A filter that only allows low frequencies to pass, chopping off the highs; used, for example, to eliminate a hiss.

magnetic tape In radio production, audiotape composed of a backing strip coated with iron oxide particles. When the particles are aligned in response to a signal in an analog or digital recording device, the signal can be stored and later played back as sound.

master pot The potentiometer (volume control) that governs the entire output of a console.

microchip A small circuit produced by a photographic process, used in computer technology.

microphone A transducer that converts sound energy into an electrical signal, which may then be amplified, recorded, or broadcast.

middle-side miking Technique for total-sound recording, involving a bidirectional mic picking up sound from the sides of the performing area and a cardioid mic in the middle; used to produce a very spacious sound.

MIDI [**pronounced "middy"**] A device for interfacing a number of sound-producing instruments with a computer and with each other.

mix To combine a number of sound sources.

modulation The electrical imprint of a sound signal on an audio or radio wave.

monaural Literally, "one-eared"; having only one channel of audio. The addition of another discrete channel gives a stereo effect.

monitor Loudspeaker in a sound studio or control room.

motional energy Energy produced by movement, such as sound. Sound qualifies as motional energy because it is produced by a physical vibration in molecules in the air or in some other medium.

mouse A device for controlling the movement of information on a computer screen.

moving-coil mic A microphone whose characteristic element is a coil that moves through a magnetic field (thereby producing an electric signal) in response to the movement of a diaphragm, which vibrates in response to sound waves.

multichannel A type of console capable of isolating a number of channels from one another; used in sound recording.

multiple A setup that allows many mics to be plugged into a sound source; useful for public events where many press people will be using tape recorders.

multitrack A device that records several audio sources, usually laid down on one tape.

music bed A segment of recorded music used as background sound in a broadcast production (usually a commercial). See also **donut**.

music wrap An editing/production

structure that begins with music, which gives way to a speaking voice in the middle, which gives way finally to concluding music.

muting system A device that automatically cuts the control room speaker when a mic is opened, in order to prevent feedback.

mylar A substance used as a backing for audiotape; it is stretchier than acetate.

needle drop The means of measuring usage of material from a licensed set of sound effects or music beds. Fees are charged "per needle drop."

network A linkage of broadcast stations in which a central programming source supplies material to the individual stations making up the system.

normal connection The way in which an engineering staff routes a signal under normal circumstances. If you want to change the pattern, you can use a patchcord to break the normal.

omnidirectional (Of a microphone pickup pattern) capable of picking up sound sources equally well from all directions.

output Anything that is fed out of an audio system.

overdub To add another audio element to an existing one. For example, a singer can listen to her or his previously recorded work while simultaneously recording (overdubbing) a harmony part.

pan pot A control that allows a producer to move a sound source from the left stereo channel to the right one, or vice versa.

parabolic mic A microphone positioned in a reflecting dish that has a three-dimensional parabolic shape; used to pick up distant sounds.

parametric equalizer A type of equalizer that allows an operator to select one particular frequency and boost or lower that frequency.

patchbay A device into which patchcords are plugged for the purpose of routing signals.

patchcord A wire with an easily inserted connection, used to reroute signals for the convenience of the operator.

patching A method of changing the routing of a signal through an audio system. Also, a connection that is temporarily placed between audio inputs and outputs.

phase Synchronicity. When two or more sounds reach a mic at the same time, the sounds are said to be *in phase,* and their amplitudes combine. When the sounds reach the mic at different times, they are called *out of phase,* and they cancel each other. A similar principle applies to electrical waves.

pickup pattern A representation of the area within which a mic effectively picks up sound, based on a 360-degree polar pattern.

pinch roller A rubber wheel, driven by the capstan on a tape deck, that keeps the tape moving at the correct speed.

pitch The ear's and mind's imprecise interpretation of the frequency of a sound.

plate The part of a turntable that holds the disc and revolves.

playback head The part of the head system in a tape recorder or deck that reads the patterns created on tape by the record head and produces an electrical signal conveying this information to the rest of the playback system.

playback only Designation for a cartridge machine or other audio unit that does not have a recording capability.

polar pattern A graph consisting of concentric circles that are assigned decreasing values toward the center of the graph; a pattern superimposed on the graph represents the area within which the microphone effectively picks up sound.

pop filter A wind-blocking screen in or on a microphone, designed to prevent the blasting or popping noise caused by announcers who pop their *p*'s and *b*'s.

popping An undesirable explosive sound caused by too vigorous pronunciation of sounds such as *p* and *b*.

pot Short for *potentiometer*—a device on an audio console that controls volume.

potentiometer See **pot.**

preamp A small amplifier that boosts a signal, usually up to line level. It generally accomplishes the first step in the amplification process.

pressure-gradient mic Another name for a ribbon mic, which operates by measuring the difference in pressure between one side of the ribbon and the other.

pressure-zone mic A type of microphone that eliminates proximity effects and phasing problems. Pressure Zone is a trade name.

producer A person who manipulates radio equipment to construct a program and achieve an effect.

production The process of manipulating sound elements with radio equipment in order to transmit a message and achieve an effect.

production library A collection of music or sound effects used in production. Production libraries are generally leased but sometimes bought outright; increasingly they are appearing on compact discs.

program A mode of operation in which sound can be channeled through the console to the on-air transmitter.

proximity effect A property certain mics have of accentuating lower frequencies as sound sources move closer.

public-affairs programming Program elements in the general public interest.

public-service announcements Program elements designed to provide the public with needed information.

quarter-track A method of recording in which individual channels are laid down on each of four tracks of a tape.

RAM Random access memory; in a computer, the area into which software can be loaded and information can be loaded and retrieved.

range The portion of the frequency spectrum that a microphone or other audio element can reproduce.

rarefaction An area in which air molecules become less dense; the opposite of a compression. Sound waves are carried through the air by a series of rarefactions and compressions.

record head The part of the head system in a tape recorder that imprints the sound pattern on the magnetic tape.

release time The length of time it takes for an audio processing unit to let a signal return to its previous level.

remote Production done on location, as opposed to in a studio.

reverb Short for *reverberation*—an effect produced with an electronic device that adds a time delay to a sound source and then adds it back to the signal.

ribbon mic A microphone with a paper-thin element that vibrates in response to the velocity of sound waves. The element is suspended in a magnetic field that converts the sound into an electrical signal.

riding levels Keeping close watch on the strength of signals to ensure that the program is not overmodulated. Also known as *riding gain.*

ROM Read only memory; the area of a computer where information (which has been factory installed) can be read but not accessed.

routing Channeling an audio signal.

sampling frequency The number of

times per second (expressed in Hz) a digital recording unit takes a sample of a sound source.

satellite An orbiting device that, among other things, retransmits signals to a broad portion of the earth's surface.

segue The transition between two recordings played consecutively without interruption.

shape As a component of frequency response, the level of response at various frequencies within a mic's range; basically, the form of the graph that indicates the mic's sensitivity at various frequencies.

shotgun mic A long, narrow mic that has a very narrow, highly directional pickup pattern.

sibilance The noticeable prominence of hissy *s* sounds.

signal-to-noise ratio The ratio (expressed in decibels) between the intended sounds of a recording or broadcast and the undesirable noise of a system.

sine wave A visual representation of a sound wave as it moves through its various values of compression and rarefaction.

slipcueing Finding the starting point of a disc by slipping it back and forth on the turntable plate (without allowing the plate to move). Also often used synonymously (though somewhat inaccurately) with *slipstarting.*

slipstarting Starting a record on a turntable by holding the record at the proper starting point as the turntable spins and then releasing the record to get instant startup. The term is often used interchangeably with *slipcueing.*

slug A heading used by a wire service for quick identification of a story. (Example: WEATHER FOR SEVEN WESTERN COUNTIES.)

software The programs run by a computer.

solid-state (Of electronic equipment) operating without using vacuum tubes.

solo A control on a multitrack console that mutes other inputs so that the remaining channel can be heard alone.

sound The perception by the ear or by some other instrument of waves resulting from the vibration of air molecules.

sound bite A piece of sound recorded at the scene of a story and integrated into a newscast. Often used synonymously with *actuality,* but the term *sound bite* is more commonly used in radio if the piece of sound is a sound effect, such as a siren screaming.

sound effect Any sound other than music or speech that is used to help create an image, evoke an emotion, compress time, clarify a situation, or reinforce a message. Abbreviated as *SFX* in scripts.

sound envelope The waveform that represents a sound. In modern usage, the term usually refers to the waveform representation on a computer screen produced by means of a MIDI or other digital editing device.

sound shapers Devices on a recording console that can be used to change the physical characteristics of the audio signal.

spaced-pair mics Two microphones set up parallel to each other, 1 or 2 feet apart; used in stereo recording to produce a very broad sound.

spatial enhancers Devices used to alter the stereo signal to give the impression of a larger physical environment—that is, to create the impression of a very large hall.

splicing The process of joining together two pieces of recording tape, usually with the aid of an editing block and adhesive tape made specifically for this purpose, in order to edit recorded material or to repair broken tape.

spot A prerecorded announcement (usually a commercial).

stereo Using two channels for sound reproduction in order to create the illusion of depth and spaciousness.

stinger A brief musical opening designed to attract attention. Increasingly, stingers are produced by digital technology.

stripping the wire Taking printed information off the teletype and organizing it into various categories, saving what is needed for later use and throwing away what is not needed.

stylus The portion of a phonograph that makes contact with the grooves in a record and vibrates in response to the shape of the grooves. The vibrations create an electrical signal in the cartridge, and this signal is subsequently fed into an amplifier and distributed within an audio system.

submixer A miniature console through which several sources can be output to one of several submasters on a full-size multichannel console.

supercardioid A microphone pickup pattern that is narrow, heart-shaped, and unidirectional and falls somewhere between a cardioid pattern and a hypercardioid pattern.

supply reel The reel on a tape recorder from which tape spools off during play.

syndicators Firms that distribute programs or program material to individual radio stations, for a fee.

synthesizer An electronic musical instrument that resembles an organ, but can produce a wide range of sounds.

takeup reel The reel on a tape recorder that pulls and collects tape during play.

tape guide Equipment on a tape deck that keeps the moving tape in a precise position.

task-oriented sequence The arrangement of radio production tasks in the most convenient and efficient order for accomplishing them within the confines of the production studio. Thus, doing

the ending of a commercial first may actually be preferable under some circumstances.

telco drop The point at which the telephone company terminates a transmission line for carrying a remote signal back to the studio from the site of a remote broadcast. The station's remote equipment is connected to the drop.

teletype A machine that prints the output of a wire service. The old-style typewriter teletype has almost universally been replaced by the computer printer.

tonearm The moveable arm on a turntable unit that holds the stylus and cartridge.

total-sound recording Recording the entire sound output of, for example, a musical group, as a single sound source—rather than recording separate sections or instruments with separate mics (see **isolated-component recording**).

touchscreen A system that allows the operator to execute commands by touching the appropriate display on a video terminal.

track The portion of a strip of magnetic tape that is used for recording sound information. Also, of a phonograph cartridge, to trace with accuracy the grooves of a record.

transducer Any device that performs the function of converting energy from one form into another.

transmitter The device responsible for producing the radio waves that carry a station's signal.

trim control An adjustment control that makes very fine changes on the volume level on a console.

turntable A system consisting of a plate, a drive mechanism, a tonearm, a speed control, and an on–off switch; used to play conventional disc recordings.

two-track See **half-track**.

unidirectional (Of a microphone pickup pattern) capable of picking up sound sources clearly from one direction only. Also called *one-directional*.

uplink The piece of equipment that sends a signal up to the satellite.

vertical/slide fader A pot that slides up and down a linear slot, rather than turning on a projecting axis (as does the traditional circular pot).

voice actuality A report from a journalist with an actuality segment inserted in its midst.

voicer An oral report of a news item, spoken by a journalist who signs off with his or her name, sometimes the location from which the report emanates, and sometimes the name of the news organization. (Example: ". . . Bob Roberts reporting from Capitol Hill for WAAA News.")

voice wrap An editing/production structure that begins with one voice, which gives way to a second voice, which gives way finally to the first voice until the conclusion of the spot.

volume The level of sound, perceived as varying degrees of loudness.

volume-unit meter (VU meter) A device that provides a visual readout of loudness. The most important use of a VU meter is for taking zero on the scale as a reference level for the proper audio-level output.

wave A complete cycle of electrical or sound energy.

waveforms Visual representations of physical waves.

wild sound Ambient sound used to enhance the atmosphere of an actuality or sound bite.

wind filter A filter that fits inside or outside a mic and blocks the blasting noise caused by wind.

wire service A news-gathering organization that supplies news copy and audio reports to subscribers, who use the wire-service material to supplement their own news-gathering resources. The name is something of an anachronism, since most of the material is delivered by satellite today, rather than by wire.

wow The sound a record or tape makes when the audio portion is heard before the playback device has reached full speed.

XLR A type of three-pin connector commonly used in radio.

Suggested Readings

Listed in this supplemental section are books and periodicals that will be of particular help in understanding radio in general and production in particular. Some may be out of print, but many of the older books are readily available in libraries.

■ Production and Technical Works ■

▶ Stanley R. Alten. *Audio in Media,* 2d ed. Belmont, Calif.: Wadsworth, 1986. The most comprehensive guide available on audio; much of the content is applicable to radio production.

▶ Joseph Carr. *The TAB Handbook of Radio Communications.* Blue Ridge Summit, Penn.: TAB Books, 1984. Not exactly a guide to engineering operations of a radio station, but a good self-teaching approach to radio electronics.

▶ E. B. Crutchfield, ed. *The NAB Engineering Handbook,* 7th ed. Washington: National Association of Broadcasters, 1985. Frequently updated and very comprehensive book.

▶ Robert McLeish. *The Technique of Radio Production,* 2d ed. Stoneham, Mass.: Focal Press, 1988. Primarily a production book, but also deals with ethics, societal issues of radio, and general station operations.

▶ Alec Nisbett. *The Technique of the Sound Studio,* 4th ed. Stoneham, Mass.: Focal Press, 1979. A comprehensive look at recording, with an extensive glossary.

▶ Alec Nisbett. *The Use of Microphones,* 2d ed. Stoneham, Mass: Focal Press, 1983. A very thorough study of mics and mic placement. Useful for radio, although probably more useful to recording-studio engineers.

▶ Robert S. Oringel. *Audio Control Handbook: For Radio and Television Broadcasting,* 5th ed. New York: Hastings House, 1983. Good reference for audio operators; less useful for producers.

▶ Randy Thom and others. *Audio Craft: An Introduction to the Tools and Techniques of Audio Production.* Washington: National Foundation of Community Broadcasters, 1982. A practical guide.

■   General Radio, Radio Operations,   ■
and Surveys Dealing Substantially
with Radio

‣ Eric Barnouw. *A History of Broadcasting in the United States*. New York: Oxford University Press, 1966, 1968, 1970. Three-volume history; comprehensive and readable.

‣ Linda Busby and Donald Parker. *The Art and Science of Radio*. Boston: Allyn & Bacon, 1984. Broad in scope but many interesting details; a good and easily accessible reference.

‣ George H. Douglas. *The Early Days of Radio Broadcasting*. Jefferson, N.C.: McFarland Publishing, 1987. Narrative of radio's troubled birth and childhood.

‣ Sydney W. Head and Christopher H. Sterling. *Broadcasting in America: A Survey of Electronic Media*, 5th ed. Boston: Houghton Mifflin, 1987. The well-known all-in-one guide to understanding the complexities of the broadcasting world.

‣ Michael C. Keith and Joseph M. Krause. *The Radio Station*. Stoneham, Mass.: Focal Press, 1986. A heavily illustrated guide to radio.

‣ Lewis B. O'Donnell, Carl Hausman, and Philip Benoit. *Radio Station Operations: Management and Employee Perspectives*. Belmont, Calif.: Wadsworth, 1989. A comprehensive guide to many aspects of radio, including physical facilities, station programming, operations, production, sales/advertising, and management.

‣ Christopher H. Sterling and John M. Kittross. *Stay Tuned: A Concise History of American Broadcasting*. Belmont, Calif.: Wadsworth, 1982. More than just a history—an easy-to-use, quick-reference guide to many aspects of broadcasting.

■   Radio Programming   ■

‣ Susan Tyler Eastman, Sydney W. Head, and Lewis Klein. *Broadcast/Cable Programming: Strategies and Practice*, 3d ed. Belmont, Calif.: Wadsworth, 1989. A broad but concisely analytical study of programming with specific references to radio.

‣ Herbert H. Howard and Michael S. Kievman. *Radio and TV Programming*. New York: Macmillan, 1983. Coverage of programming, primarily from a historical point of view.

‣ Michael C. Keith. *Radio Programming: Consultancy and Formatics.* Stoneham, Mass.: Focal Press, 1987. An in-depth analysis of strategies for commercial radio formats.

‣ Murray B. Levin. *Talk Radio and the American Dream.* Lexington, Mass.: Lexington Books, 1987. An exhaustive study of radio talk shows. Includes transcripts of broadcasts.

‣ Edd Routt, James B. McGrath, and Frederic A. Weiss. *The Radio Format Conundrum.* New York: Hastings House, 1978. A dated but nonetheless thoughtful view of how and why formats work.

■   Radio News   ■

‣ Barbara Dill. *The Journalist's Handbook on Libel and Privacy.* New York: Free Press, 1986. Includes analyses of recent cases; a practical guide for journalists.

‣ Irving Fang. *TV News, Radio News,* 4th ed. St. Paul, Minn.: Rada Press, 1985. An authoritative working guide.

‣ Carl Hausman. *The Decision-Making Process in Journalism.* Chicago: Nelson-Hall, 1989. A guide to principles of news judgment.

‣ Ted White, Adrian J. Meppen, and Steven Young. *Broadcast News Writing, Reporting and Production.* New York: Macmillan, 1984. An incisive guide that goes beyond writing and shows the entire range of radio (and, of course, television) news operations. Excellent examples of how news is gathered and scripted for broadcast.

■   Announcing/Performing   ■

‣ William Hawes. *The Performer in the Mass Media . . . in Media Professions and in the Community.* New York: Hastings House, 1978. Particularly useful for those interested in the dramatic aspects of TV performance.

‣ Stuart W. Hyde. *Television and Radio Announcing,* 5th ed. Boston: Houghton Mifflin, 1987. A durable book, now updated.

‣ Lewis B. O'Donnell, Carl Hausman, and Philip Benoit. *Announcing: Broadcast Communicating Today.* Belmont, Calif.: Wadsworth, 1987. Many of the techniques discussed are applicable to radio; some chapters deal specifically with radio announcing.

■ Commercials and Advertising ■

› Elizabeth J. Heighton and Don R. Cunningham. *Advertising in the Broadcast and Cable Media,* 2d ed. Belmont, Calif.: Wadsworth, 1984. Integrates advertising and research in an understandable way. More relevant for sales and management, but still informative for writers and producers of commercials.

› Jonne Murphy. *Handbook of Radio Advertising.* Radnor, Penn.: Chilton, 1980. A hands-on approach.

› David Ogilvy. *Confessions of an Advertising Man.* New York: Atheneum, 1980. A revealing insight into the world of professional advertising by the founder of one of the world's most successful advertising agencies. Useful for anyone who wants to design advertising of any type.

› Charles Warner. *Broadcast and Cable Selling.* Belmont, Calif.: Wadsworth, 1986. A very useful guide primarily aimed at selling time, but much insight is provided into producing effective advertising.

› Sherilyn K. Zeigler and Herbert H. Howard. *Broadcast Advertising: A Comprehensive Working Textbook,* 2d ed. Ames, Iowa: Iowa State University Press, 1984. Step-by-step guide; a good reference for a producer.

■ Periodicals ■

› In addition to the preceding books, the following periodicals are recommended as ongoing references for anyone interested in any aspect of radio.

› *Billboard.* 1515 Broadway, New York, N.Y. 10036. A source of in-depth information on the music industry, both broadcast and music stories.

› *Broadcasting.* 1735 DeSales St., N.W., Washington, D.C. 20036-4480. A trade journal of the industry; heavy emphasis on business aspects.

› *Broadcast Management/Engineering.* 820 Second Ave., New York, N.Y. 10017. A resource designed for engineers but comprehensible to managers. Excellent source for keeping up with latest technologies; special attention is paid to production equipment.

› *Cash Box.* 330 W. 58th St., Suite 5-D, New York, N.Y. 10019. Comprehensive coverage of the coin machine, music, and radio industries.

› *The Pulse of Broadcasting.* 150 E. 58th St., New York, N.Y. 10022. Covers radio from all angles: news, music, programming, buying and selling of stations, and interviews with radio's movers and shakers.

› *Radio and Records Weekly.* 1930 Century Park W., Los Angeles, Calif. 90067. Especially good for coverage of music in the radio industry.

‣ *RadioActive*. Published by the National Association of Broadcasters, 1771 N St., N.W., Washington, D.C. 20036. Insightful articles on a broad range of radio topics; good coverage of promotion and AM radio.

‣ *Radio World Newspaper*. P.O. Box 1214, Falls Church, Va. 22041. Offers updated news and interesting feature material to radio professionals.

‣ *Variety*. 154 E. 46th St., New York, N.Y. 10036. Coverage of theater, TV, radio, music, records, and film.

Index